THE INTERNATIONAL
WINE AND FOOD SOCIETY'S GUIDE TO

German Cookery

Other books in the series

THE INTERNATIONAL
WINE AND FOOD SOCIETY'S GUIDE TO

German Cookery

BY

HANS KARL ADAM

translated from the German by
NORAH TOMKINSON

with colour photographs by
NORBERT AMANN

and wood engravings by
HELMUTH WEISSENBORN

The International
Wine and Food Society

DAVID & CHARLES
NEWTON ABBOT

A publication of
The International Wine and Food Society Limited
Marble Arch House, 44 Edgware Road, London W.2.

President : André L. Simon

© The Wine and Food Society Publishing Company, 1967

This book was designed and produced by
Rainbird Reference Books Limited
Marble Arch House, 44 Edgware Road, London W.2.

Phototypeset in Monophoto Plantin by
Oliver Burridge Filmsetting Limited,
Crawley, Sussex
Printed and bound in Yugoslavia

Editor : Robin Howe
Designer : Ronald Clark

First published 1967
2nd edition, revised 1970

SBN 7153 4809 4

Contents

Colour Plates

Stories and Legends about Eating and Drinking

In every age and in every language books have been written about this subject. I have read many, and learnt much from them, but the things I remember best are to be found in no book. They are stories and vivid descriptions of eating and drinking for which I am indebted to my old Scripture master. Many years have passed since I was in the schoolroom, but I still see this much-admired teacher of mine before me and hear his melodious voice. He was a well-built man, around fifty, whose high forehead, framed by dark hair, was accentuated by horn-rimmed spectacles, behind which sparkled lively eyes. The sensuous lips formed whatever he told so convincingly that there remained no room for doubt. He used to wear his old black frockcoat open (if he had buttoned it over his plump stomach it would have been drawn into folds), and was given to emphasizing his words most eloquently with short squat hands.

So much for what our Scripture master looked like. He was a very learned man, a member of the Board of Education, but none the less very willing to enjoy all God's good gifts. He went to the heart of things and tried to discover their historical origins. He told us not only about what he

had read in old chronicles but would also recall his own experiences of
eating and drinking, intermingled with 'culinary dreams'. Yet despite this,
he could be content with the simple things of life. When he was a mere
chaplain in a small village near the Polish border he had taken a keen
interest in cooking. He had discovered, for instance, that green beans do
not discolour if a copper coin is added to the water they are boiled in. And,
much to the villagers' surprise, he had planted artichokes to delight his
palate.

Perhaps my readers can also remember a tutor who combined a diligence
in teaching his subject with the relation of all sorts of other anecdotes
that interested him, in such a way that they have remained in the memory
and roused their own interest. But let me invite him to speak for himself.

Gentlemen, [he would begin,] when we start discussing the history of eating and
drinking we must, as is customary in school, begin with the Greeks. First of all
I must cite Homer: 'And they came unto the house of Odysseus, like unto a god,
slaughtered sheep and goats, fat pigs and one of the oxen, roasted the innards and
divided them between themselves. Others mixed wine in the jugs. But the head
herdsman Philoitios handed the citizens bread in dainty baskets, Melanthios
poured the wine. And they lifted their hands to the tastily prepared meal'. So
you see, even in those days eating and drinking played an important role. In the
foremost Greek families the heroes enjoyed the privilege of being allowed to
roast their meat on the spit.

If we go forward some 800 years we find ourselves in the middle of the Roman
Empire. The Romans had a great many well-trained cooks, and the first known
cookery book, written by Apicius, dates from this period. No trouble, no expense
was too great to prepare a banquet, and one which became famous was given by
Trimalchio. For those who are interested, Petronius describes it.

The cooks were responsible not only for unusual dishes, but for the works of art
produced in the kitchen and also for striking and amusing table decorations.
Besides food and drink, pleasant entertainment was ensured. At Trimalchio's,
for instance, they not only served a host of dishes and delicacies, but an enormous
platter with a roast wild sow suckling a litter of piglets made of baked bread.*
All the guests watched a huntsman cut open the sow, and what happened? A
whole flight of fieldfares flew out into the hall, but their short spell of freedom did
not last long for birdcatchers had been engaged to catch them in nets. Later on
during the meal, a pig was roasted whole and brought in. When it was opened,
different kinds of sausages came rolling out, to the delight of the guests.

So you see that the meal evolved into an entertainment. People were in need
of 'bread and circuses' as they are today. As Epicurus – who knew how to enjoy
life to the full – wrote, there is a connection between eating and health, food and

---

* Something similar is still known in South Germany, where at Easter time 'Easter Hares'
are baked – made from yeast dough – with an egg under each tail. These eggs are later coloured.

temperament, even between the soul and the stomach. Epicurus, himself a modest man, invariably chose the best dish, not the biggest: he much preferred quality to quantity. 'What use are wisdom and riches to an invalid?' is still a valid question nowadays. We shall all grow older, and I can but give you the advice to guard your health as the greatest treasure God has blessed you with. 'To be rich and healthy is better than poor and ill', said the jester!

However, I would like to dally with the Romans a little longer. They had spices at their disposal, from different parts of their world-wide Empire. For instance, pepper and marjoram, nutmeg and bay-leaves, lemons and oranges were not unknown to them. They even had rice, although they did not appreciate it much, probably because they did not know how to boil it. The choice of fish from the Mediterranean was wide; and there were sole from the Channel (via Britain) and oysters from France. Lucullus, whom you have learnt about in history as a great military leader, is in truth more renowned because he imported cherries into Rome from Persia. His was a luxurious home, in whose kitchens the most exquisite delicacies were prepared. The following amusing anecdote has come down to us. One day he was dining at home, in the yellow dining-room of his villa, but was not in the least pleased with his repast. He called for his chef and couched his complaint in these words: 'Did you not know that Lucullus was dining with Lucullus today?'

The Romans had ice-cream, which the Sicilians knew how to prepare so well. In winter, snow could be shovelled into deep trenches and covered with brush-wood so that the sun could not melt it too soon. Large blocks of ice from rivers and lakes were deposited in deep, cool cellars and used in summer, both for the making of ice-cream and to cool drinks. Even nowadays, many of the peasants chop ice from their fishponds in winter and store it in their cellars for later use.

Marco Polo brought noodles (macaroni) over from China – the Romans, and later on the Italians, made all sorts of different kinds of noodles.* Nowadays Italy is considered to be *the* country for macaroni – so much so that a foreigner wrote to a travel agency in Milan saying he wanted to visit Italy to see for himself where spaghetti grew and could they write and tell him when it was harvested!

But we must not be led into thinking that simple folk were able to afford plentiful meals; their table was and probably always will be – plain and frugal. For instance, the early Germans, whose culture had by no means reached the standards of the Roman Empire, not surprisingly felt an urge to go to that country 'flowing with milk and honey'.

Apart from that, culturally it was a most important period in which a nation that had so far been itinerant and relied on hunting, settled down. Every new culture was founded in this way, and so the ancient Germans began building houses, started to farm and breed their own cattle. I know people still go hunting and shooting, but it is no longer of prime importance and they no longer live entirely on animal products. Fats and albumen were terms unknown to them, nor did they know that vegetables provided the body with precious carbohydrates.

*The Italians call them *pasta asciutta*, i.e. dried paste or dough, of which they have an enormous variety.

You have all no doubt seen pictures of your ancient forefathers, wearing rams' heads on their own, the horns polished, and looking most belligerent. They would hold a good solid cudgel in one hand, with which to defend themselves, and probably a bone in the other to stuff into their mouths. The latter was probably a pork chop roasted on the spit over a charcoal fire, on which pine cones were also thrown at times.

Mead was occasionally poured over the meat. This drink was made from honey, water and barley, a mixture from which, later, beer was evolved. Basting made the meat crisp and brown, and lamb, venison, veal, even whole oxen, were cooked in this way. The lack of pots and pans meant that cooking, let alone boiling, was almost impossible. For winter storage they salted and pickled meat and vegetables and hung the pork up to dry. Potatoes were unknown, and cutlery had not yet been invented. But there was a great variety of food, even if the quality of their crops did not compare with what we are used to today. Everything grew wild, and grafting was as yet unknown. At annual fairs – such as the famous October Fair in Munich, when we watch whole oxen being roasted over open fires – memories of our forebears are conjured up. Apart from the excitement that we derive from the sight, I suppose that a little bit of atavism still slumbers in most of us!

Plates, too, were unknown in those days. Bread, baked in large, round, flat pieces, took the place of plates, as is still the case in Arabia. But of course it was unleavened bread, for yeast had not yet been heard of in those parts. In 800 B.C. it seems to have been in use, but when it was first used, and by whom, has not been passed down to us. Bread baking was left to the womenfolk; the men lit the fires. Mixing the dough was left to the women, and the dough-mixer was called *hlæfdige* by the Anglo-Saxons, from which word 'lady' eventually derived.

Salt was rare. One had to be very sparing with it and that is probably why it is still considered to be unlucky to spill salt. But it is essential to men's well being. Even in those days they were aware of this fact, as they are today; but that we need 5 grammes per day is something that has only been known to us for the last twenty years or so.

No, the Germans did not live in need, but tales of the affluent life led in Italy had reached their ears. Tempting descriptions of the sumptuous food and heady wines had been brought to them. On long winter evenings they had dreamt of this much-praised country and, in spring, a few brave men would set out on horseback to cross the dangerous Alps and find out for themselves if these rumours were true. Not all of them returned, but those who did were able to report that everything was finer and better even than they had been led to expect. They were able to describe at first hand what they had seen, heard and tasted.

Cooking evolved from Roman times grew finer and better in the many palaces throughout the country and their traditions survived the Dark Ages so that when Catherine de' Medici married the Duke of Orleans (later King Henry II of France) in 1533 she became the first Medici queen of France and brought her own master cooks with her from Italy. The foundation stone of France's famous cuisine was laid in those days. Slowly but surely they have developed their own tastes, their own recipes, but have based them on those which first came to them from Italy.

But let us once again return to our own forefathers, to the days of Charlemagne who certainly appreciated good food. Above all, he liked fried meat, and especially venison. Boiled meat, known by then, he considered dull and tough. (The chronicler does not mention whether perhaps his teeth were to blame!) Charlemagne spent half his life in the saddle, riding through his vast empire with his chancellor. He himself liked to arrange where they were to stop, eat and spend the night, and had a pronounced preference for monasteries. Here, the centres of interest, besides the Church and religious problems, were the library, the kitchens and the cellars. How much we are indebted to those old cooks and cellar masters for all the good things that appear at table today! There would have been no Champagne, no liqueurs, no spirits, no spiced pastries, nor many other things besides. We must also thank the monasteries – who had to rely on them during Lent – for recipes on how to prepare fish; and most especially, for wines. These they needed for Mass, and hence the monks saw to it that vineyards were planted and wine made. In the days before Christianity the Romans had already brought vines over the Alps and grown them with great success.

Charlemagne advised the monasteries to keep herb gardens. They were to grow parsley, lovage, pimpernel, borage, caraway, chives, garlic and, most important of all, dill, which, chopped finely, is excellent with fish and crabs.

When Charlemagne set out again in the morning, he would take with him in his saddlebags a solid hunk of bacon, salt, spirits and bread for his day's ration, saying as he did so: 'Bread from the plant, salt from the earth, bacon from an animal, and spirits from the realms of bliss – truly a heavenly combination!'

Around the year A.D. 1000 the nobility had developed the habit of serving large baskets full of different kinds of bread at table. Red-cheeked apples, nuts and the different fruits in season were also put out in wooden bowls to tempt the guests. In the course of a banquet enormous dishes with whole roast sucking pigs, saddles of beef or lamb were served. Inside, the meat was more often than not still raw, and each guest sawed his own slices off the joint. The kitchen staff (and the many dogs) looked forward to the bones, with the meat that had been left on them. Wine was drunk out of pewter or earthenware mugs and provided a gaiety which all too often degenerated to a point when people would start throwing rotten apples and pears at one another's heads. These brawls usually took place under the table, by which time the guests would be drunk and truculent.

Charlemagne's successor, Henry (the Saxon king) had to take precautionary measures against the continual Hungarian invasions. He hit on the shrewd idea of building castles throughout the country as strongholds from which the enemy could be repelled. The people who lived in these castles were called *Bürger* (burghers) in contrast to the peasants. The burghers were given their food from the castle kitchens. In German, good simple cooking is still called *gut bürgerlich*.

Besides the burghers, 'knights' came to the fore. They were the king's officers and soldiers-at-arms. In days of peace they held banquets and tourneys. The dish 'poor knights' was first heard of in those days. When the king, on his travels through the country, spent a night at Regensburg, he could look forward to those tasty local sausages served with white and black radishes. All three specialities are still for sale.

The first Crusaders brought perfumes from Arabia, as well as spices, oils and ointments. But they were so expensive that only the very rich could afford them. However, artisans and burghers by then lived better than their forefathers. Their fruit and vegetables were of better quality, cattle and poultry had improved through breeding, and cooking too was far better. Cauldrons were hung over the open fire on pot-hooks, and filled with meat, vegetables and herbs. Those who had a kitchen range put their pans on metal rings over wood fires.

Lentils, peas, green and yellow (haricot) beans, cured and smoked pork and (especially in winter) white beans in a white sauce, were favourite dishes. From a mixture of milk, eggs and flour, many kinds of cake were made. During the cold months, dried fruit was served with cured meat. Pears, apples and plums were put into the oven to dry after the bread was done.

In the well-to-do burgher families (as, for instance, the famous banking Fuggers in Augsburg) food was quite as good as at court, if not better.

Luther is purported to have said: 'If every nation has its own devil, the Germans must have the devil drink'. A contemporary of his answered him: 'Oh, Luther, Rome is the only place you have ever visited; you have not travelled the wide world, otherwise you would have learned that everywhere where man suffers under life he turns to drink'. As late as 1773, a decree was issued by Leipzig aldermen that any woman found drunk was to be brought into the market square with a notice tied across her brow proclaiming her to be 'a drunken mugwife'.

When the Duke of Saxony's wife had given birth to a child her husband gave orders that the master of the cellars was to send five buckets of beer up to her. She was to drink them in childbed, he wrote to her, for while herring and milk are good for the morning after, it is better still to sleep it off.

The discovery of America brought in its wake all kinds of additions to food in western Europe. The seafaring English brought potatoes and tomatoes from South America. Frederick the Great introduced the former to Prussia, but it took a long time before the citizens grew accustomed to them, and today hardly anyone remembers that it was he who brought potatoes into the country.

At the same time the turkey, so popular nowadays in America, came to us as well as coffee and cocoa. Maybe you are familiar with Adolf von Menzel's picture *The Coffee Sniffers*, made as an illustration for a book about the life of Frederick the Great. This depicts an incident that is but part of the turbulent story of coffee. At his castle of Sans-souci the king could not deny himself the pleasure of drinking a cup of coffee, poured from a silver coffee-pot, after meals. He liked to live well and abundantly, in spite of his physicians' warnings.

Voltaire, too, was a connoisseur not only of literary but of culinary matters. His *chef de cuisine* had standing orders to show him the menu for the following day. There were always several courses exquisitely prepared. His favourite was eel pie, of which he invariably ate so much that he could not sleep at night. At table wisdom forsakes even great men, and they too are proved to be but human.

Kant, who lived at about the same time as Frederick the Great, was proud of his establishment. His valet had to prepare simple but select dishes, his favourite being Königsberg mincemeat balls. But the most famed gourmet of his day was

Goethe, in Weimar. For someone who lived in such exalted intellectual spheres, it might have seemed natural that his food should correspond with his daily work, and be simple but really good. He had been used to excellent food at home. His mother was a noted and charming cook who had written a book on cookery, later to be printed. His grandfather came from Lyons, where he had been much sought after as a tailor but had, as a sideline, run a wineshop, which often leads to a good kitchen.

In Strasbourg, Goethe had tasted snails for the first time, cheese from Munster and the pithy wine from Alsace, whose people set much store by natural products such as ham baked in the oven, pigs' tongues cured and boiled in their own juices, and chicken boiled in white wine with fresh mushrooms. Even in his youth, truffled *pâté de foie gras* had been such a favourite of his that he over-ate himself. His friends coined the phrase that 'intelligence drinks, but stupidity gorges'. Goethe taught them better. He proved that one could feast *and* enjoy oneself. Once he had his own *ménage* in Weimar, he always offered hot soup, beef or game with vegetables and, as dessert, pastry or some other sweet with fruit or sugar. After he had been to Italy, he grew fond of fish, boiled or fried, for lunch, with lettuce and fresh herbs or with vegetables. His wife Christine was adept at making the dumplings so popular in Thuringia, and she seems to have been an excellent cook. Only when very many guests were expected was the local Swan Inn called upon to provide a cold buffet, accompanied by pastries from the confectioner. Goethe's many poems on wine were inspired mainly by wines from Franconia, obtained from the Julius Hospital in Würzburg in the pouch-shaped bottles still current today and known as *Bocksbeutel*. His cellars contained the finest French red wines, along with Champagne and noble Rhine wines. His friends knew of his weakness for rare specialties in wine and food and so he was much delighted when one winter his friend Marianne sent him a small tub of caviare from Vienna. He set great store by elegant table decoration and fine clothes, as well as good food, as we know from a letter written by Major von Marwitz, describing Goethe as a tall, handsome man, invariably clad in embroidered court dress, his hair powdered and worn in a hair bag, and at his side a dress sword worthy of his standing.

Prince Louis Ferdinand (who was killed at the Battle of Jena) wrote of Goethe 'I have now really met Goethe. He came home with me late last night and sat by my bed. We drank Champagne and punch and the conversation was most enjoyable'.

Goethe was capable of drinking enormously, while the close relationship between his work and his food is illustrated by the following lines from his pen:
'The ship in which we sail is laden with colourful
birds whose bright tails hang overboard and glitter
in the sunlight. They are not only beautiful, but
beautiful to eat'.

The poet Grillparzer, whom he often invited to table, said 'Goethe has occasionally written, but never eaten, anything of inferior quality'.

About 1800, four-fifths of the German population consisted of peasants. Their own pigs were naturally the mainstay of their diet. Bread and fruit, and spirits and cider to drink, were served with the meat. Towards the end of the century, potatoes were such a regular item that smoke coming from a cottage chimney at night was an almost certain sign that, inside, potatoes, bacon and onions were being fried.

At the Prussian court of William I and Frederick III there were two famous French chefs, Bernard and Dubois. Each compiled, in French, a fine book on cooking. They both handed down the recipes which they and their colleagues had used at court. Still later Bismarck, whose preference for good and plentiful food was always known, became a connoisseur. His home town always delighted him by sending plovers' eggs for his birthday in April, and he was capable of eating dozens at a sitting. But, as he not only ate but also drank too much, his physicians often felt moved to reprove and to warn him.

I could tell you a host of other stories, [continued the old Scripture master,] but your mothers will be waiting at home to give you lunch and I can imagine how hungry you must be and how glad to leave the schoolroom.

At this juncture, we schoolchildren would scamper home to lunch, and he would stroll away to his own. The point at which he ended his history should, however, perhaps be developed just a little further and brought down to days which, happily, he did not live to see.

To return briefly to the last century: simple folk lived quite well in those days and were able to afford far more than their forefathers. In fact, a certain standard of living had been reached.

At Court, under William II, whose mother was a daughter of Queen Victoria, English customs had taken root. Breakfast was therefore the main meal of the day. The Kaiser enjoyed it enormously and was kept going very well till lunch at which he ate very little, as guests found to their cost. They never had enough to eat and consequently would be seen afterwards in *Weinstuben*. (According to Count August Eulenberg, the then controller of the royal household, no alcohol was served at luncheon.)

At the royal palace in Berlin, cooks and servants worked under difficulties before the building was altered. The kitchens were in one wing, the banqueting halls in another. All the food had to be carried across the courtyard and warmed up again before serving, which of course detracted from its quality. A menu served at court in 1893 consisted of the following courses:

Oysters as hors d'oeuvre
Princess soup
Carp in Olives
Sirloin of Lamb with Vegetables
Lobster Soufflé

Grouse in Aspic
Venison with Fruit and Lettuce
Artichokes with Rice
Hot Chocolate Dessert
Ice Cream - Cheese Straws

The navy was highly esteemed by William II, who often invited a certain much-honoured admiral to table. The admiral, however, was extremely annoyed that the waiters tended to remove his plate long before he had finished his food, merely because the Kaiser had finished his. One day he was on the *qui vive*. The Kaiser was just going to say something when the waiter tried to take the admiral's plate. The latter rapped him over the knuckles with his knife and said, 'Be off with you'. The Kaiser was greatly amused.

Court habits and court tastes began to find their way into the hotels. In Berlin's famous Unter den Linden, Adlon had founded the luxury hotel which was to become world-famous. It was here that Escoffier invented his *sauce diable*. Many cooks who later became famous were trained at the Adlon. Crowned heads, aristocrats, artists and tycoons, all dined at the Adlon in the white and gold dining rooms.

At the same time, a whole series of first-class inns (*Weinstuben*) sprang into existence in Berlin and became famous for their excellent food: Borchardt, Hörcher, Walterspiel, to mention but a few.

During the inflation in Germany, kitchens suffered too. Not until Hitler came were banquets in vogue again. Hitler, like so many other fanatics, was a vegetarian. His favourite meal consisted of an omelette with rice or boiled potatoes; he drank little or nothing at all. On the other hand, it was generally known that Göring gave enormous banquets at Karinhall. The best hotels had to fly out cooks bearing specially prepared dishes with which to regale him, his family and his guests. When the annual exhibition was opened in Munich's Museum for German Art, a cold buffet was served which was without equal in the whole of Europe. The long tables, covered with white cloths and strewn with rose petals, looked like satin cushions. On these stood the different cold dishes, each more beautifully decorated than the last.

Goebbels, too, was very fond of pomp and magnificence, although he was inclined to be modest, but by this time, the war had begun, many of us had exchanged the schoolroom for the barracks, and had to make do with the simplest fare. As long as we were served a warm meal and a slice of bread to go with it, we were content.

I never saw my favourite master again, but since he used to start with the Greeks, I would like to end my description of him with a phrase coined by Democritus. 'Religion is a prism, from whose seven colours each can choose the one he likes best. All of them, however, derive from a single ray of sunshine'.

My readers will no doubt be able to remember how we fared after the war as far as eating and drinking went; after the all-too-meagre rations, bakers', butchers' and grocers' shops and shop windows slowly but surely started to fill up again and all of us were only too willing to turn to all these good things. A general affluence developed and came to the point where the most exotic and expensive delicacies from all over the world were being imported. But saturation set in. It was Wilhelm Busch who wrote 'Nothing is harder to bear than a series of good days'. And so today's gourmet has turned back to simplicity in cooking - natural, normal and healthy food.

Let one and all eat and enjoy what suits and pleases them; and, like my Scripture master, let them gratefully enjoy all God's good gifts, including food and drink.

HISTORICAL RECIPES

STUFFED CABBAGE CHARLEMAGNE (*Kräuterroulade Karl der Grosse*)

Place leaves of white cabbage, without any of the stem, upon a board well sprinkled with salt and caraway seed so that for each *roulade* three of four leaves overlap. Sprinkle salt and caraway on top. Heap chopped parsley, chives and dill with 3 tablespoonfuls of chopped boiled onion and bacon on top. Place on each portion 5 oz. of mince (half pork, half beef) seasoned with salt, pepper, nutmeg, the whole to be blended with beaten egg and shaped like a cigar. Close the cabbage leaves round the meat so as to form a solid *roulade*. Melt lard in a flattish pan, scatter over it rounds of carrot, onion, garlic and celery and on them lay the *roulades* packed closely together. Pour on ¾ pint (2 cups) of meat stock and place on each *roulade* a thin slice of lean bacon. Cover and simmer for about 30 minutes. Take out the *roulades* and keep them hot. Thicken the sauce a little with cornflour, stir in some fresh cream cheese and after adding more seasoning, cover the *roulades* with the sauce, sprinkling over the top fresh chopped herbs including dill, parsley, chives and borage. Serve with steamed potatoes and accompany with a light white wine.

COLD CUTLETS OF WILD BOAR CHARLEMAGNE
(*Wildschweinschnitzel Kalt Karl der Grosse*)
Cut slices weighing 7 oz. from a well-hung leg. Season with salt and pepper and sprinkle with crushed juniper berries. Seal both sides by frying quickly in hot fat, then place in a flat pan and cover with a mixture of meat stock and red wine. Add chopped bacon, onion, a bay leaf and a clove, cover and simmer till the meat is tender. Remove the cover, and pour in 4 tablespoonfuls of brandy per cutlet; taste and set aside to cool. The sauce will solidify and produce one cutlet in aspic for each person.

Serve with roast potatoes and cranberries. Drink red wine with it.

COLD EEL PIE FREDERICK THE GREAT (*Aalpastete kalt Friederich der Grosse*)
Take 4 lb. of eel, boned and skinned, and cut into slices; 1 lb. of fresh mushrooms, sliced; 10 oz. of boiled shallots finely chopped; 2 tablespoonfuls of chopped dill, 1 of chopped parsley; salt and lemon juice.

For the fish stuffing: 2 lb. of pike, boned, skinned and passed through a fine sieve; 5 eggs; about 5 oz. of white bread; 6 tablespoonfuls of brandy; 3 oz. of onions, the same of chopped bacon, both boiled. Stir everything together, add 5 tablespoonfuls of cream, season with salt, pepper and nutmeg.

Line a piedish with pastry and spread the fish stuffing over the sides and the base. Fill with alternate layers of eel and mushrooms topped with fish stuffing until the dish is almost full. The top layer of all should be stuffing. Make sure that the pastry cover to the pie is made fast to the edge of the dish. Decorate the top with a little of the pastry and make two holes so the steam can escape.

Bake for about 35 minutes. Eat cold. Drink a powerful white wine with it.

CHICKEN FREDERICK THE GREAT (*Poulet Provençal Friederich der Grosse*)
For two people cut an oven-ready chicken into eight pieces; bind a strip of lean bacon round each piece. Sprinkle with salt and paprika. Dip in flour and fry quickly in very hot olive oil.

In a casserole simmer 10 tablespoonfuls chopped onion, 10 table-spoonfuls of chopped tomato, 3 crushed cloves of garlic in a little oil. Season, place the pieces of lightly fried chicken on top, cover with white wine and cook with the lid on for 30 minutes in a moderate oven. Remove the pieces of chicken and keep them hot, reduce and thicken the sauce a little, stir in some fresh cream cheese, bring to the boil and pour over the chicken. Accompany it by rice and a stout red wine.

STEWED PARTRIDGE GOETHE (*Rebhuhn Goethe*)

Wrap one oven-ready partridge per person in thin strips of bacon, lightly salted, and quickly brown them in a frying pan. When they have coloured, fit them tightly together in a casserole.

Spread over them 1 lb. chopped mushrooms, 4 fl. oz. ($\frac{1}{2}$ cup) dry white wine, 3 oz. bacon cut up small and 2 oz. finely chopped onions. Add 5 crushed juniper berries and 8 fl. oz. (1 cup) meat stock. Cook in the oven for 40 minutes. As soon as the partridges are ready, remove them and keep them hot. Boil up the mushroom sauce again, adding 4 tablespoonfuls brandy and 4 tablespoonfuls sour cream. Stir; pour over the partridges.

Serve with creamed potatoes and red wine.

PLOVERS' EGGS BISMARCK (*Kiebitzeier Fürst Bismarck*)

Plovers' eggs should be boiled for 10 minutes and served in their shells because of their decorative markings. Wash a handful of morels, cut them into little pieces and fry them with finely chopped onion. After 5 minutes stir in salt, lemon juice and sour cream.

Serve with new potatoes or buttered rice, and drink white wine with it.

SPARE RIB OF PORK AND SPRING VEGETABLES BISMARCK (*Schweinenackensteak in Junggemüse Bismarck*)

For four people, take four sections of spare rib each weighing 7 oz.; salt and pepper lightly, colour quickly in a hot frying pan and place the meat on a bed of vegetables in an ovenproof casserole. Use the following vegetables: 9 oz. savoy cabbage, 7 oz. sliced carrots, 7 oz. sliced potato; lightly salt everything and add about 2 oz. chopped fried bacon. Cover with 8 fl. oz. (1 cup) white wine and put the dish, covered, into a slow oven for 40 minutes. When ready sprinkle chopped parsley over all. Drink white wine with it.

Cookery in Berlin

'Food tastes so good in Berlin'. 'A well-roasted goose is a fine gift of God!' Or so they say in Berlin. Even if this particular roast was no discovery of the Berliners, at least the best saying about it was coined here.

In Berlin, as in other places, they prefer to cook what they like best. These sometimes extremely pungent dishes are suited to the climate of North Germany. There are strongly flavoured soups, such as pea soup with bacon, or haricot beans with pork, and, as is to be expected in a region close to the sea, eel and other fish provide a welcome variation in the diet. The rich soil of the neighbourhood provides sturdy asparagus, crisp beans, and ivory white cauliflowers. Goethe made famous the small Teltower turnips, which he received on one occasion from his friend Zelter. From the North Sea and the Baltic freshly caught fish arrive in a very short time, packed in ice and carried by express train to the market . . . above all herrings. It does not surprise me at all that it was a smart Berlin cook who first prepared piquant rollmops.

Several gastronomic discoveries which have achieved world-renown are named after Berlin butchers, pastry-cooks and hostelries.

Master Kassel is supposed to have discovered the dish named 'Kassler' after him – pickled, smoked pork cutlets – and an inventive pastry-cook devised *Baumkuchen*, cakes in the shape of a pyramid or tree-trunk. Even Berliners, whom people are ready to call '*Schnauze mit Herz*', cut themselves thin slices of this cake and eat it just as it is; they do not cut it lengthways as evil Bavarian tongues have humorously maintained. The latter too have given rise to the legend that gigantic birch trees grow in Berlin in order to provide mouth-organs.

Doughnuts or 'Berliners' were the invention of another genius. These delicate balls are cooked in hot fat until golden brown but white at the centre. An old master of his trade revealed to me the secret of success: they should be cooked in horse fat.

Finally a landlord, by the name of Scholz, discovered *Bockwurst* (a beef sausage for boiling). Like many inhabitants of Berlin he probably came from Silesia. With rucksacks on their backs these Silesians arrived at the 'Catholic Station', as the Silesian Station was formerly called, and brought a host of good recipes with them, such as *Mohnspielen*, carp in gingerbread sauce, and Viennese sausage in raisin sauce. It is hard to decide which dish has acquired the greatest following, but it is certain that leg of pork with pickled cabbage and purée of peas should head the list. The fact that pickling is so popular with Berliners is attributed to old Fritz (Frederick the Great). He ordered his citizens to buy so much salt that they could not possibly use it all. So they came to preserve pork, vegetables and gherkins in salt. And Berliners have made a proverb out of it: 'Pickled gherkins are also a dessert'.

As regards wine, a sweetish, light one is preferred, as everywhere in the North. It agrees with people better.

Beer and clear *Schnaps* are the usual accompaniment for most favourite dishes. On this account one can best get to know these dishes in large restaurants, where beer is served.

The excellent air and water of Berlin contribute to the mild beer. Drawn from the barrel straight into the glass, it is called *Molle*.

The Berlin 'white' beer is renowned, a beer that foams on top in a bowl-shaped glass. *Mit Schuss* indicates with a dash of raspberry syrup. A most refreshing drink on a hot day.

Mit Strippe indicates either with brandy or with Kümmel. *Schnaps* plays an important role in Berlin.

People say that when anyone sells anything, he '*verkümmelt*' it, i.e. he quickly spends the proceeds of his sale on Kümmel.

In every bar there is bottled Kurfürstlicher Magenbitter, a bitter cordial for the stomach. Briefly, this is what is told about it. When an inexperienced customer orders a cordial, the landlord pours out a large one, a double. The customer says that he only wanted a small one. 'Sir', says the land-lord, 'have you ever heard of a *small* Kurfürst?'

Whoever eats in Berlin with Berliners, shares their favourite dishes and beer, and laughs heartily with them, will learn more about them than ever he could from books.

SOUP

PEA SOUP WITH BACON (*Löffelerbsen mit Speck*)

1 lb. dried split peas
3 tablespoons (3¾) fat
1 each carrot, onion and
  leek, sliced
1 stick celery, chopped
3 pints (3¾) boiling
  seasoned meat stock
½ lb. fat bacon, diced
1 small onion, diced
marjoram or thyme

Soak the peas overnight in plenty of cold water to let them swell. In the morning drain them in a colander and rinse well. Melt the fat in a large saucepan, add the vegetables and cook gently, without water, for 10 minutes. Add the peas, cover with the meat stock and allow to simmer until the vegetables are tender. Brown the bacon in another pan; as the fat runs, add the diced onion. When this is brown, stir it into the soup. Add either marjoram or thyme to taste. Stir but do not sieve it. Serve with sliced, hard German sausage (Drink: beer)

PEA SOUP WITH PIGS' EARS (*Erbsensuppe mit Schweinsohren*)

Cook 4 fresh or pickled pigs' ears in the Pea Soup (above). When tender, take the ears from the pan and cut into thin slices. Return these to the soup. If preferred, the soup may be passed through a sieve or put into a liquidizer and the sliced pigs' ears returned as a garnish.

Do you know the legend about the origin of this soup? Willibald Alexis recounts it in his renowned novel *Der Wehrwolf*.

The Emperor Charles IV once came to a monastery, tired and ravenously hungry from hunting, and demanded food for himself and his followers. There was, however, not a morsel of meat in the house and the Abbot re-fused to kill his pigs as they represented his winter provisions. What then should the cook do? When the peas were tender in the pot, and he was diligently stirring the soup and sprinkling in pepper by the handful, inspiration came to him and he served a soup at table in which small pieces of meat were floating, as sweet and tender as cream. 'What meat is that then?' asked the Emperor, and went on, 'It tastes like pork'. Then the Abbot demanded: 'Cook, have you deceived me?' But he answered, 'Count the pigs and you will see that none is missing'. The Abbot and his guests went with all haste to the pigsty, and behold, all the pigs were there . . . only they no longer had their ears. Until that time, pigs' ears had been thrown on the rubbish heap. Brother Kagelwind was thus a great inventor – only now the pigs are slaughtered first. (Drink: beer)

FISH

EEL IN A GREEN SAUCE (*Aal grün*)

2 lb. eel, cut in 2 in. lengths
1 small onion, chopped
1 pint (1¼) fish stock
½ pint (1¼ cups) white wine
1 oz. (2 tablespoons) butter
1 bunch parsley, chopped
1 tablespoon (1¼) each of chopped chervil, chives, dill, spinach and sorrel
1 oz. (4 tablespoons) flour
4 tablespoons (5) sour cream

Put the eel into a pan with the onion, stock and wine, bring to the boil, lower the heat and cook until tender. Heat the butter in a saucepan, add the herbs, sprinkle with flour and stir to keep the mixture smooth. Take the eel from the stock and keep hot. Reheat the liquid, then gradually pour this over the butter and herb mixture. Stirring all the time, bring the sauce to the boil. Add the sour cream and pour the hot sauce over the eel, making sure the pieces are covered. Serve with boiled potatoes, a gherkin salad, sour cream and chopped dill as a garnish. (Drink: white wine)

HERRINGS WITH FRENCH BEANS (*Matjes Heringe mit grünen Bohnen*)

fresh herring fillets
cooked French beans
butter
salt, grated nutmeg
chopped hard-boiled eggs
finely chopped parsley

The beans should be cooked, tossed in butter and flavoured with salt and nutmeg. Arrange a layer of eggs on a platter and cover with the herrings. Serve with the beans, sprinkled with parsley. (Drink: beer)

JELLIED EEL (*Aal in Gelee*)

2 lb. eel, cut in 2 in. lengths, skinned
Stock:
3 pints (3¾) cold water
½ pint (1¼ cups) herb vinegar
1 onion stuck with 2 cloves
1 bay leaf
1 medium-sized carrot, sliced
1 small leek, sliced
Aspic:
3 egg whites
4 tablespoons (5) cold water
2 envelopes gelatine, dissolved in water

Combine the stock ingredients and cook for 10 minutes. Add the eel, bring once to the boil, lower the heat, continue cooking for 20 minutes or until it is tender. Take out the eel and put aside to cool. Sieve the stock, skim off the fat, also put aside to cool. Beat the egg whites in a pan with the cold water. Add 2 cups (2½) of the stock and cook over a low heat. Stir the gelatine into the stock, continue stirring until the egg white sets. Strain the aspic through a cloth and pour enough into the bottom of a shallow dish to make a layer about ½ in. deep. Put this in a cold place to set. Arrange the eel on top and cover with the rest of the aspic. Let this set. Serve with boiled potatoes. (Drink: beer or *Schnaps*)

ROLLMOPS (*Rollmöpse*)

8 salt herring fillets
2 tablespoons (2½) German mustard
2 gherkins, sliced
pinch mustard seeds
1 onion, thinly sliced
Marinade:
1 cup (1¼) mild vinegar
1 cup (1¼) water
1 small onion, sliced
sugar to taste
1 bay leaf
3 cloves
4 allspice corns
1 teaspoon (1¼) German mustard
5 white peppercorns

Combine all the marinade ingredients, bring to the boil, strain and leave until cold. Lay the herring fillets skin downwards on a board and spread each fillet with the remaining ingredients. Roll each one up and fasten with toothpicks. Lay them in a shallow bowl and cover with the cold marinade. Leave for a few days in a cool place. Serve with boiled potatoes in their jackets.
Variation: Mix sour cream with soft herring roes, put through a sieve and add cream cheese or mayonnaise. Spread this mixture over the herring fillets and roll up.
(Drink: beer)

BERLIN EELS (*Aal Berliner Art*)

2 lb. eel, cleaned, skinned
  and salted, cut in 2 in.
  lengths
2 pints (2½) pale ale
1 cup (1¼) white wine
1 onion stuck with 2 cloves
1 bay leaf
½ lb. black bread, crumbled
1 tablespoon (1¼) lemon
  juice

Put the beer and wine into a pan, add the onion, bay leaf, bread and lemon juice. Cook for 10 minutes over a moderate heat, add the eel and cook until tender. Leave it in the sauce for 20 minutes, keeping it warm. Take out the eel, arrange on a dish, sieve the sauce and pour it over the eel. Serve with boiled potatoes.

(Drink: beer)

MEAT

BRISKET OF BEEF WITH HORSERADISH SAUCE
(*Rinderbrust mit Brühkartoffeln und Meerettichsauce*)

Cook 2 lb. brisket of beef in plenty of water with 1 stick celery, 2 carrots, 1 leek and onion, 2 cloves and parsley to taste. Cook until just tender. Slice thinly and serve with horseradish sauce and boiled potatoes, sprinkled with parsley.

Horseradish sauce:

2 cups (2½) white sauce
4 tablespoons (5) grated
  horseradish
2 tablespoons (2½) cream
juice 1 lemon
pinch salt and sugar
1 oz. (2 tablespoons) butter
a little diced carrot, celery
  and leek
2 lb. potatoes, peeled
finely chopped parsley

The sauce should be made with half milk and half meat stock. While it is still hot, beat in the horseradish, cream, lemon juice, salt and sugar. Keep hot but do not cook any further (to keep it hot, place in a pan of hot water).

Heat the butter and gently fry the carrot, celery and leek. Add the potatoes and cover with stock from the meat. Cook until soft but not broken. Drain and sprinkle with parsley.

If a lighter, milder sauce is preferred, 4 tablespoons (5) of stiffly whipped cream may be added to the sauce just before serving.

(Drink: red wine)

LEG OF PORK WITH SAUERKRAUT AND PURÉE OF PEAS (*Eisbein mit Sauerkraut und Erbspüree*)

2 lb. knuckle half leg of pork

2 lb. sauerkraut

1 lb. yellow peas, whole or split

6 peppercorns

1 onion stuck with cloves

1 bay leaf

1–2 onions, quartered

¼ lb. fat bacon, diced

1 small onion, finely diced

Soak the peas overnight in cold water. Put the meat with plenty of cold water in a pan, add peppercorns, cloved onion and bay leaf. Cover and cook gently for 1½ hours. Take from the pan. Keep hot. Add the *sauerkraut* to the pan and continue cooking another hour. Rinse the peas, cover with water, add the quartered onions, cook until tender. Rub through a sieve. Fry the bacon, add the diced onion and cook until golden. Serve the meat surrounded by the *sauerkraut*, and the purée separately, sprinkled with fried bacon and onion.

(Drink: beer)

ASPIC CUTLETS AND ROAST POTATOES (*Sülzkoteletten mit Bratkartoffeln*)

Cook 6 pork cutlets in plenty of water with 2 calves' feet, mixed soup vegetables, salt and pepper. Cool the meat in its own liquid. Cut the pork flesh into neat pieces, discarding excess fat and bones. Strain the stock.

2 pints (2½) stock from cutlets

¼ cup (⅓) each white wine and vinegar

salt, pepper

2 envelopes gelatine

1 egg white

Garnish:

sliced hard-boiled egg

sliced carrots and gherkins

Cook the stock over a low heat, add wine and vinegar and season well. Dissolve the gelatine in cold water, add with the egg white to the stock. Whisk well. When the egg white sets, pour the liquid through a fine cloth. Rinse a shallow mould in cold water. Cover the base with half the aspic and set in a cold place. Lay the garnish on top, add the meat and the rest of the aspic and leave to set. Hold the mould under warm water and turn out on to a plate.

Serve with roast potatoes.

(Drink: beer and *Schnaps*)

SWEETS

BERLIN DOUGHNUTS (*'Berliners'*)

1 lb. (4 cups) flour
1 oz. (1½ cakes) yeast
3 oz. (scant ½ cup) sugar
½ cup (⅔) sugar
pinch of salt
grated rind 1 lemon
3 eggs
3 oz. (6 tablespoons)
   melted butter
fat for deep frying
plum or apricot jam
icing (confectioners') sugar

Sieve the flour into a bowl and make a well in the middle. Cream the yeast with 1 tablespoon (1¼) of sugar and milk. Pour this into the well and gently cover it with flour. Cover and leave in a warm place for about 20 minutes or until it has doubled its bulk. Add sugar, salt, lemon rind and eggs. Work the dough and add the butter. Knead the dough and continue working until bubbles appear and the dough leaves the sides of the bowl. Cover and leave again to prove, about another 1 hour.

Roll the dough into an even sausage, cut it into 20–25 pieces and roll each piece into a ball. Leave the balls to prove on a lightly floured board covered with a cloth. When they are spongy, fry them in deep hot fat in a deep small pan. When they are a golden brown on one side, turn them and brown on the other side. Drain the doughnuts on absorbent paper. As soon as it is possible to handle, squirt a blob of jam (using a forcing bag) into the centre of each doughnut. Toss the doughnuts into icing sugar or dip into a sugar glaze. If using the latter, drain before serving.

POOR KNIGHTS (*Arme Ritter*)

Soak 8 slices of thick white crustless bread in milk, then dip into beaten egg yolk, toss in breadcrumbs and fry until a golden brown in a little fat. Sprinkle with cinnamon sugar (i.e. powdered cinnamon mixed with sugar) and spread with apple purée. Serve with apple purée or stewed fruit.

Or :

Dip slices of crustless white bread in pancake batter, drain and fry.

Cookery in
North and East Germany

On the coasts of the North Sea and the Baltic it is the fruits of the sea which determine the character of the cooking. No one prepares fish better than the inhabitants of these shores. As a young cook, I learnt the preparation of fish in Westerland auf Sylt. I enjoyed it then and I enjoy it even more today, for what is more delicious than fresh fish? In the evening, after the netting, Hinrichs the fisherman would bring us his catch of turbot, sole, plaice and other fish. They smelt of seaweed, salt water and sea air. I had to behead and bone the fish, setting aside the fillets and pieces and washing them clean in cold water. Heads, tails and fins were washed separately and set aside for the making of a highly spiced fish stock from which sauces and soups would be derived. Let us have no nonsense about *bouillabaisse* being the only fish soup in the world. It is certainly splendid, but our own German fish soup is its equal. When you have tried the recipe we will discuss the subject further!

Our fish cook saw to it that the powerful stock cooked at a fast boil on the stove. Into it he would throw an onion stuck with cloves, parsley stems and tops, cloves of garlic and celery roots, along with a lot of salt, which sea fish require. Hinrichs the fisherman once told me over a stiff grog that in the days when he had 'gone deep sea' in larger vessels, the cook used to boil the fish in sea water, and that they tasted best of all that way. Turbot we used to lay in highly aromatic water, so that it was covered. We would bring the water to the boil just once, then withdraw the pan from the fire and let the fish stand for 20 minutes. Turbot should be firm and its white flesh should have some bite to it. A linen napkin would be placed on a silver dish and the fish laid on top, decorated with sprigs of parsley and quarters of lemon. As garnish we served steamed potatoes with drawn butter and a sprinkling of chopped parsley. But I am forgetting something, a speciality of our master: *Reine claudes*. When I first saw this addition I could not imagine what the combination would taste like, but once I had experienced it, I was enchanted. Plaice were fried in odds and ends of bacon fat and served with a moist potato salad. Soles were served *meunière*, with chopped parsley, lemon and Worcester sauce. At the last minute frothing melted butter would be added and the whole made into an incomparable dish.

Every morning the postman would deliver baskets of live Heligoland lobsters. They would be displayed to the guests, still alive, on a large dish. Everyone could choose his own. On a small lobster menu were listed the different ways in which they could be served. Boiled with melted butter, cold with mayonnaise, *à l'Américaine*, or grilled. On Sundays we used to serve Heligoland lobster soup with asparagus tips, *fines herbes* and lots of well-seasoned fresh lobster meat.

From List, on the northern tip of the island of Sylt, we obtained fresh fiscal oysters ('fiscal' because the oyster beds were managed by a government department). Admittedly, they were a little smaller than the famous Linfjord oysters, but they tasted just as good.

So far, I have sung the praises of North Sea fish, but I must not forget that fish from the Baltic are as good – or better, in many knowledgeable opinions. The reasons for this lie in the salt content and the temperature of the water. The whole coastline abounds in fish, and in every village delicacies are prepared from recipes handed down and perfected over the centuries.

Meat, however, is not neglected hereabouts. The broad meadows, with their wiry grasses over which the sea wind blows, develop healthy cattle. Veal, particularly, compares in quality with the best Dutch and Danish. I well remember that in our hotel kitchens we used to receive ninety-pound legs of veal. Cut up, the joints would lie impeccably carved, on fresh cloths in the cool room, all pink and extremely appetizing. The *Schnitzel* could not be squeezed into the pan like laundry into a basket. On the contrary, they seemed to swell up like yeast dumplings, and it was a pleasure to fry them.

One fine day when we had worked well in the kitchen and the chef was pleased with us, he invited us on an afternoon's excursion by bus. He enjoyed pointing out to us the beauties of the island and introduced us, in a tavern, to Tea Punch. On the bar stood little cups and saucers as if ready to have coffee poured into them. For three marks in those days one could order some twenty cups. Hot tea was stood on the bar in a handsome blue teapot, and beside it a bowl of coffee crystals and a full bottle of *Kümmel*. First we all had to put a few crystals into the cup, then the tea was poured over them and one could hear the crystals cracking as they dissolved in the heat. Then the cup was topped up with *Kümmelschnaps* (the *eau de vie*, not the sweet liqueur). Anyone who filled his cup to the brim was advised to tie a bootlace round the top so that nothing would be wasted. Even so, he would have to leave the cup on the bar, stoop down and suck some up. Only then could he lift the cup safely to his lips. In this way we would consume five or six little cups, which meant our boss had to pay for five or six rounds of the punch, after which everyone went home and carried on working more merrily than ever!

Here in the north, grog is a great drink. To make it one uses Flensburg or Bremen rum, and still more rum, with as little hot water as possible and some sugar. Let no one think of grog as an exclusively winter drink, for it tastes fine in summer too. Naturally, beer is drunk as well. Here, as everywhere else in Germany, life would be unthinkable without it. Wine is appreciated too, and especially red wine. Burgundy and Bordeaux have been shipped since medieval times to Bremen and Lübeck to mature there in the shippers' cellars. There are many cellarmasters and *sommeliers* to look after these vintages, and at table of an evening you may see many an old gentleman whose nose bears witness to his devotion to red wine.

HAMBURG

Hamburgers are gastronomically very spoiled. They know how to judge the freshness of a fish. People say that they buy their *Matjes* herrings direct from Altona since by doing so they are an hour fresher than in Hamburg. When they are in the neighbourhood of the fishing harbour, they will go to Selmer's fish restaurant and enjoy a plaice, a turbot or one of the other countless dishes that are to be had there. They prepare a fish soup there which belongs by right in any Golden Book of cookery, and if anyone is prejudiced against salt-water fish, then let him eat there. He will undergo the same sort of experience that St Paul did on the road to Damascus. But we cannot confine our praises to salt-water fish alone. Tench and carp from Schleswig-Holstein and eels from Finkenward are equally tasty delicacies.

The Hamburgers are not fond of composite dishes, nor of offal, but prefer straightforward cooking. Not for them the kidneys, lungs, hearts, sweetbreads or other innards. Their prejudices, however, are mostly due to incorrect preparation of the dishes, and I know Hamburgers who have been delighted with tripe in Stuttgart and pickled lung in Munich.

This part of Germany is famous for its poultry, and for its ducks in particular. The quality of veal and beef is excellent too. Strangers to Hamburg may be interested to know that in some of the greatest restaurants women chefs stand at the stove and grill the tender and juicy rump steaks and lamb cutlets. In such an international city there is of course no lack of good foreign restaurants offering the specialities of their various countries. Seamen, however, after many months away from their home port, prefer to eat a good dish of salted pig's trotters with sour cabbage. Hamburg is the home port of the Hamburg-American Shipping Line whose passengers are spoiled by a really exceptional cuisine and service. A young cook who wishes to learn more of his art and to see the world at the same time could hardly do better than sign on as a cook at sea. Not for nothing is Hamburg called 'the gateway to the world'.

BREMEN

Every visitor to Bremen should call in on the Ratskeller with its wonderful murals by Slevogt. They are so impressive that no reproduction can convey them and words can only attempt their description. They have served as models for many a German Ratskeller and even for American and Canadian versions.

In the banqueting hall of the old Rathaus or City Hall they hold a celebrated banquet every year, dating back to the thirteenth century and called the *Schaffermahlzeit*, or Artisans' Banquet. The participants may come and go, but the ceremonial has not changed since the Middle Ages. It forms, in a sense, an introduction to Bremen cookery. The sequence of dishes has hardly altered over the centuries. Granted that in the leaner times of 1947 they were reduced to Lobscouse or Seaman's Hotpot (*Seemanngericht Labskaus*). The traditional menu is as follows:

Bremen chicken soup

Stockfisch, drawn butter, steamed potatoes

Cabbage, sausage, smoked meat, chestnuts, fried potatoes

Roast veal, celery salad, katharine plums, steamed apples

Riga flounder, sardines, sausage, tongue

Cheese, hard and soft

Fruit

Coffee

The Bremen chicken soup is a cream soup with a little butter added into which crabmeat has been pounded, imparting a slightly rosy hue and a piquant flavour.

The *Stockfisch* is dried Norwegian cod. *Pinkel*, the sausage in the third course, is an oatmeal sausage and the smoked meat is beef. The veal is a back-roast, boned to facilitate carving. Katharine plums are a large Argentine species, which are lightly stewed, first alone to soften them, then with lemon peel and a stick of cinnamon. They are served cold, like the apples.

With the coffee the banquet is concluded. Ladies are never admitted but sit together in a neighbouring room where an orchestra plays dance music. The first dance is a formal one, opened by the wife of the senior Artisan and the Head Chef. Everyone present claps as a way of expressing their thanks to everyone concerned in the preparation of this magnificent occasion.

We should not leave Bremen without a mention of the Norddeutsche-Lloyd Shipping Line, whose home port it is. The kitchens of the line are renowned, and the sea-going chefs are familiar with delicacies from the four corners of the world. They and their assistants look after passengers so thoughtfully that a passage on a Lloyd vessel is not only restorative and sociable, but also a culinary experience.

Should any of my readers visit North Germany, they are sure to make more discoveries of their own and I hope will forgive me for any omissions I may have made. The very wealth of material prevents me from describing all the fascinating contents of the country's kitchens and cellars. I should be happy, however, to feel that I have given a brief survey of this good regional cuisine and I hope the recipes will be successful and enjoyable.

SOUP

BREMEN EEL SOUP (*Bremer Aalsuppe*)
Preparation as for Hamburg eel soup. The only difference is in the presentation. The soup is eaten first and the pieces of eel and the dumplings are served separately.
(Drink: beer)

HAMBURG EEL SOUP (*Hamburger Aalsuppe*)

1¾ lb. fresh eel
herb vinegar
6 pints (7½) meat stock
1 ham bone
½ lb. each chopped celery, carrots, onions, hamburg parsley
½ lb. fresh green peas
¾ lb. small pears
½ lb. cooking plums
bouquet garni
pinch of sugar

Wash and skin the eel and cut into 2 in. lengths. Put into a pan with a little salt water and herb vinegar and bring once to the boil. Lower the heat and simmer until tender. Take out the pieces of eel. Cook the remaining ingredients in the meat stock until tender. Remove the ham bone, return the pieces of eel to the pan and continue cooking gently until reheated. Serve with tiny dumplings.
(Drink: beer)

HANOVER BARLEY SOUP (*Hannöversche Gerstensuppe*)

1½ oz. (3 tablespoons) fat
½ lb. fat bacon, diced
¾ lb. mixed diced carrots, leeks, onions, celery
3 pints (3¾) meat stock
8 oz. (1 cup) barley, soaked in water
2–3 cooked sliced potatoes
5 slices black pudding
finely chopped parsley

Heat the fat, add the bacon and vegetables and brown. Add the meat stock. Bring to the boil. Drain the barley and add to the boiling stock. Cook over a moderate heat until the soup is thick and crumbly, add the potatoes and black pudding; sprinkle with parsley and serve.
(Drink: beer)

HUSUM CRAB SOUP (*Husumer Krabbensuppe*)

1 lb. fresh crabmeat
1 oz. (2 tablespoons) butter
1 onion, diced
3 pints (3¾) hot meat stock
1 tablespoon (1¼) cornflour (cornstarch)
½ cup (⅔) sour cream
1 tablespoon (1¼) lemon juice
½ cup (⅔) white wine
finely chopped parsley
croûtons

Heat the butter and gently fry the onion until soft but not brown. Add the crabmeat and continue frying for a few minutes. Stir in the stock. Bring to a gentle boil. Mix the cornflour to a thin paste with water, add this to the boiling stock. Add cream. Stir until the soup thickens, add the lemon juice and wine. Bring again to the boil, sprinkle with parsley. Serve with croûtons. As a variation the soup can be flavoured with about ½ cup (⅔) of mayonnaise.
(Drink: dry white wine)

KÖNIGSBERG SOUP (*Königsberger Fleck*)

1 lb. finely chopped ox stomach
5 pints (6¼) meat stock
½ lb. leeks, sliced
1 stick celery, chopped
salt, peppercorns to taste
1 bay leaf
finely chopped marjoram

Cook the ox stomach in the stock with the leeks, celery, salt, peppercorns and bay leaf. When the meat and vegetables are tender, serve the soup lightly sprinkled with marjoram.
(Drink: clear white *Schnaps*)

FISH

EEL WITH POTATOES (*Tuckeraal*)

1 lb. small eels
salt, pepper
¾ lb. potatoes, sliced
pinch of allspice
½ cup (⅔) meat stock
chopped parsley

Clean the eels and cut into 2 in. lengths. Put into a pan with seasoned water to cover and cook for about 10 minutes. Take out the eel and keep warm. Add the potatoes, allspice and meat stock to the pan. Return the eel to the pan and cook for a few minutes. Arrange the potatoes on a plate and cover with the eel. Sprinkle with parsley.

(Drink: beer and *Schnaps*)

FRIED FISH (*Pfannfisch*)

1 lb. cooked cold fish,
  skinned, boned and
  shredded
1½ oz. (3 tablespoons) fat
½ lb. onions, sliced
1½ lb. cooked potatoes,
  sliced
salt
German mustard

Heat the fat in a shallow pan. Add the onions and when they begin to change colour, add the potatoes. Fry until well browned. Add the fish, heat it thoroughly and stir well into the onions and potatoes, adding salt and mustard. Serve with a green salad.

(Drink: beer)

COD WITH ONIONS AND CHIVES (*Kabeljau mit Schnitt-lauchzwiebeln*)

½ lb. cod fillet
1 tablespoon (1¼) oil
1 small onion, sliced
1 tablespoon (1¼) finely
  chopped chives
salt
juice ½ lemon
¼ cup (⅓) white wine

Heat the oil and fry the onion and chives gently without browning. Salt lightly. Sprinkle the fish with lemon juice. Place the fish on top of the onion, add the wine, cover and simmer over a low heat for 15 minutes. Serve with boiled potatoes.
(Drink: beer)

FILLET OF PERCH WITH PARSLEY TOMATOES (*Gold-barschfilet mit Petersilien-Tomaten*)

½ lb. perch fillets
½ oz. (1 tablespoon)
  margarine
2 tomatoes, sliced
1 small onion, diced
salt
lemon juice
finely chopped parsley

Heat the margarine in a pan, add the tomatoes and onion and cook for 3 minutes. Lay the fish on top. Sprinkle lightly with salt and lemon juice. Cover and simmer over a low heat for 15 minutes. Sprinkle with parsley and serve with boiled potatoes.
(Drink: beer)

GRILLED SALMON (*Salm oder Lachs vom Grill*)

½ lb. slice salmon, 1 in.
  thick
olive oil
lemon slices
1 sprig parsley
salt
herb or anchovy butter

Place the salmon in olive oil, cover with lemon slices and parsley and stand for 1 hour, turning the salmon once. Take the fish from the oil, sprinkle lightly with salt and grill on both sides, about 8 minutes each side. Serve with a herb or anchovy butter, boiled potatoes and a green salad.
(Drink: red wine)

PLAICE WITH FRIED BACON (*Scholle mit Speck gebraten*)

1 plaice, cleaned
2–3 slices fat bacon, diced
salt
lemon juice
Worcestershire Sauce
finely chopped parsley

Fry the bacon in a shallow pan until the fat runs, add the plaice, lightly sprinkle with salt and lemon juice. Fry the plaice on both sides until brown, arrange on a hot plate. Sprinkle again lightly with lemon juice, a little Worcestershire Sauce, parsley and the bacon with its fat. Serve with a potato salad, dressed with mayonnaise.
(Drink: white wine)

FISH HOTPOT (*Fischlabskaus*)

1½ lb. fish fillets
pinch salt, pepper
2½ lb. potatoes, boiled
3 oz. (6 tablespoons) butter
1 onion, chopped
2 teaspoons (2½) anchovy
   paste
2 teaspoons (2½) German
   mustard
pickled gherkin, sliced

First cook the fish in a little salted water until tender. Mash the potatoes. Crumble the fish and mix with the potatoes. Heat the butter and fry the onion until golden. Mix with salt, pepper, anchovy paste and mustard. Put the potato and fish mixture onto a hot dish, spread with the sauce and garnish with gherkins.
(Drink: beer and *Schnaps*)

STUFFED ROLLED PLAICE (*Schollenröllchen gefüllt*)

2–3 fillets of plaice
salt
lemon juice
anchovy paste
1 teaspoon (1¼) capers
1 tablespoon (1¼) oil
½ cup (⅔) white wine
2 tablespoons (2½) sour
   cream

Lightly sprinkle the fillets with salt and lemon juice and spread with anchovy paste. Scatter the capers on top and roll up each fillet. Secure with toothpicks. Place in a shallow pan with the oil and wine, cover and simmer for 10 minutes. Take out the fish, put aside but keep hot. Stir the cream into the sauce, reheat gently and pour this sauce over the fish. Serve with boiled rice.
(Drink: beer)

MEAT

POT-ROASTED LEG OF VEAL (*Milchkalbskeule*)

4 lb. leg of veal

2 oz. (4 tablespoons) fat

½ cup (⅔) white wine

1 tablespoon (1¼) tomato
purée

2 cups (2½) meat stock

salt, pepper

2 teaspoons (2½) cornflour
(cornstarch)

Heat the fat in a large wide pan, add the meat and cook until it is brown and crisp. Add the wine, baste often. When the veal is almost ready, place it on a rack in the same pan to prevent the bottom getting soft. Mix the tomato purée with the stock, season and stir it into the gravy. Continue cooking slowly until the gravy is reduced, the meat tender. Take out the meat, put aside but keep hot. Bring the gravy to the boil, mix the cornflour with enough water to make a thin paste, stir this into the pan, bring to the boil, stir and cook for 5 minutes. Serve the veal with the sauce separately and with boiled potatoes.
(Drink: white wine)

KÖNIGSBERG DUMPLINGS (*Königsberger Klopse*)

1 lb. pork

2 lb. beef

6 rolls, soaked in water
and squeezed dry

5 onions, quartered and
fried until brown

6 anchovy fillets

4 eggs

salt, pepper

1 pint (1¼) stock

2 teaspoons (2½) cornflour
(cornstarch)

4 egg yolks

½ cup (⅔) sour cream

1–2 tablespoons (1¼–2½)
capers

finely chopped parsley

Grind the meat, mix with the bread, onions and anchovies, grind again. Add the 4 whole eggs, salt and pepper. Knead well, break off small pieces and shape into balls. Bring the stock to the boil, lower the heat, add the meat balls and cook for 20 minutes. Take out the meat balls, put aside but keep warm. Strain the stock, bring again to the boil. Mix the cornflour with water to a thin paste. Stir this into the pan, bring to the boil and cook for 3 minutes. Blend the egg yolks with the sour cream and stir this mixture into the sauce. Cook over the lowest heat, stirring all the time until hot. Pour this sauce over the meat balls, sprinkle with capers and parsley.

FRIED SAUSAGE MEAT (*Würzfleisch Niedersächsisch*)

1 lb. lean spiced pork
  sausage meat
1 oz. (2 tablespoons) fat
1 medium-sized onion,
  diced
¾ lb. fresh mushrooms,
  sliced
2 pints (2½) hot meat stock
4 potatoes, grated
salt, pepper

Heat the fat and fry the meat and onion until brown. Add the mushrooms, fry for a few minutes, then add the stock, bring to a gentle boil, reduce the heat and cook gently until the meat is tender. Thicken with the potatoes and continue cooking until these are soft. Add salt and pepper to taste and serve with semolina dumplings.
(Drink: beer)

SMOKED PIG'S HEAD WITH GREEN CABBAGE (*Geraucherter Schweinskopf mit Grünkohl*)

1 smoked pig's head
1 onion stuck with 2 cloves
1 bay leaf
salt to taste
1 large cabbage, shredded

Boil the head in plenty of water with the onion, bay leaf and salt. Just before the head is ready, take out enough stock to cook the cabbage, drain and arrange on a hot platter. Keep hot. Take the head from the pan and bone; arrange the meat on the cabbage and serve with sautéed potatoes.
(Drink: beer)

STUFFED BREAST OF PORK (*Gefüllte Schweinebrust*)

4 lb. boned breast of pork
salt
½ lb. tart apples, sliced
½ lb. stoned prunes
pinch each sugar,
  cinnamon
6 tablespoons (7½)
  breadcrumbs
4 egg yolks
3 oz. (6 tablespoons) fat
1 onion, diced
chopped green herbs to
  taste
¾ pint (2 cups) meat stock

Sprinkle the inside of the meat with salt and fill with the apples, prunes, sugar and cinnamon. Mix the breadcrumbs with the egg yolks and push into the meat and sew up. Sprinkle with salt. Heat the fat, brown the onion and herbs, add the meat, brown it all over, add the stock, bring to a gentle boil and cook over a moderate heat until tender. Serve with red cabbage and boiled potatoes.
(Drink: red wine)

VEAL WITH CAULIFLOWER (*Kalbsfleisch mit Blumenkohl*)

1 lb. diced veal
1 pint (1¼) meat stock
1 onion stuck with 2 cloves
1 bay leaf
1 medium-sized cauliflower
salt
2 teaspoons (2½) cornflour
  (cornstarch)
1 tablespoon (1¼) lemon
  juice
½ cup (⅔) sour cream
3 egg yolks, beaten
finely chopped parsley

Cook the meat in the stock with the onion and bay leaf. Divide the cauliflower into flowerets and cook in boiling salted water. Mix the cornflour with water to make a thin paste, add to the meat, stir and cook until the sauce is thick. Add the juice. Combine the sour cream and egg yolks and stir into the sauce – do not cook any more. Drain the cauliflower and mix it with the meat and sauce. Sprinkle with parsley.

(Drink: white wine)

POULTRY

GOOSE GIBLETS WITH TURNIPS (*Gänseklein mit weissen Rübchen*)

1 set goose giblets
salt, pepper
1 oz. (2 tablespoons) fat
1–2 onions, diced
1 lb. white turnips, sliced
finely chopped parsley

Cook the giblets until tender in seasoned water to cover. Heat the fat and gently fry the onions and turnips. Add these to the giblets and simmer until tender. Sprinkle with parsley and serve with boiled potatoes.

(Drink: beer)

GOOSE LEGS IN CABBAGE (*Gänseschenkel in Schmorkohl*)

2 goose legs
salt to taste
1 oz. (2 tablespoons) goose
  fat
2 large onions, finely
  chopped
1 large white cabbage,
  shredded
4 tablespoons (5) vinegar
2 tablespoons (2½) sugar

Wipe the legs with a damp cloth, rub with salt. Heat the fat and brown the legs, add the onions and water to cover. Cook over a low heat until tender. Add the cabbage 1 hour before the legs are tender and continue cooking. Add the vinegar and sugar, test for salt. Strip off the meat from the legs, mix gently with the cabbage and serve hot with boiled potatoes.

(Drink: beer)

EGG DISHES

EGG NOG (*Eiergrog*)

1 egg yolk
1 tablespoon (1¼)
  powdered sugar
½ cup (⅔) hot rum

Whisk the egg yolk and sugar until frothy. Slowly add the rum, stirring all the time. A similar drink is made in summer with cold rum. Less sugar is used.

SCRAMBLED EGGS WITH SMOKED EEL (*Rührei mit Räucheraal*)

Place scrambled eggs on a warm plate and on top lay fillets of smoked eel, boned and skinned. Offer lemon juice, salt and pepper so that the dish may be seasoned to taste. Serve with toast.

SCRAMBLED EGGS WITH SMOKED BUCKLING (*Rührei mit Bücklingen*)

3 eggs per serving
buckling fillets (smoked
  herring)
salt
butter

Beat the eggs well and cook in an omelette pan with a little salt and butter. In another pan toss the buckling fillets in hot butter with a little salt; then place in the middle of the scrambled eggs.
(Drink: beer)

SMOKED EEL OMELETTE (*Räucheraal in Omelett*)

Chop fillets of smoked eel in very small dice, and toss quickly in warm butter. Add sliced mushrooms. Fill a prepared omelette with this mixture.
(Drink: beer with all eel dishes)

VEGETABLES

'TURKISH BEANS' WITH PEARS (*Türkische Bohnen mit Birnen*)

1 lb. French (snap) beans
½ lb. pears
¾ lb. smoked belly pork
2 cups (2½) stock
salt, pepper
nutmeg
cornflour (cornstarch)

Trim the beans, peel and quarter the pears and cut the meat into medium-sized pieces. Put these ingredients into a pan, add the stock, salt, pepper and nutmeg to taste. When the meat is tender, thicken the stock slightly with cornflour (first mixed to a thin paste with water). Serve with boiled potatoes.

BREMERHAVEN CABBAGE (*Bremerhafener Grünkohl*)

2 lb. green cabbage
salt to taste
2 oz. (4 tablespoons) pork
 dripping
1 large onion, diced
1 cup (1¼) meat stock
1 tablespoon (1¼) flour
1–2 oz. (2–4 tablespoons)
 goose fat
nutmeg to taste

Strip the cabbage leaves and wash thoroughly. Boil in salted water until tender, drain and chop. Heat the pork dripping and fry the onion until soft but not brown. Add the cabbage, salt and stock. Cook gently until the cabbage is soft. Mix the flour with enough water to make a thin paste. Stir this into the cabbage. Stir well until the sauce thickens. Add the goose fat and nutmeg. Serve with boiled potatoes, *Pinkelwurst*, *Mettwurst*, or roast goose.
(Drink: *Schnaps* and beer)

ROLAND POTATOES (*Rolandkartoffeln*)

Take small round, peeled new potatoes: boil them in salted water, drain, dry and fry in deep fat until brown and crisp. Sprinkle with breadcrumbs.

SWEETS

RED CREAMS (*Rote Grütze*)

2 pints (2½) redcurrant juice
 or half each redcurrant
 and raspberry juice
sugar to taste
1½ oz. (¼ cup) cornflour
 (cornstarch)
cream as garnish

Bring the juice to the boil adding sugar. Mix the cornflour with water to make a thin paste; stir into the juice, bring again to the boil, cook and stir for 5 minutes. Pour into small moulds, previously sprinkled with sugar. Cool and then chill. Turn out to serve garnished with cream. These creams must be sharp in flavour and cool. If using only raspberry juice, also add a little lemon juice.

Cookery in Hesse

This handsome countryside, with its timbered houses and gay peasant costumes, round the little town of Marburg where the brothers Grimm collected and wrote their fairy tales, is rather overshadowed by the brilliance of Frankfurt where Goethe was born. The splendid church of St Paul does further honour to the town. In the house of Goethe's parents one can still visit his mother's kitchen. She was well known as an outstanding cook and baker, and the whole place has an atmosphere of good food. In the old days, Frankfurt's important Museum of Culinary Art was cared for by the German Cookery Guild which now has its headquarters here, from which it organizes with passionate devotion the International Cookery Fair which is held in Frankfurt every four years.

During the period of the Fair, great artists from many lands come to display their skills. At the end of their day's work they slip out to dinner, perhaps to the *Appelwoi* at Sachsenhausen, where they can enjoy *Rippchen und Kraut*, cutlets and cabbage. Cooks seldom eat what they have cooked themselves, because by so doing they might lose their objectivity and sense of proportion. They turn, therefore, to simple things, to the dishes of the local countryside which suit them so well. Many foreign visitors to Frankfurt do the same, for they like to sit with the local regulars, gossiping, joking, eating and drinking. Here the landlord stands in his shirt sleeves behind the bar, pouring cider into fluted glasses out of a grey and blue measuring jug. At the first sip it seems rather astringent, but the second glass tickles the tongue not unpleasantly and by the third glass one is looking forward to the fourth. In the end one is convinced that the stuff is not really strong after all, despite an increasing tendency to talk, but after really quenching one's thirst the street swims before one's eyes. Moderation in all things, however, including cider, which is best as an accompaniment to the special local *Pretzels*, the *Rippchen* and *Handkäse mit Musik*, as described in our recipes.

In this area one can enjoy both the simplest and the most refined cuisine. Frankfurt, so it seems to me, parallels Strasbourg in this respect. There, too, Goethe lives in the hearts of the students and populace alike, as much a part of their lives as *pâté de foie gras*.

To Frankfurt came Eugen Lacroix, a native of the Black Forest and here from the humblest beginnings he built up his *pâté de foie gras* business to international dimensions. His son carries on the business skilfully and in the old tradition, to the lasting pleasure of gourmets the world over. Another international gastronomic organization is based on Frankfurt, for here Lufthansa has a giant kitchen which cooks and bakes both for its passengers and for the general public. If the visitor to Frankfurt wanders down the streets looking into shops loaded with delicacies, he may well wonder how they can all be sold and eaten. Let him rest easy: the gifts of God are prepared with loving cunning, and nothing goes to waste.

SOUP

HESSE SAUSAGE SOUP (*Hessische Metzelsuppe*)
This is stock in which sausage is cooked. The more they burst, the better it is. In Hesse it is thickened with mashed potato.

MEAT

BEEF SAUSAGE (*Rindfleischwurst*)
Beef sausages dropped into a pan of boiling water and simmered for 15 minutes. Serve with mustard and brown bread or potato salad.
(Drink: beer)

BAKER'S STEW (*Bäckerskrummbeere*)

2 lb. potatoes, peeled and quartered
1 lb. pork, diced
1–2 onions, sliced
1 cup (1¼) sour cream
salt
freshly ground nutmeg

Put everything into an earthenware casserole (or other type) and bake in a moderate oven. This stew is called baker's stew because it was usually taken to the baker who put it in his oven. It takes 3 hours to cook and is delicious.
(Drink: buttermilk or wine)

BREAD, SAUSAGE AND WINE (*Weck, Worscht und Woi*)

The three holy 'Ws' of the Rhine. By this are meant Wasserweck (a small loaf), meat sausage and wine. Frequently the small cheeses from Mainz are used instead of sausages. The poor *Rentner* or vineyard labourer, who works in the cellars in winter used to bewail his lot, crying 'all day long on a hard bench, drinking cold wine'.

GIPSY ROAST (*Zigeunerbraten*)

2 lb. smoked meat, ham or beef boned, preferably from the leg
bread dough (from the baker)

Wrap the meat in greaseproof paper, then wrap both in dough. Bake slowly in the oven for about 3 hours. One can also bake this 'parcel' over a fire in the open. It is always a treat. Serve with potato salad.
(Drink: red wine or beer)

SPARERIBS FRANKFURT STYLE (*Rippchen Frankfurter Art*)

Sprinkle the spareribs lightly with salt and cook in stock until tender –
and still on the bone. Or they can be cooked in a dish of *Sauerkraut*. When
tender, but still fairly firm, separate the spareribs. Serve with *Sauerkraut*
and boiled potatoes. If any are left over, keep in the stock so that they
remain succulent.

FRANKFURTER SAUSAGE (*Frankfurter Würstchen*)

Cook the sausages gently in hot water for 10 minutes. Serve with brown
bread, German-style mustard or grated horseradish. They can also be
served sliced in potato, lentil or pea soups, excellent in all. America
has christened her sausages after 'Frankfurters', so one may well call them
world-famous.

KASSEL SPARERIBS (*Kasseler Rippchen*)

A great dispute exists between the people of Kassel and Berlin. The latter
maintain that it was master-cook Kassel who invented this dish; the
people of Kassel that it was they themselves. In any event, a laurel wreath
to both, for this dish tastes marvellous everywhere if it is correctly
prepared.

2 lb. smoked pork spareribs
2 cups (2½) meat stock
1 onion stuck with 2 cloves
1 bay leaf
salt to taste

Boil the spareribs without separating in
the stock with the onion and bay leaf. Add
salt. Cook gently until tender, about 1
hour. Separate the spareribs and serve
with *Sauerkraut* and boiled potatoes.
Variations:

1. Cook the spareribs as above but serve
   in a Burgundy sauce with mushrooms
   and potato croquettes.
2. Cook as above, leave to cool, separate
   and serve with a mixed salad.
3. Separate the spareribs before cooking,
   beat until thin. Dip in beaten egg and
   roll in fine breadcrumbs and fry. Serve
   with mayonnaise.
4. Take the meat uncooked from the
   bones, wrap in a dough and bake for 2
   hours in a moderate oven. Serve with
   asparagus.

VEGETABLES

ASPARAGUS SALAD (*Lampertheimer Spargel als Salat*)

1 lb. cooked asparagus
1 tablespoon ($1\frac{1}{4}$) mild
  vinegar
3 tablespoons ($3\frac{3}{4}$) olive oil
$\frac{1}{4}$ teaspoon ($\frac{1}{3}$) each salt,
  sugar
finely chopped parsley
2 chopped hard-boiled eggs
sour cream (optional)

Make a dressing with the vinegar, oil, salt and sugar. Add the parsley and mix well. Pour this mixture over the asparagus. Sprinkle with the eggs. A little sour cream may be mixed into the dressing. Serve with cooked ham or plain or pickled tongue.

(Drink: white wine)

BRAISED SPRING (GREEN) ONIONS (*Zwiebelgrüngemüse*)

1 lb. spring (green) onions
$1\frac{1}{2}$ oz. (3 tablespoons) butter
4 tablespoons (5) stoneless
  raisins
$\frac{1}{2}$ cup ($\frac{2}{3}$) white wine
4 tablespoons (5) fine
  breadcrumbs

Cut the onions into slices including the green portion. Heat the butter, fry the onion, add the raisins and simmer for a few minutes. Add the wine, cover and cook gently until tender. Mix in the breadcrumbs to slightly thicken the onion mixture. Serve with chops and boiled potatoes or indeed almost any meat or fish.

LEEKS WITH GOOSE (*Gans mit Lauch*)

Roast the goose as in the recipe given on page 81. Instead of apples, place 5 leeks, cut in slices, inside the bird. The rich flavour of the leeks naturally penetrates the bird, and the leeks made the fat more digestible.
(Drink: beer)

RADISH AND TOMATO SALAD (*Rettich und Tomatensalat*)

3 radishes, thinly peeled
  and sliced
10 tomatoes, thinly sliced
1 tablespoon ($1\frac{1}{4}$) vinegar
3 tablespoons ($3\frac{3}{4}$) oil
$\frac{1}{4}$ teaspoon ($\frac{1}{3}$) sugar
salt, pepper to taste

Place the radishes and tomatoes in separate bowls. Make a dressing with the vinegar, oil, sugar, salt and pepper. Pour this over the tomatoes. Sprinkle the radishes with salt. After 30 minutes, wipe the radishes dry and mix them with the tomatoes. Serve with Swiss cheese and bread.

(Drink: beer)

SAUCES

GREEN SAUCE (*Grüne Sauce*)

1 tablespoon (1¼) each finely chopped parsley, sage, cress, sorrel, borage, chives

a little finely chopped dill, tarragon and savory

1 tablespoon (1¼) vinegar

3 tablespoons (3¾) oil

¼ teaspoon (⅓) sugar

salt

4 finely chopped hard-boiled eggs

Mix all the herbs together. Make a dressing with the vinegar, oil, sugar and salt. Mix well. Stir the eggs into the sauce. Some people add lettuce or leeks, others a little mayonnaise. This sauce is good with boiled beef, fish, poultry, hard or soft eggs, and is a delicacy with cooked asparagus.

CAKES AND DESSERTS

HESSE DOUGHNUTS (*Kräppel*)

In Hesse, where pigs are frequently killed at home, there is plenty of pork dripping available. This is heated and the *Kräppel* are deep-fried in it.

PLUM FLAN (*Zwetschgen* or *Quetschenkucken*)

1 lb. yeast dough (page 26)

2–3 ripe plums

sugar to taste

powdered cinnamon

Topping:

3 tablespoons (3¾) chopped almonds

3 tablespoons (3¾) coarse breadcrumbs

3 tablespoons (3¾) sugar

¼ cup (⅓) plum cordial

Prepare the yeast dough and roll it out thinly to an oblong. Grease a baking sheet and line it with the dough. Stone the plums and make incisions on the inside of each of the halves so they will lie flat on the pastry. Lay them neatly in rows, cut side uppermost, very close together on the pastry. Sprinkle lightly with sugar and cinnamon. Leave to prove. Bake in a hot oven for 30 minutes. Mix the remaining ingredients and spread over the top of the flan after it has left the oven.

(Drink: not coffee, but cider)

FRANKFURT WREATH (*Frankfurter Kranz*)

Batter:

4 oz. (½) cup butter
4 eggs, separated
4 oz. (scant ½ cup) sugar
5 oz. (1¼ cups) cake flour
3 oz. (½ cup) cornflour
  (cornstarch)
1 teaspoon (1¼) baking
  powder
1 tablespoon (1¼) vanilla
  sugar or grated lemon
  rind

Butter-cream:

½ lb. (1 cup) unsalted butter
½ lb. (scant 2 cups)
  powdered sugar
1–2 egg yolks
vanilla essence to taste
3 tablespoons (3¾) brandy

Topping:

3 oz. (full ⅓ cup) sugar
2 oz. (⅓ cup) slivered
  almonds

Beat the butter until creamy adding alternately 1 egg yolk and 1 tablespoon (1¼) sugar until the mixture is creamy. Add the flour, cornflour, baking powder and vanilla sugar. Beat the egg whites until stiff and fold in. Pour the mixture into a well-greased ring-form and bake in a moderate oven for 30 minutes. Turn and leave to cool. To make the butter-cream, beat the butter until creamy, mix with the other ingredients and beat thoroughly until completely blended. Cut the cake through the middle; spread the bottom portion with two-thirds of the cream; cover with the top half and spread this with the remaining butter-cream.

To make the topping, heat the sugar in a thick pan until it melts, quickly add the almonds and cook until they brown. Take from the pan, cool and crush with a rolling pin. Sprinkle these over the top of the cake.

CREAM CAKE FROM HESSE (*Hessischer Sahnekuchen*)

1 lb. yeast dough (page 26)
2 cups (2½) sour cream
3 tablespoons (3¾) sugar
1 teaspoon (1¼) powdered
  cinnamon

Roll out the yeast dough finger-thick and line a baking (cookie) sheet. Leave to prove. Bake in a hot oven for 15–20 minutes. While still hot spread with sour cream, sprinkle with sugar and cinnamon.

SMALL CHEESES WITH MUSIC (*Handkäse mit Musik*)

These cheeses, small enough to fit into a man's hand, used to be made at home, but now are mass-produced. Of a curd basis, they are matured in an earthenware pot until truly ripe, and served with bread and butter or goosefat and a dressing made from finely chopped onions, oil, vinegar, salt and pepper. This last is the 'music' which makes itself heard a few hours later.

A Berlin speciality: knuckle half leg of pork with sauerkraut and purée of peas
(*Eisbein mit Sauerkraut und Erbspüree*)

Cookery in Westphalia

The agricultural character of Westphalia and its proximity to Holland are reflected in its famous, savoury casseroles. One should not, however, be led into thinking that just anything can be put into them. At the very heart of such a stew there is always pork. Potatoes and vegetables serve only as a garnish.

From this district originated the long rectangular table, with its thick boards in which the plates are formed by round hollows carved into the wood. In the middle of the table is a larger round hollow, which serves as a casserole. When the meal is ready in the cauldron that hangs from the chimney hook over the open fire, the steaming spicy contents are emptied into the middle of the table, and everyone can fill his 'wooden plate' from it to his heart's content.

But it is not only in Westphalian casseroles that pork takes pride of place; it occupies the same position in the heart of every true Westphalian. Above all it is the hams which he loves. What would he not give to have pigs with four hindquarters? In North Germany they have already managed to breed a pig with thirteen ribs; perhaps we shall not have to:

51

A Westphalian dish:
broad beans and smoked pork
(*Dicke Bohnen mit Rauchfleisch*)

wait too long for one with four hams! Westphalian butchers, kings of the realm, have won world renown for themselves with their Westphalian hams. The ham with the bone – in fact with practically the whole hind leg – is pickled and later smoked according to jealously guarded recipes. Should you ever come to the exhibition of Food and Luxuries in Cologne (ANUGA – *die Allgemeine Nährungs- und Genussmittel-Ausstellung*) which takes place every two years, do not delay a visit to the wooden display stands. There you will see magnificent examples of these hams, which make the visitor's mouth water.

One cannot speak, however, of the *Skinken* (as the hams are called locally) without mentioning *Pumpernickel* – mellow black rye bread, cut in slices – and *Steinhäger*. They belong together like bacon and eggs. And if there are a few radishes to nibble as well, one can wish for no greater happiness. The ham could be called Westphalia's gift to mankind. It is laid on a wooden frame, on which it is held fast by four wooden pegs, so that it can easily be carved into even slices.

No less excellent are the various kinds of sausage, for example, the *Knackwürst* and *Metwurst*.

Corn liquor from the region of Münster is called *dat reine Woord Guods* – the true word of God! It is amber in colour and is often drunk from pewter spoons. *Steinhäger* is a spirit made from juniper berries which does the stomach good.

In Münster in the old tavern of Pinkus Müller we can still find a small island of true Westphalian comfort. At an open fire surrounded by old tiles one can sit by the crackling logs and drink the beer that he and his sons brew themselves – a beer that foams on top, refreshing and cooling in summer, and marvellous, as Müller has discovered, with strawberries. Ham and beer combine splendidly too!

When Napoleon's brother was king of Westphalia, in the first decades of the nineteenth century, the following is supposed to have happened: the king loved to take a morning bath in Burgundy. For this his servants emptied 20 bottles of warmed wine into his bathtub. After the bath these rogues put the Burgundy back in the bottles, and behold, there were 21 bottles which, without batting an eyelid, they tipped down their thirsty throats.

Westphalian saying: 'If anything is left, first the mice get it, and then the owls'. Now for some genuine recipes:

MEATS AND ENTRÉES

BROAD BEANS AND SMOKED PORK (*Dicke Bohnen mit Rauchfleisch*)

2 lb. shelled broad beans
2 lb. smoked pork
1 onion stuck with 2 cloves
salt, 1 sprig summer
  savory
¼ lb. diced fat bacon
1 small onion, diced
¾ pint (2 cups) meat stock
3 tablespoons (3¾)
  cornflour (cornstarch)
milk
1 cup (1¼) single cream
chopped parsley to taste

Cook the pork slowly with the whole onion in unsalted water until tender, about 2½ hours. Cook the beans and summer savory in salted water until tender. Fry the bacon, as the fat runs add the diced onion, let this change colour, add the beans and stock. Mix the cornflour with milk to a thin paste. Add this with the cream to the pan, stir until the stock thickens. Sprinkle with parsley and simmer for a few minutes. Pour the beans and sauce into a deep dish, slice the pork, place it on the beans and serve with boiled potatoes.

SPICED BEEF STEW (*Pfefferpotthast*)

A favourite dish for men on club evenings, especially in the bowling clubs in Dortmund. It gives a good lining to the stomach before quenching one's thirst with the renowned Dortmund beer.

2 lb. beef (ribs or brisket)
1 oz. (2 tablespoons) fat
4 onions, sliced
stock or water
salt, pepper
2 cloves, pinch allspice
1 bay leaf
1 tablespoon (1¼) capers
breadcrumbs

Heat the fat in a large pan and fry the onions for 5 minutes. Cut the meat into finger-length pieces, add to the pan, cook for 5 minutes, add stock to cover. Add the remaining ingredients (except breadcrumbs) and cook gently until the meat is tender. Add the breadcrumbs, stir well until blended. Serve with boiled potatoes, beetroot, pickled gherkins, salad.

BRATWURST SAUSAGE (*Bratwurst*)

½ lb. sausage per person
milk
fat

Pour hot water over the sausages to prevent bursting. Rinse in milk and fry until brown in hot fat. Serve with boiled potatoes and green or red cabbage.

BEEF WITH APPLES AND ONIONS (*Rindfleisch mit Äpfeln und Zwiebeln*)

1 lb. cooked beef, thinly sliced
4 apples, peeled and sliced
3 onions, thinly sliced
1 oz. (2 tablespoons) fat
salt, sugar
½ cup (⅔) white wine
1 cup (1¼) meat stock

Heat the fat in a casserole and lightly fry the onions. Lay the meat on top and cover with the apples. Add salt to taste, a little sugar, the wine and stock. Cover the casserole and cook in a moderate oven for 30 minutes. Serve with puréed potatoes. (Drink: beer)

BRATWURST IN BEER SAUCE (*Bratwurst in Biersauce*)

3 pairs Bratwurst
¾ pint (2 cups) beer
½ lb. crumbled gingerbread
3 oz. (6 tablespoons) fat

Pour hot water over the sausages to prevent bursting. Dry. Bring the beer to the boil, add the gingerbread, bring again to the boil to make the sauce slightly lumpy. Heat the fat, fry and brown the sausages. Take from the pan, drop into the sauce, simmer for 10 minutes. Serve with boiled or puréed potatoes, gherkins and mustard.

Tip for the sauce: soak the cake in beer and rub it through a mincer, then the sauce will cook quicker.
(Drink: beer)

FRIED BRATWURST SAUSAGE (*Geschmorte Bratwurst*)

1 lb. Westphalian Bratwurst
flour
3 oz. (¼ cup) fat
2 onions, diced
meat stock
1 teaspoon (1¼) cornflour (cornstarch)
½ cup (⅔) red wine

Pour hot water over the sausages, dry and roll in flour. Heat the fat, fry the onions until they change colour, add the sausages and brown them all over. Add stock to cover and cook gently for 30 minutes. Take out sausages, put aside but keep hot. Mix the cornflour with water to make a thin paste, stir into the gravy, bring to the boil and cook for 3 minutes. Add wine. Pour the sauce over the sausages and serve with potato purée, salad or red cabbage.

CASSEROLE OF CALF'S HEAD (*Töttchen*)

1 half-boned calf's head
½ lb. calf's lung
½ lb. calf's heart
1 onion stuck with 2 cloves
1 bay leaf
Sauce:
2½ oz. (5 tablespoons) butter
2 onions, diced
2 tablespoons (2½) flour
2 tablespoons (2½) white wine
¼ teaspoon (⅓) sugar

Cook the meats with the onion and bay leaf in water to cover until tender. Strain, cool the meats and cut into small pieces. Heat half the butter in a pan and lightly fry the onions. Add the flour, stir until blended, then add enough of the meat stock to make a sauce. Add wine and sugar. Heat the remaining butter in another pan, add the pieces of meat and reheat. Pour the sauce over the top, bring again to the boil. Serve with mustard, black bread or rolls.
(Drink: beer)

HAM IN BURGUNDY (*Schinken in Burgunder*)

1 whole 4 lb. ham
1 cup (1¼) bouillon
1 pint (1¼) Burgundy
1 tablespoon (1¼) cornflour (cornstarch)
Madeira

Soak the ham overnight in cold water. Drain, cover with hot water and boil gently for 1½ hours. Drain and put in a baking pan. Combine the bouillon and wine and pour it over the ham. Bake in a hot oven for 50 minutes. Take out the ham, drain but keep hot. Mix the cornflour with stock from the pan to make a thin paste. Bring the rest of the stock to a boil, stir in the paste and cook until the sauce is thick. Add enough Madeira to give a good flavour and pour the sauce over the ham. Serve hot with puréed potatoes and spinach.

SALT LEG OF MUTTON (*Hammelkeule sauer eingelegt*)

4 lb. pickled leg of mutton
4–5 slices fat bacon
salt, pepper
4 oz. (½ cup) fat
1 cup (1¼) sour cream

Cover the meat with bacon. Season. Heat the fat in a large baking pan and fry the meat until brown. Transfer to a hot oven and roast until tender, basting often. Just before serving, pour the cream over the meat. Serve with boiled potatoes and cranberries.

MOCK CHICKEN CASSEROLE (*Blindeshuhn*)

1 lb. haricot beans,
   previously soaked
2 lb. gammon
½ lb. carrots, cubed
½ lb. green beans, sliced
½ lb. potatoes, cubed
1 onion, sliced
1 lb. tart apples
salt
a little mixed spice

Boil the haricot beans in the liquid in which they soaked. Add the gammon. Cook until the gammon is tender. Add the carrots, beans, potatoes and onion. Without peeling, core and quarter the apples. Add to the pan and take out the gammon. Cut the meat into cubes, return to the pan, add salt and spice and cook another 15 minutes. Serve with boiled potatoes.
(Drink: beer)

WHITE PUDDING (*Panhas*)

4 pints (5) sausage stock
salt, pepper
2–3 slices fat bacon, diced
   and fried
about 1 lb. buckwheat
   flour
hot fat

Sausage stock is the liquid in which fresh black, white or liver sausages have been cooked. Bring to the boil with the salt, pepper and bacon. Add the buckwheat, stirring all the time until the stock is thick. Cook for 15 minutes, then take the pan from the heat and leave until the buckwheat becomes thicker. Fill the mixture into bowls and leave until cold and stiff. Turn out, thickly slice and fry in plenty of hot fat until brown on both sides. Serve with potatoes, tomato salad, gherkins and bread.
(Drink: beer)

Variations: *Möppkenbrot* or *Würstebrot*

5 pints (6) sausage stock
½ cup (⅔) pig's blood
½ lb. seedless raisins
½ lb. bacon, diced
½ lb. rye flour
1 sound pig's bladder

Put the stock, blood, raisins and bacon into a large pan. Mix the flour with a little cold stock or water to a thick paste and stir into the pan. Bring to the boil and continue cooking until it is thick. Fill the mixture into the bladder, close the opening and leave to get cold. Slice and fry as above.

SAUSAGE ROLLS (*Würstebrot*)

1 lb. risen yeast dough
1 lb. sausage meat
1 egg yolk, beaten

Roll out the pastry to ⅛ in. thick. Cut into 8 rectangles, roughly 5 by 2 in. Roll out the sausage meat, cut off 8 pieces (or same number as pastry pieces). Put a 'sausage' in the centre of each rectangle and roll over. Wet the edges to seal, pinch firmly and leave in a warm place to rise, lightly covered. Paint with egg and bake in a hot oven for 20 minutes on the top shelf. Serve with salad.

HEAVEN AND EARTH (*Himmel und Erde*)

1 lb. puréed potatoes
1 lb. puréed apples
salt, sugar, nutmeg

Mix the potato and apple purées while both are still hot and season with salt, a little sugar and freshly grated nutmeg. Serve with fried blood or liver sausage. (Drink: beer)

APPLE TART (*Äpfeltorte*)

1 lb. risen yeast pastry
2 lb. peeled, grated apples
5 tablespoons (6¼) sugar
5 tablespoons (6¼) seedless raisins
2 oz. (⅓ cup) ground almonds
cinnamon
1 tablespoon (1¼) grated lemon rind

Break off one-third of the pastry and put aside. Roll out the larger portion to ⅛ in. thick and line a flan tin. Mix the remaining ingredients, spreading them evenly over the pastry. Roll the remaining pastry out thinly and cover the mixture. Wet the edges to seal, press firmly all round and leave covered in a warm place until the dough has risen. Bake in a hot oven until the pastry is a golden brown. While still warm, sprinkle with sugar.

YEAST FRITTERS (*Böllebäuschen*)

Take tablespoonfuls of yeast dough and fry quickly in deep hot fat until they are brown and crisp. Drain and toss in sugar.

WHITE BREAD MEN (*Stutenkerl*)

**white bread dough
currants**

Roll out as much dough as required about half-a-finger thick. Cut out shapes of men, either with arms hanging or in imaginary pockets. Mark the face with currants and stick a tiny clay pipe in the mouth. Let the dough rise and then bake in a hot oven until a golden brown. These are made at home and in bakers' shops during Advent.

Cookery in Thuringia

At a time when tourism was still in its infancy, Thuringia coined a most appealing slogan: 'Thuringia – the green heart of Germany'. It did not lack success. Guests from all over the world came to her spas in summer and winter. First-class hotels offered not only comfortable accommodation but also the exceptional products of their kitchens.

Erfurt, the world-famous town of flowers in which Napoleon and Goethe once met, really belongs to Prussia, but was formerly the capital of Thuringia. My cooking career began here and I therefore know what importance is attached to the famous potato-balls known as *Klösse*. Every Thursday was *Klösse* day. This meant that we apprentices had to peel and grate raw potatoes by the hundredweight, fill sacks with them, and squeeze the juice from them with the aid of a press. The potatoes were grated in warm water so that they stayed white. The squeezed-out paste was put in a large bowl and blended with a hot potato purée prepared from mashed cooked potatoes mixed with boiling milk. The whole mixture was seasoned with salt and stirred briskly with a wooden spoon.

Meanwhile starch would begin to drift to the bottom of the bowl which collected the water from the pressed potatoes. This was also mixed in with the paste for the *Klösse*. As the *Klösse* were shaped in rounds, 4–6 small toasted cubes of white bread were put in the middle of each, in order to absorb the moisture in the *Klösse*. The paste has to be quite spongy. During these preparations, large pans stood on the stove, filled with salt water, and the shaped *Klösse* were then put into the boiling water. They were brought to the boil once and allowed to soak for 20 minutes. When they floated to the surface, they were ready. If ever the paste failed to bind, so that the *Klösse* disintegrated in the water, a little semolina or raw potato paste would be mixed in, so that the mixture had a better consistency. For this reason it is advisable to make a test *Kloss* before shaping all the others and only proceed further when all is in order. The true Thuringian *Kloss* must be white and light as down. When one opens it on a plate one is not far from the Thuringians' Paradise.

What tastes best with them? In my time in Erfurt on *Kloss* days we would have roast goose with red cabbage, crisp roast duck, pork or lamb, even brisket, according to the season. In other words, always a meat that produces a rich sauce, so that the *Klösse* set this off and slip down all the better.

Anyone well acquainted with the secrets of Thuringian cookery will know that the Rennsteig up in the Thuringian Forest is a *Kloss* boundary. On one side the pressed raw potatoes are mixed with hot potato purée; on the other side, with semolina. It is hard to decide which are the better *Klösse*. Daughters learn the art of making *Klösse* from their mothers, and hand it on to their children from one generation to the next.

Whenever they had a little time, Thuringian soldiers on active service in the two World Wars, rubbed their few potatoes on home-made graters and made their own *Klösse*.

The second renowned speciality of Thuringia is *Rostbratwurst* – a roast sausage. It is made of top quality ham and seasoned with salt, pepper, nutmeg and caraway. It is not very thick and over nine inches long. It is roasted over the embers of a wood fire, so that the juices drop into the cinders and a seductive smoke is sent up into the sky. Even at a distance one is aware that fresh sausages are being roasted. To serve the sausages, a long roll is cut lengthwise and a sausage placed inside. A line of mustard over the sausage makes it still tastier, and a beer completes one's pleasure. On another side of the grate, *Rostbrätel* still go on cooking. These are slices of pork from the neck, well-pounded, salted, and peppered, which can be cooked slowly according to the time they will be needed.

Thuringian sausages are famous: the butchers in these parts have thoroughly mastered the art of seasoning, and are proud to make sausages of every possible kind.

The marvellous dishes that have pride of place in Thuringia are also available in neighbouring Saxony and are of excellent quality. But in Saxony people take more pleasure in sweet pastries, and several varieties from Dresden and Leipzig have achieved world-renown. Dresden *Stollen*, Thuringian *Schittchen*, *Eierschecke*, or Leipzig *Lerche* – whoever has had the good fortune to taste these pastries, made according to the original recipes, knows how delicious they are. Needless to say, these cakes could be obtained in Germany's first *Kaffeehaus*, the *Grüne Baum* in Leipzig.

It is well known that Goethe studied for a few terms in Leipzig. At that time there was less coffee drunk than wine or beer. *Die Gose* is a beer that foams on top, similar to the Berlin mild beer, and very refreshing.

To give the reader an opportunity to prepare dishes from Thuringia and Saxony, I should now like to introduce a few original recipes from those districts.

SOUP

LEIPZIG BEER SOUP (*Leipziger Biersuppe*)

1 cup (1¼) brown ale
2 cups (2½) milk
2 tablespoons (2½) sugar
rind of 1 lemon
pinch of cinnamon
2 tablespoons (2½)
  cornflour (cornstarch)
2 egg yolks, beaten

Bring the milk with the sugar, rind and cinnamon to the boil. Mix the cornflour with water to a thin paste. Pour into the milk and cook, stirring, until the mixture is thick. Warm the beer, stir this into the soup. Whisk the egg yolks with a little beer and stir into the soup immediately before serving. Remove the rind and sprinkle with nutmeg.

LENTIL SOUP WITH ROTWURST (*Linsensuppe mit Rotwurst*)
A well-flavoured lentil soup served garnished with thick slices of fried Thuringian *Rotwurst*. The sausage falls apart but does no damage to the flavour of the soup.
(Drink: beer)

DUMPLINGS

THURINGIAN POTATO DUMPLINGS (*Thüringer Klösse*)

2 lb. peeled, grated potatoes
1 lb. mashed potatoes
2 eggs, beaten
3 thick slices toasted white bread
salt

Squeeze the grated potatoes in a cloth until dry, collecting the liquid that comes from them in a bowl. Mix the mashed and grated potatoes and add the eggs and liquid. Break off pieces of the potato mixture and shape into fairly large balls. Cut the toast into cubes, push one of these into each dumpling. Drop the dumplings into boiling salted water and bring to the boil. Remove from the heat and leave the dumplings uncovered in the pan for 15–20 minutes or until they float on the surface of the water. The dumplings should be served at once while they are still spongy and light. Apple purée or hot melted butter and ground sugar can be served with the dumplings.

VOGTLAND GREEN DUMPLINGS (*Grüne Klösse wie im Vogtland*)

The preparation of these is the same as for Thuringian *Klösse* except that the liquid from the uncooked, grated and pressed potatoes is mixed with cold boiled sieved potatoes. Here too toasted cubes of white bread are put inside the *Klösse* to absorb the moisture.

WATTE DUMPLINGS (*Watteklösse*)

Watte means cotton wool or wadding, and these dumplings are thus named because they are so light.

1 lb. cooked potatoes
6 oz. (1 cup) potato flour
salt, nutmeg to taste
¾ pint (2 cups) boiling milk
2 slices thick toast

Sieve the potatoes, add the potato flour, salt and nutmeg. Add the milk, stirring quickly. Make dumplings from this mixture, push toast cubes into the middle of each and cook as for Thuringian dumplings.

FRIED DUMPLINGS WITH EGGS (*Klösse geröstet mit Ei*)

Cut cold *Klösse* in slices. Brown on both sides till crisp in a little fat. Pour over them a well-beaten egg to each *Klösse*. Serve when set.

MEAT

BRATWURST WITH RAISINS AND APPLES (*Bratwurst mit Rosinenäpfeln*)

1 lb. Bratwurst
4 oz. ($\frac{2}{3}$ cup) seedless raisins
1 lb. peeled, quartered apples
2 oz. (4 tablespoons) butter
2 tablespoons ($2\frac{1}{2}$) sugar

Heat half the butter, add raisins, apples and sugar. Simmer. Heat the remaining butter, fry the sausages until brown. Place these on top of the apples, cook gently a further 10 minutes.
(Drink: beer)

KNUCKLE LEG OF PORK WITH DUMPLINGS AND HORSERADISH SAUCE (*Eisbein mit Kartoffelklössen und Meerettichsauce*)

Pig's knuckles served with horseradish sauce and potato dumplings.

KÖTHENER SHOEMAKER'S DISH (*Köthener Schusterpfanne*)

$1\frac{1}{2}$ lb. pork belly, sliced
$1\frac{1}{2}$ lb. potatoes, sliced
$1\frac{1}{2}$ lb. firm pears, sliced
salt, sugar to taste
small piece cinnamon
2 cups ($2\frac{1}{2}$) meat stock
1 teaspoon ($1\frac{1}{4}$) caraway

Arrange the meat in the middle of a casserole and surround with potatoes and pears. Add salt, sugar, cinnamon, stock and caraway. Cook in a moderate oven for 2 hours.
(Drink: beer)

MEAT AND ONIONS (*Zwiebelfleisch*)

$1\frac{1}{2}$ lb. pork belly
1 oz. (2 tablespoons) pork fat
2 lb. onions, sliced
salt, pepper, caraway
$\frac{1}{2}$ teaspoon ($\frac{2}{3}$) each sugar, vinegar
$\frac{1}{2}$ lb. white bread, sliced
chopped parsley

Cook the pork in water to cover until tender. Heat the fat, brown the onions, add salt, pepper, caraway, sugar, vinegar and enough water to cook until soft. Put the bread on top of the onions, add enough of the pork stock to swell out the bread, bring to the boil. Serve with the meat thinly sliced and with potato dumplings. Garnish with parsley.

GROUND PORK (*Hackepeter*)

A popular dish in many parts of Germany, also called *gehacktes*. Similar to Beef Tartare, it is freshly ground lean pork heavily seasoned with salt, pepper, caraway seeds and finely chopped onions. A single portion is reckoned to be about 4 oz. The seasoned meat is either served on a plate garnished with sliced gherkins, sometimes topped with a poached or raw egg yolk, and served with bread, or spread on bread and simply garnished with sliced gherkins, as an open sandwich.
(Drink: beer)

SALT SPARERIB OF PORK (*Pökelkamm mit Kartoffelklössen und Meerettichsauce*)

3 lb. salted sparerib
1 onion stuck with 2 cloves
1 bay leaf
horseradish sauce
  (page 24)
potato dumplings
  (page 62)

Cook the pork in water with the onion and bay leaf until tender. Bring to the boil, take from the heat and leave to get cold in its liquid. Cut in slices, spread with horseradish sauce and serve with dumplings.
(Drink: beer)

POT ROAST (*Topfbraten*)

2 lb. cheap cuts of pork
seasoned meat stock
¼ lb. gingerbread, crumbled
3 tablespoons (3¾) plum jam
pinch of mixed spice
2 tablespoons (2½) vinegar

Stew the pork in a little stock until tender. Add gingerbread and cook until the gravy thickens. Add the jam, spice and vinegar. Serve the meat in the sauce.

THURINGIAN FRIED PORK (*Thüringer Rostbrätel*)

1 lb. pork per portion
salt, pepper, mustard
fat
bread

The pork can be a thick slice or chop. Rub with salt and pepper. Fry the pork in a little fat until it is cooked through and is crisp and brown. Place the meat on slices of bread, spread with mustard and serve with fried sliced onions, mashed potatoes and cabbage.
(Drink: beer)

STUFFED CABBAGE LEAVES (*Kohlrouladen*)

1 large white cabbage
½ lb. each pork, beef
2 rolls soaked in milk
2 oz. (¼ cup) butter
1 onion, chopped
chopped parsley to taste
salt, pepper
caraway, nutmeg
1 onion, sliced
1 carrot, sliced
meat stock or water
6–8 slices bacon
1 tablespoon (1¼) flour

Squeeze rolls dry, reserve the milk. Put the meat with squeezed rolls through the fine plate of a grinder. Heat half the butter, fry the chopped onion and parsley, add seasoning and milk. Stir well, mix into the meat. The mixture should be loose and if a large quantity is required, cold cooked rice may be added if necessary.

Remove the outside leaves from the cabbage and cut out the hard core. Cook the head well covered in salted water for 10 minutes. Drain and rinse in cold water. Separate the leaves and cut out the centre ribs. Lay the larger leaves on the table and cover with the smaller leaves. Sprinkle with caraway and nutmeg. In the centre of each leaf put some of the filling. Fold over into rolls, tucking in both ends. Tie each roll with cotton thread to prevent them coming apart during cooking.

Heat the remaining butter in an iron casserole. Fry the sliced onion and carrot, Add stock, then the cabbage rolls and cover with bacon. Put the casserole into a hot oven and cook the rolls covered for a good hour. Uncover and continue cooking until the rolls brown.

Take the casserole from the oven. Arrange the rolls on a hot platter. Mix the flour with water to a thin paste. Bring the gravy to the boil, stir in the flour paste and cook on top of the stove until the gravy is thick.

Serve the cabbage rolls and gravy separately with boiled potatoes sprinkled with parsley.

(Drink: beer)

RED CABBAGE ROULADEN (*Rotkohlrouladen*)

Prepare as in previous recipe using red cabbage instead of white. Cook the cabbage in water generously flavoured with vinegar so that the cabbage leaves retain their fine colour.

FRIED MUTTON (*Hammelbraten*)

Prepare as for fried pork (see page 64). Serve with Thuringian dumplings. (Drink: red wine)

VEGETABLES

ERFURT BROAD BEANS (*Erfurt Puffbohnen*)

1 lb. streaky bacon,
   in 1 piece
1 onion stuck with 2 cloves
1 bay leaf
1 lb. shelled broad beans
1 tablespoon (1¼) cornflour
   (cornstarch)
2 tablespoons (2½) cream
chopped parsley

Cook the bacon with the onion and bay leaf in unsalted water until tender. Take from the pan. Add the beans and cook until soft. Mix the cornflour with water to a thin paste, stir into the beans and cook until the broth thickens. Add the cream and parsley. Slice the bacon. Serve the beans covered with the bacon.
(Drink: beer)

LEIPZIG 'ALLSORTS' (*Leipziger Allerlei*)

½ lb. carrots, diced
½ lb. shelled peas
½ lb. cauliflower flowerets
½ lb. asparagus tips
½ lb. mushrooms
1 pint (1¼) stock
salt, nutmeg, parsley

Put all the ingredients except salt, nutmeg, parsley into a large shallow pan and cook gently until tender. Add salt and nutmeg and sprinkle with chopped parsley before serving.

CHEESE AND CAKES

THURINGIAN CHEESE WITH DRIPPING AND BREAD
(*Thüringer Käse mit Gänsefett-Bemmchen*)

Thuringian cheese, like that of the Harz or of Mainz, is made from curds and shaped like a long sausage. With it is served thickly sliced bread spread with goose fat.
(Drink: beer or *Schnaps*)

Meat pie Altbürgermeister
(*Altbürgermeister Nuschhappen*)

CHEESE CROQUETTES (*Quarkkeulchen*)

1 lb. curd cheese, sieved
1 lb. cooked potatoes, sieved
3 oz. (¾ cup) flour
2 eggs, well beaten
4 tablespoons (5) sugar
½ cup (⅔) raisins
grated lemon rind
salt, cinnamon
butter for frying

Combine the cheese and potatoes and when blended add the remaining ingredients (except butter). Break off pieces and shape into croquettes. Heat the butter and brown the croquettes on both sides. Serve hot sprinkled with sugar and cinnamon mixed. They can be served with apple purée or other stewed fruits.

DRESDEN CAKE (*Dresdner Eirschecke*)

1 lb. yeast dough
2 lb. curd cheese
5 eggs, beaten
3 oz. (⅓ cup) sugar
4 oz. (½ cup) butter
4 oz. (½ cup) sugar
8 eggs, separated
1 tablespoon (1¼) flour
chopped blanched
  almonds or raisins

Line a round baking pan, with spring side opening, with the dough, let it rise then fill with the following fillings: sieve the cheese, mix with the 5 eggs and first quantity of sugar, beat until frothy. Pour into the pastry case. Beat the butter and remaining sugar until creamy, add the 8 egg yolks and flour and beat well. Whisk the whites until stiff and fold into the butter mixture. Spread this over the curd cheese, sprinkle with almonds or raisins. Bake in a hot oven for 40 minutes.

POPPY CAKE (*Mohnkuchen*)

1 lb. yeast dough
3 oz. (½ cup) semolina
½ pint (1½ cups) water
2 oz. (½ cup) poppy seeds
6 oz. (1 cup) raisins
3½ oz. (½ cup) sugar

Roll out the dough and line a baking sheet. Leave to rise. Cook the semolina with the water until thick and smooth. Beat in the poppy seeds, raisins and sugar. Spread this mixture evenly on top of the pastry. Bake in a hot oven until the pastry is a golden brown. The semolina serves to keep the cake light and moist.

Almond-coated Médaillons
(*Médaillons in Mandelrock*)

A Silesian Childhood

Silesia has two principal rivers,
Schnaps and the River Oder!

How could it indeed be otherwise, what with the dust from the mines and
the long cold winters? Neither would be bearable without *Schnaps*. And
let no one think of it as an oily drink in these parts where they will consider
nothing less than a clean, clear-grain spirit and similar pure and highly
alcoholic drinks. Many wanderers from other lands brought their recipes
with them to Silesia, Croatian beer among them. In time, in their new
homeland, they developed into even better drinks and even today they are
constantly improving.

Although I came originally from Silesia I drank no *Schnaps* in those
days, so my opinions are drawn from my fellow-countrymen. While we
are on the subject of drink, a *Schnaps* and a beer chaser are the traditional
combination, and a clever one. The stomach is warmed up by the *Schnaps*
and the cool beer cannot adversely affect it. In this way, my countrymen
could drink quite a quantity!

There used to be distilleries in every little town. On Fridays, paydays, rows of bicycles twenty deep used to stand outside them. Their owners wet their whistles with *Schnaps*, taken not from little tiny glasses but from tumblers. What's to be made of that?

The different varieties were not kept in bottles in the bar but in small barrels heaped one upon the other. The particular variety was marked in chalk on each barrel and poured out of a stopcock. There were *Weinstube* as well. In fact, my father kept one and had a hard time making a living. If it had not been for the Church and Communion wine, I hardly know how he could have raised us all. Simply on account of Communion wine, grapes were grown almost as far north as Königsberg. In Silesia the wine of Grünberg was well known. It was supposed to be so sour, however, that the following story is told of it. Outside the Post Office in Grünberg two postmen are said to have spilt their litres of *Grünberger* over the mail coach – by accident, of course. It was so sour that before their very eyes the coach shuddered, contracted and turned into a postman's bicycle. *Se non e vero, e ben trovato.* The truth of the matter, unhappily, is that although both a *Sekt* and a brandy of sorts were made from this wine, by itself it was barely drinkable.

Silesia is a country which, above all other parts of Germany, might have set out to become independent. It had its great river, the Oder, coal, minerals, a healthy agriculture and a population of notably industrious and undemanding workers. We knew little in the way of luxury, even in our diet. The linen-weavers cooked with linseed oil, and ate curds with potatoes in their jackets. No wonder that they gave a powerful impulse to the Socialist movement around the turn of the century. Gerhard Hauptmann, with his play 'The Weavers', contributed to that impulse. People in my homeland were poor, and Breslau was wellknown as the cheapest big city in Germany.

I remember so well the *Grafschaft* of Glatz, that fortress so dear to Frederick the Great. The mountain-dwellers lived in houses with tiled roofs, and on the ground floor you would often see the simple, polished dower chests, the top and bottom of which would be full of dried fruit waiting for the onset of winter.

The kitchen ranges which, like the tiled stoves, were so much the heart of the house, were fired both by coal and wood. Their iron plates threw out their glow first thing in the morning before we went to school. In winter, of course, it was dark at this hour. In the centre of the kitchen burned one feeble rushlight. The cracks between the plates of the oven would cast a warm glow on the dark walls. On top of it there would be a plain porridge made with water and, on special days, enriched by the addition of milk, a piece of margarine or even of butter. That was breakfast. Sometimes we would toast black bread as well. Take it or leave it, this kept us going till noon.

Most families, even in towns, slaughtered a pig in the autumn. In the cool, dark cellar stood the tub of brine, beside it a barrel containing home-made *Sauerkraut*. Not far away lay at least 30–40 hundredweight of potatoes, for our family of seven. These were divided into potatoes for baking in their jackets, potatoes for salting, mealy potatoes, and very firm potatoes suitable for potato salad. In our other cellar lay hundredweights of coal and wood for heating. On the walls stood glass jars containing our own preserved fruit and vegetables. In every house these would have been the housewife's pride. From October 1st onwards, everything stood ready. Let winter come and do its worst, we were prepared and should neither freeze nor starve.

The influence of neighbouring countries is to be detected in Silesian cookery: Polish carp and cheeses, Bohemian goulash, Austrian sausage. We owe a number of cornmeal dishes, particularly cakes, to our neighbours. *Pfefferkuchen* (pepper cakes) are typical. Very likely they were brought by the Franks who migrated into Silesia – the city of Frankenstein is their witness – from the area round Nürnberg. Here it was developed into a specialized craft, the *Pfefferküchler*. Since the season for these cakes is limited to Christmas, they all ran sweetshops at the same time. Bakers, especially bakers of confectionery, knew this art too, as a sideline. Later we will outline a recipe for it.

It was not Carême and Escoffier back in Silesia but the fare was hearten-ing and honest. Noodles and roast pork dominated Sunday lunch, and various forms of pork with *Sauerkraut* were a regular feature of our meals. There was little difference in the standard of food between town and country. The yeoman farmer who ate with the rank and file of his labourers and maids was only recognizable in that he urged the men to eat curds with their jacket potatoes so as to spin out the butter: 'Eat curds, curds are cooling'. But the men would answer: 'We'd sooner eat butter, even if we burn our tongues'.

Thanks to broad meadows and extensive forests, there was a notable quantity of game. Pheasants, partridge, deer and hares abounded. So did carp, which we cooked in the Polish fashion.

If Sunday was the high point of the week, so was Christmas the great moment of the year at table. On Christmas Eve, everyone who could possibly contrive it ate carp and followed it with poppy-seed dumplings. On the first Holy Day they would eat a noodle soup, followed by a roast goose, crisp on the outside and garnished with red cabbage and *Klösse*; on the second Holy Day, roast hare larded with bacon fat and served with a cream sauce and *Sauerkraut*. On New Year's Eve, too, there would be carp, but cooked *au bleu* because of the scales which (if you kept them) meant money for a whole year. And on New Year's Day there used to be another goose.

On January 2nd, whatever might still be left over was warmed up for the last time and then everyday life resumed its usual rhythm. Nobody grumbled. What was there to grumble about? The simple dishes that we did have, such as garlic sausage, Polish sausage, *Wellwürste* when a pig was slaughtered, all these were unbeatable of their kind. Nevertheless, we were not insensitive to higher things. Crabs were enjoyed in many ways when the month has no 'R' in it, and over in Ohlau there was a master cook renowned for his goose-liver pasties, prepared exclusively from Silesian *foie-gras*. But a humble star of moderation hangs over the Silesian kitchen. The best proof of this is that wherever you meet a Silesian he thinks himself in heaven merely by having some dried fruit with bacon and *Klössen*. *Schlesisches Himmelreich* (Silesian Heaven) is the name of the dish: the recipe for it will be found among many others here.

SOUP

POTATO SOUP (*Kartoffelsuppe aus rohen Kartoffeln*)

¾ lb. potatoes, grated
2 oz. (4 tablespoons) bacon fat
1 large onion, sliced
1 large carrot, sliced
1 leek sliced
1–2 sticks celery, sliced
3 pints (3¾) meat stock
milk or cream (optional)
salt, pepper
chopped marjoram to taste
chopped parsley

Heat the bacon fat, add the sliced vegetables and fry for 5 minutes. Add the stock, bring to the boil, add the potatoes. Cook gently until all the vegetables are soft. As the colour becomes an insipid grey, milk or cream may be added to improve it. Flavour with salt, pepper and marjoram and sprinkle with parsley before serving.
(Drink: beer)

CRAYFISH SOUP (*Krebsuppe vom frischen Krebsen*)

12–16 crayfish
3 pints (3¾) fish stock
¼ cup (⅓) brandy
½ lb. (1 cup) butter
2 pints (2½) clear meat stock
2 tablespoons (2½) cornflour (cornstarch)
cold milk
½ cup (⅔) white wine
4 egg yolks, beaten
½ cup (⅔) single cream
12 asparagus tips or finely chopped mushrooms

Bring the fish stock to the boil, add the crayfish, lower the heat and simmer for 12 minutes. Take from the heat, cool the crayfish in their liquid. Pull off the tails, clean the fish. Pour the brandy over the tails and put aside. Put the rest of the fish through an electric blender, adding enough fish stock to make a thick purée. Heat the butter, add the purée, cook gently for 10 minutes. Pour off the surplus butter, strain and put aside. Bring the meat stock to the boil, add the fish purée, stirring, then the fish stock and continue cooking gently for 30 minutes. Strain the soup, return it to the pan. Mix the cornflour with milk to make a thin paste. Stir this into the soup, add wine and continue stirring until the soup thickens. Beat the egg yolks into the cream, stir into the soup and at once remove from the heat. Heat the reserved crayfish butter, toss the crayfish tails and asparagus into it, add brandy, stir well and turn into the soup. Serve at once.

BOILED PORK SOUP (*Wellfleischsuppe*)

This particular soup is only made in the country at pig-killing time. The name stems from the German word *wellen* which means to boil – also curiously to wallop. To make the soup, various odd portions of the freshly-killed pig, which are not salted or cut into expensive joints, are taken and boiled at once while the flesh is still body-warm. When the meat is tender it is drained from the pan, put aside and kept hot to be used as the main course for a *Wellfleisch* dinner and the liquid is brought again to the boil. Pork sausages, also made from fresh pork, are added, the heat reduced and the sausages cooked until tender. The reason for lowering the heat is to prevent the sausages bursting as they cook, but even so it is considered desirable that a few should burst to add flavour to the soup and thicken it.

To prepare a *Wellfleisch* dinner, it is important that the pork is, as mentioned above, truly body-warm when it is put into the pan. It is this warmth which is said to give the fresh pork its special flavour. If the pork were allowed to cool before being cooked, then all pork dishes could be justly called *Wellfleisch*, which is far from being the case. The sausages too are of a particular size, being 1 in. thick and 6 in. long, and closed on both sides with sausage skins, not tied with thread.

For a *Wellfleisch* dinner the sausage soup is served first and this is followed by a hot platter filled with the freshly-boiled pork. In this will be included the head, kidneys, heart and even the snout, preferably still with a few hairs shining on it. With this will be served *Sauerkraut*, pickled gherkins, liver sausage just warm and even some fried black pudding.

Both *Schnaps* and beer are served during the meal, which is hearty to say the least.

FISH

POLISH CARP (*Polnischer Karpfen*)

2½ lb. carp

2 pints (2½) water

2 carrots, sliced

1 leek, sliced

2 onions, sliced

4 sticks celery, sliced

6 sprigs parsley, chopped

1 onion stuck with 2 cloves

2 slices lemon

salt to taste

1 bay leaf

1 pint (1¼) brown beer

¼ lb. gingerbread, crumbled

2 oz. (⅓ cup) almonds, blanched

2 oz. (⅓ cup) seedless raisins

Put the water, vegetables, lemon, salt and bay leaf into a pan, bring to the boil, lower the heat and simmer for 10 minutes. Add the fish and the beer. Cover and simmer for 30 minutes or until the fin on the head can be easily pulled out. Take out the fish, keep it warm, and strain the stock. Return it to the pan, add the gingerbread, almonds and raisins and cook for 10 minutes. Spoon the sauce over the fish and serve with boiled potatoes.

A few scales from the Christmas carp kept in a purse indicates money the whole year through.

(Drink: red wine)

BLUE TROUT (*Forellen Blau*)

4 trout, freshly killed
5 tablespoons (6¼) white wine
5 tablespoons (6¼) vinegar
4 oz. (½ cup) butter
salt
lemon wedges
chopped parsley

The trout should be thoroughly cleaned inside, particularly along the backbone. The black streak should be carefully removed but when washing the fish take care not to remove the outer natural slime which mixes with the vinegar to give the beautiful blue sheen to the fish skin.

Mix enough water to cover the fish with the wine, vinegar and a little salt. Bring these ingredients to the boil and place the trout in the pan. Take the pan at once from the stove and leave for 12 minutes – if the fins are easily removed, the fish is ready. Trout should be cooked thoroughly so that when eaten, the flesh comes easily from the bones.

Heat the butter until it melts and then whisk with a wire whisk until frothy. Pour into a sauceboat. Garnish the trout with lemon wedges and parsley and serve with boiled potatoes which have been tossed in butter and then sprinkled with parsley.

(Drink: a sparkling Moselle)

EGGS

SOLEIER CREAM (*Soleiercreme*)

Soleier are hard-boiled eggs, shelled and pickled for 8 days in a brine. To make the cream, the eggs are chopped, rubbed through a sieve and then mixed with salt, mustard, a little oil, finely-chopped onions, chives, parsley and anchovy paste. The flavourings are all to taste and the mixture the consistency of well-beaten butter. It is then served on hot toasts.

(Drink: beer)

MEAT

HAM BAKED IN BREAD DOUGH (*Schinken in Brotteig gebacken*)

4–6 lb. uncooked ham
1 onion stuck with 2 cloves
1 bay leaf
baker's rye bread dough
1 egg, well beaten

Soak the ham overnight, cook next day with the onion and bay leaf in boiling water 1 hour. Skin and cool. Roll out the dough ¼ in. thick and paint with egg. Place the meat top side underneath on the dough and wrap the dough round the ham. Smooth down and place on a greased baking tin. Garnish with 'dough leaves', paint with egg and make 2 holes on top. Bake 2 or 3 hours in a hot oven – time depends on size of ham. Break open the dough, slice the ham and serve with asparagus or a salad.
(Drink: mild red wine)

PEASANT BREAKFAST (*Bauernfrühstück*)

1 lb. cooked potatoes, sliced
3–4 slices fat bacon, chopped
1 onion, diced
1 oz. (2 tablespoons) butter
6 eggs, beaten
salt, chopped chives

Fry the bacon, onions and potatoes until crisp. In another pan heat the butter, add the eggs and make a thin omelette in the usual way. Put the potatoes, bacon etc. down the middle, sprinkle lightly with salt and chives and fold over. Serve garnished with sliced tomatoes and lettuce leaves.
(Drink: beer)

STEWED BEEF WITH POTATOES (*Rindfleisch mit Brühkartoffeln*)

1 lb. stewing beef
salt, pepper
2 carrots and leeks
2 sticks celery
1 lb. potatoes, sliced
chopped parsley

Cook the meat with salt, pepper, carrots, leeks and celery in water to cover. When tender take the meat and vegetables from the pan. Cook the potatoes in the same liquid. Cut the meat into cubes, chop the vegetables and reheat in the pan. Serve sprinkled with parsley.

RUSSIAN ROAST PORK (*Russischer Schweinebraten*)

3 lb. spareribs
salt, pepper
garlic, gherkin, salami
smoked ham
1 tablespoon (1¼)
 cornflour (cornstarch)
sour cream

Sprinkle the pork with salt and pepper and stick with shredded garlic, strips of gherkin, salami and ham and continue cooking as for Silesian Pork (see below). Thicken the sauce and add sour cream just before serving.
(Drink: beer)

SILESIAN ROAST PORK (*Schlesischer Schweinebraten*)

3 lb. leg of pork
salt, pepper
2 cups (2½) hot water
3 onions stuck with cloves
1 bay leaf
1 clove garlic
2 cloves
1 tablespoon (1¼) tomato
 purée
1 stick celery, diced
1 carrot, diced
1 lb. chopped pork bones
1 tablespoon (1¼) cornflour
 (cornstarch)

Sprinkle the pork with salt and pepper, place in a deep baking pan skin side down. Add the water and cover. Cook on top of the stove until the skin is soft, about 10 minutes. Score the soft skin with a sharp knife into squares – do not cut too deeply or the squares will fall out while cooking. After 30 minutes add the onions, bay leaf, garlic, cloves, half the tomato purée and the bones. Now put the pan in the oven and roast uncovered, basting frequently until the bones have browned. Take the pan from the oven, rearrange the bones at the bottom of the pan and place the meat on top. Continue roasting, still uncovered, another 2½ hours.

Take the meat from the pan, put aside but keep hot. Add the carrot and celery to the pan and cook on top of the stove until brown. Add the remaining tomato purée and meat stock. Stir well and simmer for 30 minutes. Rub the sauce through a sieve, return it to the pan. Mix the cornflour with water to a thin paste, bring the sauce to the boil, stir in the cornflour paste and cook over a good heat until the sauce is thick. Serve the sauce in a sauceboat.
(Drink: hock or beer)

SILESIAN HEAVEN (*Schlesisches Himmelreich*)

1 lb. mixed dried fruit i.e.
  prunes, apples,
  pears
1 lb. smoked pork
1 onion stuck with cloves
2 oz. (4 tablespoons) butter
1 tablespoon (1¼) flour
pinch salt
1 tablespoon (1¼) sugar
1 tablespoon (1¼) lemon
  juice

Soak the fruit overnight in plenty of water. Remove stones. Cook the meat with the onion in just enough water to cover for 1 hour. Add the fruit and its liquid. Continue cooking slowly for 2 hours. Take out the meat, slice it and keep warm. Discard the onion. Melt the butter, stir in the flour, when blended gradually add the broth from the meat and fruit. When the sauce is thick, stir it back into the fruit. Bring to the boil, add salt, sugar and lemon juice and pour the sauce over the meat. Serve with dumplings. The Silesians say those who have never eaten *Himmelreich* have not lived.

SPICED SAUCE FOR SAUSAGES (*Pfefferkuchensauce ·für Würste*)

½ lb. gingerbread
1 pint (1¼) malt beer
small root hamburg
  parsley, chopped
1 stick celery, chopped
1 carrot, chopped
1 onion, chopped
1 leek, chopped
1 pint (1¼) meat stock
salt, pepper
2 sprigs parsley, chopped
1 tablespoon (1¼) vinegar

Crumble the gingerbread in a bowl and cover with the beer. Leave to soak. Cook all the vegetables until tender in the meat stock, add seasoning and parsley. Squeeze the gingerbread dry, stir into the stock and vegetables. Continue cooking until the stock is thick. Add the vinegar and whisk with a wire whisk.

German sausages of the boiling type are then cooked very slowly in the sauce, to which some cooks like to add chopped blanched almonds and raisins. The sausages, with their sauce, are served with mashed potatoes.

Hamburg parsley is a root with a flavour between a parsnip and celeriac. (Drink: beer)

POULTRY AND GAME

GOOSE GIBLETS IN PARSLEY SAUCE (*Gänseklein mit Petersilientunke*)

1 set goose giblets
2 oz. (4 tablespoons) butter
1 tablespoon (1¼) flour
2 cups (2½) meat stock
2 egg yolks, beaten
1 cup (1¼) cream
chopped parsley

Under the term *ganseklein* is included the head, heart, feet, stomach and wings of the goose. These must be thoroughly cleaned, i.e. the eyes and beak taken from the head, the neck cut into two, the wings broken from the bone. The stomach must be cleaned and the thick skin removed; the claws chopped off the feet. Wash all these ingredients together and chop them coarsely. Heat half the butter and gently cook the giblets. Heat the remaining butter, stir in the flour, blend well and gradually add the meat stock. Pour the sauce over the giblets and continue cooking until tender. Beat the yolks into the cream and stir into the sauce. Do not cook the sauce any longer or it might curdle. Stir in plenty of parsley. Serve with boiled potatoes, buttered noodles, dumplings, spaghetti or buttered rice. (Drink: beer)

ROAST GOOSE (*Gänsebraten*)

1 goose about 8 lb., oven-ready

4 onions, quartered

4 apples, quartered

1 sprig wormwood

2 pints (2½) hot water

2 cloves

1 bay leaf

1 cup (1¼) apple purée

Stuff the goose with the onions, apples and wormwood. Place it breast downwards on a rack in a baking pan. Add the hot water, cloves and bay leaf. The water catches the goose fat without letting the bird dry out. Turn the goose after 2 hours. Continue roasting about 1 hour longer. Take the goose from the pan. Bring the gravy to the boil on top of the stove, skim off excess fat and thicken with the purée. Stir well, strain and reheat. Carve the goose, chop the filling, discarding the wormwood. Serve the goose with red cabbage and potato dumplings and the sauce separately.

(Drink: red wine)

STUFFED NECK OF GOOSE (*Gefüllter Gänsehals*)

1 goose neck, cut off as far down the body as possible

1 goose liver, soaked overnight in milk

2 oz. (4 tablespoons) butter

½ lb. lean pork

¼ lb. fat bacon

3 onions, finely chopped

2 oz. (⅓ cup) blanched almonds

2 oz. (¼ cup) shelled pistachio nuts

marjoram, rosemary, finely chopped

salt, pepper

3 eggs, well beaten

¼ cup (⅓) Madeira

meat stock or water

Cut off the head, remove the windpipe and gullet. Wash the neck well, pull out small bones. Dry the liver. Heat the butter and fry the liver until just cooked but not soft, take from the pan. Mince the pork and bacon together. Fry in the butter with the onions. Mince the liver. Finely chop the nuts. Combine all these ingredients, add the herbs, seasoning, bind with the eggs and add Madeira. Push this mixture into the goose neck and firmly sew up both ends. Cook gently in stock for 40 minutes, not letting the liquid boil. Put the neck between 2 boards with a weight on top to flatten it. Remove threads and slice to serve. The stuffed neck can also be fried until crisp and brown in goose fat and eaten hot with rice and cooked green cabbage.

HARE IN CREAM SAUCE (*Hasenrücken in Sahne*)

**1-2 saddles of hare,
    skinned well-hung**
salt, pepper
8 thin slices mild bacon
3 tablespoons (3¾) olive oil
3 onions, sliced
1 carrot, sliced
½ stick celery, sliced
1 leek, sliced
5 juniper berries
1 pint (1¼) meat stock
**2 teaspoons (2½) cornflour
    (cornstarch)**
½ cup (⅔) sour cream
juice 1 lemon
½ cup (⅔) white wine

Wipe the meat, sprinkle with salt, wrap in bacon and tie securely. Heat the oil in a baking pan on top of the stove, add the hare and brown all over. Add the vegetables, berries and seasoning and put the pan in a hot oven. Roast for 40 minutes for underdone meat, another 10 minutes fo⁚ well done. Take the meat from the pan, keep hot. Put the pan on top of the stove, cook the sauce for 5 minutes, add the stock. Simmer 20 minutes. Pour through a sieve, return to the pan. Mix the cornflour with water to a thin paste, stir this into the sauce, continue cooking until thick, add the cream, bring once to the boil, lower the heat and add the juice and wine. Cut up the hare with the bacon still attached, discard threads. Serve the hare on a hot dish spread with a little sauce, serve the rest in a sauceboat.
(Drink: red wine)

PARTRIDGES IN LENTILS AND CREAM (*Rebhühner in Sahnelinsen*)

4 elderly partridges
¾ lb. lentils
¼ lb. (¼ cup) butter
**1 lb. mixed onions, leeks,
    carrots, celery, finely
    sliced**
3 pints (3¾) meat stock
1 onion stuck with 2 cloves
1 bay leaf
¼ lb. lean bacon, diced
salt, pepper
1 cup (1¼) sour cream
½ cup (⅔) port

Soak the lentils overnight. Heat the butter in a casserole, add the mixed vegetables and fry them without browning. Drain the lentils and add with the stock to the vegetables. Bring to the boil, add the partridges, whole onion and bay leaf. Cover the pan and place in a moderate oven. When the partridges are tender, the lentils should be soft. Fry the bacon. Return the casserole to the top of the stove, add the bacon, seasoning and cream. Stir and add the port.
(Drink: red wine)

PARTRIDGES IN CREAM (*Rebhühner in Sahne*)

**4 young partridges, hung
  for 8 days**
salt
4 onions, sliced
2 apples, peeled and sliced
8 juniper berries, crushed
**4 large slices fat bacon,
  rind removed**
8 vine leaves, washed
4 tablespoons (5) butter
4 sticks celery, chopped
1 small leek, sliced
1 carrot, sliced
**1 large and 1 small bunch
  grapes, black or white**
**4 tablespoons (5)
  Wunschelburger Korn
  Schnaps**
¾ pint (2 cups) sour cream
**1 tablespoon (1¼) cornflour
  (cornstarch)**
1 cup (1¼) white wine

Sprinkle inside the partridges with salt and fill with some of the sliced onion, apples and juniper berries. Tie a slice of bacon and 2 vine leaves round each bird. Sprinkle with salt. Heat the butter until smoking hot, add the partridges, brown lightly all over, then add the rest of the sliced and chopped vegetables and apples. Wash and stone the grapes from the small bunch, add to the pan. Cover and cook over a low heat 10 minutes, uncover, add the *Schnaps*, ignite it and leave the pan uncovered until the flame dies down. Add the sour cream. Cover again and simmer for a further 10–15 minutes. You will be surprised at the delicious aroma that arises, which is even further improved by the addition of the *Schnaps*. When the partridges are tender, take them from the pan, remove threads and vine leaves and put the birds with the bacon on a warm dish in a warm oven. Mix the cornflour with the wine. Rub the partridge sauce through a sieve, pushing as much of the vegetables through as possible. This helps to thicken the sauce and also gives flavour. Return this to a clean pan, bring to the boil on top of the stove. Add the cornflour and cook until the sauce is thick. It should be the colour of *café au lait*. It acquires a spicy, piquant flavour from the juniper berries, the apples and the grapes, whence the nickname *Nach der schönen Winzerin* (the beautiful wife of the wine-grower).

There need not be too much sauce: 4 tablespoons (5) per partridge is sufficient, then the flavour can be concentrated.

Cut 4 small wedge-shaped pieces of bread on which the birds can rest easily. Lay the partridges on top, a slice of bacon on the breast of each bird. Arrange in a large round hot dish, the large bunch of grapes in the centre. Garnish with freshly plucked, washed vine leaves. Serve with creamed potatoes and red cabbage cooked in red wine (*Weinkraut*).

(Drink: a full-bodied Burgundy)

Weinkraut can also be prepared with *Sauerkraut* as, for example, in Bavaria. Here *Sauerkraut* is cooked with seedless or stoned white grapes and either *Sekt* (German champagne) or dry white wine is added shortly before serving. This type of *Weinkraut* is also served with partridge, pheasant or roast goose.

STEWED PHEASANT IN HARICOT BEANS (*Alter Fasan in weissen Bohnen*)

1 elderly pheasant
¾ lb. dried haricot beans
seasoned meat stock
thyme, marjoram, parsley
1 stick celery
2 onions, quartered
6 juniper berries
2 slices fat bacon
1 onion, diced
1 tablespoon (1¼) tomato
  purée
½ cup (⅔) cream
½ cup (⅔) port wine

Soak the beans overnight. Next day drain and cook until tender but still firm in a well-seasoned meat stock. Put the pheasant in another pot with the herbs (to taste), celery, quartered onions and juniper berries. Cover with water and cook very slowly until the flesh is tender. Strip the meat from the bones. Fry the bacon until its fat runs, add the pheasant meat and diced onion. When the beans are tender, pour off surplus liquid. Add the tomato purée mixed into the cream. Stir gently, add the pheasant meat, bacon and onion, again stir, then sprinkle with port wine. This makes one of the most delicious casseroles that one can imagine.

(Drink: beer)

ROAST PHEASANT IN BACON (*Fasan im Speck gebraten*)

1 pheasant, oven-ready
salt
4 slices fat bacon
4 tablespoons (5) olive oil
2 onions, quartered
1 bay leaf
4 juniper berries
1 carrot, sliced
1 leek, sliced
2 oz. (4 tablespoons) butter
1 cup ($1\frac{1}{4}$) hot meat stock
1 tablespoon ($1\frac{1}{4}$) cornflour
   (cornstarch)
milk
2 teaspoons ($2\frac{1}{2}$) lemon
   juice
$\frac{1}{2}$ cup ($\frac{2}{3}$) sour cream

Sprinkle the pheasant inside and out with salt. Wrap in bacon and tie with threads. Heat the oil in a baking pan, brown the pheasant all over. Add onions, bay leaf, juniper berries, carrot and leek and continue browning a further 5 minutes. Add the butter and put the pan into a hot oven. Baste often with the meat stock. The pheasant will be ready in about 1 hour. To test, press the flesh with the thumb and forefinger; if soft, the pheasant is ready. Another test: lift the pheasant by the leg with a fork and hold over a plate; if the juice which runs out is white, the bird is ready. Take it from the oven, keep warm. Reheat the gravy on top of the stove, diluting with the remaining stock. Cook for 5 minutes, then pour through a sieve, pushing as much of the vegetables through as possible. Return to a clean pan, bring to the boil. Mix the cornflour with milk to make a thin paste. Stir this into the hot gravy, when this is thick, add the lemon juice and sour cream. Divide the bird into two, lay the bacon on top and cover with the sauce. Serve with creamed potatoes and *Sauerkraut* flavoured with wine.

DUMPLINGS

SILESIAN POTATO DUMPLINGS (*Schlesische Kartoffelklösse*)

2 lb. potatoes cooked in
  their skins, peeled
3 oz. (6 tablespoons) butter
salt, pinch nutmeg
3 oz. (¾ cup) flour
3 egg yolks, beaten
cubes of crisply fried
  bread i.e. croûtons

Mash the potatoes with the butter, salt and nutmeg. Beat in the flour and egg yolks. Break off fairly large pieces of the mixture and shape into balls or dumplings. Push a cube or two of bread into the centre of each dumpling. Drop the dumplings into a pan of bubbling boiling salted water. Bring once again to the boil, lower the heat and cook for 20 minutes. By this time the dumplings should float to the top of the pan, tender and enticing. Take the dumplings out with a slotted spoon. Potato dumplings are served as an accompaniment to a meat dish. It is important they are served quite dry and one way to ensure this is to put a saucer upside down in a bowl in which the dumplings are to be served so that any water which still remains in the spoon or on the dumplings can drain away underneath the saucer and the dumplings remain dry.

BREAD DUMPLINGS (*Semmelklösse*)

10 stale sliced milk rolls
2 slices fat bacon, diced
1 onion, diced
1 sprig parsley, chopped
3 eggs, beaten into a
  little milk
¾ pint (1) warm milk

Fry the bacon until the fat runs, add the onion and lightly brown. Put the rolls, bacon, onion, parsley, eggs and milk into a bowl and leave until the bread has absorbed the liquid. Knead well, break off pieces and shape into balls. Drop in boiling, salted water, lower the heat and cook for 20 minutes. When they float to the top, take them from the pan with a slotted spoon and serve at once.

POLISH POTATO DUMPLINGS (*Polnischer Klösse*)

2 lb. peeled potatoes, grated and squeezed dry

1 lb. cooked potatoes, mashed in a little milk

2 eggs, beaten

fried bread cubes

salt

Mix the grated and mashed potatoes and beat in the eggs. Break off pieces and shape into balls. Put a cube of bread in the centre of each. Drop into boiling, salted water, bring to the boil, lower the heat and cook for 20 minutes or until they float to the surface.

FRIED POTATO DUMPLINGS (*Geröstete Klösse*)

Cut cold potato dumplings into thick slices and fry in hot fat until brown and crisp on both sides. Serve with a salad. Beaten eggs may be poured over the slices as they are frying.

VEGETABLES

MASHED POTATOES AND MILK (*Stampfkartoffeln*)

I first ate these after a partridge drive with my father one August. Having washed under the pump, we sat down to eat them at the well-scrubbed table in the inn.

2 lb. potatoes, peeled

salt

6 slices fat bacon, diced

diced onion (optional)

Cook the potatoes in salted water until soft. Drain off half the water and mash the potatoes to a purée. Fry the bacon and scatter it over the top of the potatoes. Diced fried onion may also be added.

POTATO PUFFS (*Kartoffelpuffer*)

1 lb. potatoes, peeled and grated

4 tablespoons (5) flour

salt

1 egg, beaten

fat for frying

If the potatoes are watery, squeeze them dry in a cloth. Mix with the remaining ingredients (except the fat). Heat plenty of fat and fry the potato mixture in small round thin puffs until brown on both sides. Serve hot sprinkled with sugar, apple purée or stewed cranberries; or cold, at coffee time, thickly sprinkled with sugar.

POTATO CAKES (*Patzek*)

From any of the potato dumpling mixtures, form small, round flat cakes, lay on a greased hotplate or in a frying pan and brown quickly on both sides. A great treat for children.

COOKED SAUERKRAUT (*Gekochter Sauerkohl oder Sauerkraut*)

2 lb. sauerkraut

3 oz. (6 tablespoons) pork fat

3 large onions, sliced

2 apples, peeled and chopped

meat stock or water

1 onion stuck with 2 cloves

1 bay leaf

3 juniper berries

salt

sugar

3 medium-sized potatoes, peeled and grated

Heat the pork fat in a pan, add the sliced onions and apples and fry until soft but without changing colour. Add the *Sauerkraut*, tearing it to shreds to look like sawdust in the pan, for then it does not form into clumps. (If the *Sauerkraut* smells somewhat sour, rinse it in cold water, but washing on the whole is not advised, as this takes away the piquant *Sauerkraut* flavour.)

Cover the *Sauerkraut* with stock. Add the onion stuck with cloves, the bay leaf, juniper berries and salt and sugar, both to taste. If water has been used to cook the *Sauerkraut*, a piece of lean bacon or pork may be cooked with it. Cook for one hour over a low heat.

When the cabbage is ready, take out and discard the whole onion and bay leaf, add the potatoes and continue cooking until the potatoes are soft and have thickened the *Sauerkraut*, about 10 to 15 minutes. If bacon or pork has been cooked with the *Sauerkraut*, take this out and serve separately.

A little white wine may be added just before serving.

The time taken to cook the cabbage varies a great deal: young cabbage is ready after 30 to 40 minutes, but older cabbage needs longer. On no account must it be cooked too long; otherwise it will go soft and lose its texture.

SORREL IN BUTTER (*Sauersamfer in Butter*)

2 lb. sorrel
2 oz. ($\frac{1}{4}$ cup) butter
salt
nutmeg

Pull the leaves off the stalks of the sorrel, wash them well and finely chop. Heat the butter in a pan, add the sorrel and cook until tender. Flavour with salt and freshly-grated nutmeg.

Cooked in this manner, the sorrel retains all its flavour. If liked, diced onion can be fried in the butter and added, or the sorrel can be thickened with flour.

RED CABBAGE WITH APPLES (*Rotkohl mit Äpfeln*)

2 lb. red cabbage, shredded
1$\frac{1}{2}$ cups (2) malt or wine vinegar
1 tablespoon (1$\frac{1}{4}$) salt
4 tablespoons (5) sugar
2 oz. ($\frac{1}{4}$ cup) fat
1 large onion, sliced
2 large tart apples, sliced
2 cups (2$\frac{1}{2}$) stock or hot water
1 small onion stuck with 2 cloves
1 bay leaf
3 tablespoons (3$\frac{3}{4}$) red wine
6 tablespoons (7$\frac{1}{2}$) redcurrant jelly or strawberry or blackberry jam

Put the shredded cabbage into a bowl and add 1 cup (1$\frac{1}{4}$) of the vinegar and half the salt and sugar. Mix it round and round and leave. This is to keep the red colour of the cabbage.

Heat the fat, fry the sliced onion and apples without browning; drain the cabbage and add to the pan. Stir well, add the remaining salt, sugar and vinegar. Heat the stock, add the onion with its cloves and bay leaf. Cover the pan and cook slowly for 2 or 3 hours. Just before serving, add the wine and the jelly. The cabbage should be very tender but not mushy.

CAKES

BRESLAU 'SWEET BITES' (*Breslauer Leckerbissen*)

For 60–70 biscuits (cookies):
**honey biscuit dough
(page 95)
raspberry jam
marzipan**

Roll out the dough $\frac{1}{8}$ in. thick and spread over 2 baking trays and prick all over with a fork. Bake in a hot oven for 20 minutes. Turn out and leave until cold.

Spread raspberry jam over one layer of pastry, cover with the second layer. Spread this lightly with jam. Roll out the marzipan to a very thin layer, the same size as the pastry. Place this on top of the jam, and press down lightly. Cut into 1 in. cubes. Place on a rack and cover.

Although it is not usual, some German cooks like to decorate the top of the *Leckerbissen* with icing.

STOLLEN from Dresden, STRIEZEL from Silesia, SCHITTCHEN from Thuringia

These cakes take their name *Stollen* from their shape. *Stollen* means sticks or posts, and these have come to serve as symbols of the Child in the wooden crib. All three, *Stollen*, *Striezel* and *Schittchen*, are fundamentally made of the same dough – the *Christstollenteig* – but for each recipe it is made in a slightly different way.

The Dresden *Stollen*, which are sent out at Christmas from Dresden to all parts of the world, are the most famous. The *Striezel* plays the same important role in Silesia, but the recipe is noticeably more modest in its ingredients.

By contrast, the Thuringian *Schittchen* is made according to the same rich and extravagant recipe as the *Stollen* from Dresden. Somewhat similar is the *Klaben* from Bremen. The dough for this is also heavy and moist.

If you wish to have true, genuine *Stollen* for your Christmas table, follow this recipe:

1. Collect the ingredients in the warm kitchen on the evening before baking, so that they will be warm. Lay the prepared fruit, nuts and almonds in a bowl and leave to stand overnight well drenched in brandy, rum, Kirsch or raspberry cordial.

2. On the following day prepare a normal yeast dough. The milk should only be lukewarm, not more than 86°F., (30°C.). Add a little sugar so that the yeast can act more easily, sprinkle with flour and leave to prove until the flour mixture cracks.

3. Now knead the dough; it must be worked well until it has lost its moist gleaming appearance, and no longer sticks to the hands or to the edge of the bowl.

4. Now add the spices and soaked fruits; press them lightly into the dough, which will otherwise become grey and unattractive.

5. It is best to divide the dough into three and to press the corresponding amount of fruit and spice into each part. Then quickly mix the three parts together.

6. Leave the dough to prove for 30 minutes.

7. Fold the dough and weigh out pieces of 1 or 2 lb.

8. Work these pieces with a little flour into balls; now make them slightly oval. Make a dent with the rolling pin lengthways, more to one side than to the other, and fold the wider side over into the dent.

9. Lay the shaped *Stollen* on a baking tin covered with greaseproof paper and leave to prove for 20 minutes.

10. Baking time: for a 1 lb. *Stollen* allow 40 minutes at 450°F., (230°C.); for 2 lb., about 60 minutes. The oven must be really hot, otherwise there is a risk of the *Stollen* becoming speckly owing to the high fat content. This must at all costs be avoided; it will otherwise be indigestible, as well as unsightly.

11. As the contents of Dresden *Stollen* are so rich, it does not rise like an ordinary yeast dough. Yet it will keep for months, and indeed in many families it is traditional to keep the last pieces for Easter.

12. If you particularly wish to decorate *Stollen* as gifts, paint them with a thick sugar glaze, garnish with candied fruits of all types and then paint once more with the sugar glaze. This last coat prevents drying out and makes the cake even more attractive.

DRESDEN CHRISTMAS CAKE (*Dresdner Christstollen*)

2 lb. (8 cups) flour
2 oz. (2 cakes) yeast
½ cup (⅔) milk
4 oz. (½ cup) sugar
1 teaspoon (1¼) salt
grated rind of 2 lemons
1¼ lb. (3½ cups) raisins
2 oz. (½ cup) sweet almonds
4 oz. (1 cup) candied lemon peel, chopped
¼ cup (⅓) rum
melted butter
vanilla sugar
icing (powdered) sugar

Preparations as described above. As soon as the *Stolle* comes out of the oven, test it with a wooden skewer to make sure it is done, paint with melted butter, sprinkle lightly with vanilla sugar and thickly with icing sugar.

YEAST CAKE (*Baba*)

1 lb. (4 cups) flour
1 oz. (1 cake) yeast
4 oz. (½ cup) sugar
½ cup (⅔) lukewarm milk
2 egg yolks
5 oz. (generous ½ cup) melted butter
pinch salt
2 oz. (½ cup) almonds, chopped
2 oz. (½ cup) raisins
icing (powdered) sugar

Get all the ingredients ready overnight and leave in the kitchen to be at room temperature when used. Put the flour into a mixing bowl (preferably earthenware) and make a well in the centre. Mix the yeast with a little sugar and the milk and very little flour. Pour into the well, lightly cover with flour. Cover and leave to rise. Beat the yolks with the remaining sugar until thick. Beat into the butter, add salt, and pour into the flour. Work to a dough and knead until bubbles form. Work in the almonds and raisins. Butter a large ring mould and fill barely ½ full with the dough. Leave to rise again until double its bulk, and bake in a moderate oven until a cake tester or knitting needle comes out clean. Take from the mould while still warm and sprinkle with icing sugar.

EASTER PLAITED LOAF (*Glasierter Osterzopf*)

1 lb. (4 cups) flour
4 oz. (½ cup) sugar
1 pkt. vanilla sugar
1 oz. (1 cake) yeast
5 oz. (generous ½ cup)
  butter, melted
½ cup (⅔) lukewarm milk
2 egg yolks
pinch salt
6 oz. (1 cup) raisins
grated rind 1 lemon
2 oz. (½ cup) almonds,
  blanched
1 egg yolk
apricot jam
icing (powdered) sugar

Prepare a yeast dough as in previous recipe, using the first 11 ingredients. Leave to rise then knead well until bubbles form. Divide in half. Let the dough rise again to double its size. Break into three portions and roll each piece into 'sausages' 12–14 in. long. Plait these neatly. Brush with egg yolk. Lay on a baking sheet, leave to rise again, and bake in a hot oven 30–35 minutes.

While still warm, paint with jam and sprinkle with icing sugar.

STREUSEL CAKE (*Streuselkuchen*)

1 lb. (4 cups) flour
1 oz. (1 cake) yeast
4 oz. (½ cup) sugar
½ cup (⅓) lukewarm milk
5 oz. (generous ½ cup)
  butter, melted
1 pkt. vanilla sugar
pinch salt
2 egg yolks, beaten
melted butter
Streusel:
3 oz. (6 tablespoons)
  butter
4 oz. (½ cup) sugar
½ lb. (2 cups) flour
1 teaspoon (1¼) ground
  cinnamon

Make a yeast dough as in Yeast Cake, using the first eight ingredients. Knead until smooth and leave to rise. Roll out thinly and spread on a greased baking sheet. Let it rise again and paint it with melted butter.

Prepare the Streusel.

Melt the butter and while still hot mix with the sugar, flour and cinnamon. Cut the paste with a knife, then crumble it to resemble breadcrumbs. Sprinkle this over the rolled-out dough and bake in a moderate oven for about 35 minutes.

This type of cake is usually cut into squares, and when baked should be about ¾ in. thick.

PRASSEL CAKES (*Prasselkuchen*)

Buy or make puff-pastry; roll it out to a thickness of a knife handle; cut out rounds, about 3 in. diameter. Then roll the rounds at each end to form ovals. Paint with milk and sprinkle with *Streusel* (see previous recipe). Bake in a moderate oven. Paint with a sugar glaze while still warm.

SILESIAN POPPY CAKE (*Schlesischer Mohnstollen*)

1 lb. (4 cups) plain (all-purpose) flour

pinch salt

1 oz. (1 cake compressed) yeast

4 oz. ($\frac{1}{2}$ cup) sugar

1 cup ($1\frac{1}{4}$) warm milk

4 oz. ($\frac{1}{2}$ cup) butter, softened

Poppy filling:

10 oz. (2 cups) poppy seeds

4 egg yolks

8 oz. (1 cup) sugar

3 oz. (6 tablespoons) butter

4 tablespoons (5) brandy

$\frac{1}{2}$ cup ($\frac{2}{3}$) milk

3 oz. (scant $\frac{2}{3}$ cup) sultanas

pinch cinnamon

1 packet vanilla sugar

3 oz. ($\frac{3}{4}$ cup) chopped candied orange peel

3 oz. ($\frac{3}{4}$ cup) chopped candied lemon peel

3 oz. ($\frac{3}{4}$ cup) chopped almonds

Glaze:

10 oz. (scant 2 cups) icing (powdered) sugar

1 tablespoon ($1\frac{1}{4}$) warm milk

1 tablespoon ($1\frac{1}{4}$) brandy

Sift the flour and salt into a bowl and make a well in the middle. Cream the yeast with 2 tablespoons ($2\frac{1}{2}$) sugar and the milk. Pour this into the well and gently sprinkle flour over the top. Cover and leave to prove. Add the remaining sugar, work the dough and add the butter. Knead and beat the dough until bubbles appear. Once again cover and leave to prove. Roll out the dough into two rounds and spread on baking tins. Let it rise to double its size.

Mix the ingredients for the poppy filling together in a thick pan over a low heat on top of the stove, gently stir until all the ingredients are hot but not cooked. This is important as there are eggs in the mixture. Take from the heat and leave to cool. Spread this mixture on top of the dough and bake in a hot oven for 1 hour. Take from the oven and at once put on a cake rack.

To make the glaze, sieve the powdered sugar into the milk and brandy, beating it hard, until it is of a consistency to coat the spoon thickly. Spread the glaze over the cakes while they are still hot.

HONEY BISCUITS (*Honiggebäck*)

About 150 biscuits:

1 lb. (1½ cups) honey
½ cup (⅔) water
3 oz. (⅓ cup) butter
¾ lb. (3 cups) rye flour
¾ lb. (3 cups) plain (all-
  purpose) flour
pinch ground ginger
2 teaspoons (2½) baking
  powder
8 oz. (1½ cups) currants
8 oz. (1½ cups) raisins
4 oz. (1 cup) each candied
  orange and lemon peel,
  chopped

Boil the honey, water and butter and then leave to get cold. Mix both flours with the remaining ingredients, add the honey mixture and stir to a thick dough. Roll out on a floured board and cut into strips 1 in. wide. Place on a greased baking sheet and bake for 15 minutes in a very hot oven. When brown cut into wedge-shaped pieces which can be decorated or iced. Serve cold. These biscuits are hard but when left for a few days soften, as they should. Half the quantity of ingredients is enough for most families.

SILESIAN GINGERNUTS (*Schlesische Pfeffernüsse*)

1 lb. (1½ cups) honey
3 oz. (⅓ cup) butter
10 oz. (1¼ cups) sugar
2½ lb. (10 cups) plain (all
  purpose) flour
1 teaspoon (1¼) ground
  ginger
grated rind 3 lemons
2 eggs, beaten
2 teaspoons (2½) baking
  powder
a little rum
1 lb. (4 cups) icing
  powdered sugar

Cook the honey, butter and sugar over a low heat to dissolve the sugar and melt the butter. Leave to cool. Put the flour into a bowl, add the ginger, lemon rind and eggs, then pour in the cooled honey mixture. Dissolve the baking powder in rum and stir into the dough. Roll in flour and form the dough into 'sausages'. Cut into ½ in. thick slices. Place on a greased baking sheet and bake in a hot oven until brown.

Boil the powdered sugar with ½ cup (⅔) of water until it forms fine threads. Put the gingernuts in a bowl and pour the icing slowly over them, stirring with a wooden spoon. When the icing has spread, lay the gingernuts on a cake rack so they do not stick together. Store in an airtight tin as soon as dry.

LIEGNITZ HONEY CAKES (*Liegnitzer Bomben*)

50-60 pieces:

1 lb. (1½ cups) honey
½ lb. raspberry jam
½ lb. (1¾ cups) roasted
   hazel nuts, ground
½ lb. (scant 2 cups)
   almonds, chopped
½ lb. (1 cup) each
   currants, raisins
rum
½ cup (⅔) water
3 oz. (⅓ cup) butter
¼ lb. (3 cups) each rye and
   plain (all purpose) flour
2 teaspoons (2½) baking
   powder

Mix the jam, nuts, currants and raisins in a bowl, add rum to flavour. Cover and leave overnight. Boil the honey, water and butter, leave until cold. Add the flour and baking powder, mix to a firm dough. Roll out on a floured board to a rectangle, spread with the jam mixture, roll up tightly and cut into 1 in. thick slices. Place in greased 3 in. diameter rings, making sure the mixture does not come more than half way up. Bake for 30 minutes in a very hot oven. These cakes can be served hot with a warm chocolate sauce or iced when cold.

HONEY AND ALMOND BISCUITS (*Gewürztaler*)

For 50-60 biscuits:

½ lb. (¾ cup) honey
1 teaspoon (1¼) baking
   powder
½ cup (⅔) milk
2 oz. (½ cup) candied peel,
   diced
12 oz. (1½ cups) sugar
½ lb. (1 cup) butter
1¾ lb. (7 cups) plain (all
   purpose) flour
1 teaspoon (1¼) ground
   ginger
2 oz. (⅓ cup) almonds,
   ground
¼ lb. whole candied peel
chocolate icing,
   about ¾ lb.

Dissolve the baking powder in the milk. Mix with the remaining ingredients, (except whole piece of peel and icing). Work to a paste and knead well. Roll out the dough very thinly and cut into rounds. Place on a greased baking sheet and bake in a hot oven for 10–15 minutes. Cool, spread with icing and decorate with thin strips of candied peel.

DRINKS

WOODRUFF AND MOSELLE CUP (*Aromatische Waldmeister-bowle*)

Emperor Maximilian II's famous doctor, Rembert Dodoens, who was also an enthusiastic botanist, wrote that wine could be poured over woodruff. In 1664 there is further mention of this in the *Jacobus Theodorus Herbal*; beneath a picture of woodruff, we find: 'In May, when the herb is still fresh and in flower, many people are accustomed to place it in wine, and then to drink it; it is supposed to strengthen and refresh the heart'.

Pour two bottles of sparkling Moselle into a punch bowl, standing in broken ice. Tie two small bunches of woodruff without flowers and hang them by a thread in the wine, so that only the leaves and not the stalks are immersed (otherwise the bowl would taste too strongly of grass).

The woodruff must only stay 15 minutes in the wine; too strong a flavour spoils the drink. Bring $\frac{1}{2}$ lb. (1 cup) of sugar with 1 cup ($1\frac{1}{4}$) of water to the boil, remove the froth and leave to cool. Stir in $\frac{1}{2}$ bottle of light white wine, mix well, then pour into the punch bowl. Stir gently and serve.

For children, dilute with mineral water.

PUNCH (*Schneeschipperpunsch*)

A *schneeschipper* is a snow sweeper, and this is a punch for a cold day.

1 bottle red wine
1 bottle white wine
$\frac{1}{2}$ bottle brandy
1 cup ($1\frac{1}{4}$) water
8 oz. (1 cup) sugar
3 cloves
small piece cinnamon
1 spiral each orange and
　lemon peel

Bring the water, sugar, cloves, cinnamon and peel to a gentle boil. Lower the heat, simmer for 5 minutes. Add the wines and brandy, heat gently until a white foam forms. Sieve and pour into glasses while still hot.

Cookery in Bavaria

Bavaria means beer to most of us, and nowhere else has food been so contrived to marry happily with it. I must therefore be excused a slight digression into this subject.

The Bavarians say they need no ordinary calendars since they already have a calendar of beer. The Munich New Year begins in March with the brewing of strong ale. Much sampling goes on to determine whether the beer is strong enough. Strong ale is drunk while sitting on wooden benches. Strong men in *Lederhosen* take their places at the benches. If after a while they remain hopelessly anchored to them, the beer has passed muster. On May Day, the *Maibock* leaps from the barrels and into the glasses. By this time of year one can sometimes sit outside in the beer gardens, just as one does in summer, under the open sky. The landlords provide pretzels and radishes artistically carved into spirals, whilst in the *Hofbräuhaus* in Munich, girls in traditional costume move from table to table offering radishes.

Where beer is consumed in such quantity, there is no great place for *Schnaps*. One or two creep in, however. For instance, *Enzian*, a dry, rather earthy but honest *eau de vie* which goes very well with cool light beer. From Franconia too comes its fine plum brandy, *Zwetsch*. These spirits have been known to help a somewhat overloaded stomach through a difficult hour or two! Many a peasant, too, converts the last of his fruit-pickings into *Schnaps*, the so-called *Obstler* or fruit brandy. It warms the heart and helps the digestion of rich food. Hardly is summer over before the *Oktoberfest* makes its appearance. This is a tremendous occasion, one of the world's great folk festivals. Here one is a human being, here one can achieve humanity. This great throng is proudly headed by heavy-laden beer waggons, often drawn by teams of eight horses. The horses' brasses are highly polished and at their destination the *Oberbürgermeister* of Munich personally taps the first barrel of beer. Additional attractions are provided by oxen roasted whole on the spit, poultry roasted over charcoal fires, calves' knuckles, innumerable kinds of sausage, cheeses, roasted almonds, spiced breads, Bavarian malt cookies and all the other little bits and pieces contributing to the main event.

Year after year, people come from all over the world to see this show. They join in, they drink, they dance, they conduct the bands and are delighted to eat and drink to their hearts' content. As for the balance sheet, every year the previous year's record is broken. Millions and millions of litres of beer, tens of thousands of roast chickens and calves' feet are demolished. Sausages are worth counting only in tons, so supreme-ly welcome are they to so many hungry and thirsty people. The whole affair is a monumental Gaudy.

There is only one slight pause in the calendar of beer, from Christmas time until it starts up again with *Fasching*, the carnival just before Lent. Readers of this digression may well wonder when the Bavarians find time to do any work. Let us not forget that these little celebrations in the way of eating and drinking require some preparation. Quite a lot of work is done in spite of it all! Everywhere in the world where people celebrate there is work to be done on their behalf by others, and vice versa.

Among the sausages, *Weisswürste* deserve a special mention. They were invented in Munich. At the Peterhof in the Marienplatz one day they suddenly beamed out at the world. Since then there is no computing what an infinite number must have found their way into the human frame. Even at 4 o'clock in the morning they slip down gullets exhausted by dancing, eased on their way by the last gulp of beer. By 11 in the morning there are no more to be found: they must disappear by noon. Only in the fore-noon, with pretzels and French mustard, are they in full perfection.

This is the kingdom of the sausage, and the varieties to be found are innumerable. One must visit Bavaria to realize that every village has its own private and patent brand. Franconia, too, contributes handsomely with its native *charcuterie*, and with its incomparable wines. Although white wine is made in much greater quantity and is held in the highest esteem – an *Iphöfer* warmed the hearts of the guests at the coronation of Queen Elizabeth II – one must not neglect the reds, which are among the best in Germany.

It is said that the Main is the frontier of the *Weisswurst* country. To the north of it only a sprinkling is to be found. The Main is also the frontier between *Klösse* to the north and *Knödel*, to the south. Similarly, Nürnberg is the watershed (if the phrase be permissible) between wine and beer in Bavaria. To the north of Nürnberg wine outsells beer, although the situation is imperceptibly changing, and the quantity of wine now drunk in Munich is no longer negligible. On the other hand, the sale of beer is also rising steadily with the rising thirst of the city's inhabitants.

We cannot be said to have dealt satisfactorily with Bavaria's cooking unless we look in on Nürnberg. It was formerly, after Breslau, the cheapest big city of Germany in which to live. Today Nürnberg is unique, though greatly changed by force of circumstance. On the whole *Nürnberger Lebkuchen* are the city's best-known food, but the inhabitants quite understandably claim a place of honour for their *Bratwurst*, particularly the tiny ones the size of a little finger. Only the very best neck of pork goes into them, even meat from the hams, so that these sausages are a matter of real civic pride. They are cooked over wood fires and served on tin platters with cabbage, salads of asparagus or potato or with hot asparagus. In the Erlangen district Nürnberg enjoys a wonderful hinterland for asparagus, and that of a quality to that of Schwetzingen or Lampertheim. In another district garlic flourishes, as do sea-kale and horseradish. In the autumn, you will often see the peasants, with blue aprons round their waists, carrying in them the fresh, long juicy stems and leaves of sea-kale on their way to market.

Two final words about *Bratwurst*: first, that in 1658 the Butchers' Guild in Nürnberg had a sausage of this sort weighing five hundredweight brought before them; second, that it has a history of more than 600 years. To cook them, the little ones should be gently and slowly baked in a pan with very little fat, or placed on tinfoil in a hot baking oven and there roasted.

There is still another kind, and that is the thick Franconian sausage.

These are first put in hot water so that they swell, then dipped in milk, and fried till brown in hot fat. Known as *Blaue Zipfel*, they taste particularly good after a very merry evening.

FRANCONIA

Any of my readers who has visited Aschaffenburg and Würzburg will sympathize with my wish to dedicate a small chapter to this district. The landscape of the Main is delightful, gay and well tilled, but it is none the less a little overpowered by the sun of Munich, whose inhabitants travel south to Rome and Venice but seldom to their northern neighbours who, to some extent, feel that they are regarded as poor relations.

This area has much to offer: asparagus from Volkach; fish from the Main, the little white *Mainfischle*, fried golden in hot fat; eels stewed in a broth of herbs so tasty that one could drink a cupful, while from the clear streams come the trout praised by Viktor von Scheffel; and, finally, the noble wines of Franconia, centred in Würzburg.

Frankenwein ist Krankenwein, a wine to heal the sick. My notebook records this agreeable inscription, seen in a *Weinstube* near the *Residenz*:

> If someone is eating, eat with him;
> if someone is drinking, drink too;
> if someone is working, leave him to it!

The traveller can make a short detour to Coburg. The closeness of Thuringia may be the reason why the local hams and *Bratwürste* are developed to such a delicious point; and of similar excellence is the *charcuterie* from Schweinfurt. On the sideboards lie all those excellent variations on the theme of pig, accompanied by salads, cold cabbage, salt and pepper. Cider and plum brandy counteract the fatty dishes and help digestion.

In Bamberg there is *Schlenkala* to be had, a smoky-tasting beer which is served in wooden mugs lined inside with pitch, and the local specialities accompany it well. All these dishes from Franconia seem to suit the local landscape – almost to grow out of it; they truly form a rounded whole with God and the world.

There are good fish here, too: the *Renken*, the *Waller*, and the *Wels*, or sheet-fish. These should be prepared in the same way as Lake Constance pike or salmon (see Württemberg/Baden section). The best wine to drink with them is a dry white wine from Franconia.

And here are a few recipes, both Franconian and Bavarian, starting with soup, for, as they say in Bavaria: '*Ohne mei Suppen bin ich krank*', which translated, means, 'without my soup I am ill'.

SOUP

HOT BEER SOUP (*Heisse Biersuppe*)

2 pints (2½) ale
2 oz. (¼ cup) sugar
2 cloves
small piece cinnamon
1 strip lemon rind
2 tablespoons (2½) cornflour (cornstarch)
½ cup (⅔) beer
4 eggs

Bring the ale, sugar, cloves, cinnamon and lemon rind to the boil. Mix the cornflour with the beer to a paste. Stir this into the hot ale. Bring to the boil and stir until the soup thickens. Beat the eggs in a large bowl until frothy. Pour the hot soup over the top, stir well and serve.

BROTH WITH BREAD (*Bruhe mit Brot*)

Any meat broth is suitable. Put one slice of black bread, chopped small, into each plate, and pour the boiling meat broth over it. Sprinkle finely chopped fresh chives on top.

MEAT

PORK WITH SAUERKRAUT (*Schweinefleisch mit Sauerkraut*)

1 lb. pork belly with rind
2 lb. sauerkraut
1 oz. (2 tablespoons) pork fat
2 onions, sliced
3 cloves, 1 bay leaf
4 juniper berries
½ teaspoon (⅔) caraway
1 cup (1¼) meat stock
salt, sugar to taste

Melt the pork fat in a casserole, add the *Sauerkraut*. Put the pork on top. Add the remaining ingredients, cover and cook slowly in a hot oven. Serve with boiled potatoes or bread dumplings.
(Drink: beer)

POT-ROAST (*Schweinebraten mit Knödeln*)

2 lb. leg pork
salt, pepper
1½ oz. (3 tablespoons) pork fat
1 cup (1¼) stock or water
1 each carrot and onion

Sprinkle the meat with salt and pepper. Heat the fat in a pan, add the pork, skin side downwards. Cook over a moderate heat until brown and tender, add stock, vegetables and cook until soft. Remove the meat, slice and put on a hot dish. Sieve the sauce, pour it over the pork. Serve with potato dumplings, lettuce, tomato and gherkin salads.
(Drink: beer)

ROAST SHIN OF PORK (*Schweinehaxe*)

Shin makes a favourite dish in Bavaria, roasted until crisp with good clear fat and served with a green salad and sliced tomatoes.
(Drink: beer)

BOILED BEEF WITH HORSERADISH (*Kronfleisch mit Meerettich*)

Kronfleisch is meat cut from the area round the heart and the lungs. It is cooked in lightly salted water with *Suppengrün*, i.e. carrot, onion, celery, leek and Hamburg parsley, for 20 minutes. The meat is sliced and served on wooden plates with a generous portion of horseradish sauce or sliced gherkins.

KIDNEYS IN VINEGAR (*Saure Nieren*)

3 pigs' kidneys
3 tablespoons (3¾) fat
1–2 onions, finely chopped
1 tablespoon (1¼) flour
2 tablespoons (2½) vinegar
meat stock
salt
2 tablespoons (2½) sugar

Skin the kidneys, discard the hard white centre and thinly slice. Heat the fat, add the onion, cook until soft, add the sliced kidneys for 2 minutes, no longer or the kidneys become tough. Arrange the kidneys on a hot plate, keep hot. Stir the flour into the onion, add the vinegar and enough stock to make a medium-thick sauce. Add salt and sugar, bring once to the boil and pour the sauce over the kidneys. Serve with sautéed potatoes. (Drink: red wine)

LIVER IN VINEGAR (*Saure Leber*)

This is thinly sliced liver cooked as in previous recipe.

LIVER DUMPLINGS (*Leberknödeln*)

1 lb. ground pigs' liver
8 bread rolls soaked in
   water and squeezed dry
1 slice fat bacon, ground
salt, pepper to taste
1 tablespoon (1¼) chopped
   fresh marjoram
1 onion, diced
2–3 eggs, beaten
1 onion stuck with 2 cloves
1 bay leaf

Mix the liver, bread, bacon, salt, pepper, marjoram, diced onion in a bowl, add the eggs, knead thoroughly and form into small dumplings. Put these into a pan of boiling water with the onion and bay leaf. Bring once to the boil, lower the heat and simmer for 15 minutes. When the dumplings float to the top they are ready. Serve with cooked cabbage, the broth poured over it and boiled potatoes. (Drink: beer)

BACON DUMPLINGS (*Speckknödeln*)

8 bread rolls
3 eggs
½ cup (⅔) milk
3 slices fat bacon, diced
chopped onion, parsley

Cut the soft part of the rolls into dice. Beat the eggs with the milk, pour the mixture over the bread. Fry the bacon until the fat runs, add onion and parsley. Pour this over the bread, knead to a dough. Make into small dumplings and cook as above.

LUNGS SERVED WITH BREAD DUMPLINGS (*Lüngerl mit Semmelknödeln*)

1½ lb. pigs' lungs and ½ lb. heart
1 whole onion
1½ oz. (3 tablespoons) fat
1 onion, chopped
1 tablespoon (1¼) flour
marjoram, parsley to taste
1 bay leaf
pinch salt, sugar
2 tablespoons (2½) vinegar

Wash the lights, put into a pan with salted water, 1 onion and cook slowly until the lungs are tender – the heart takes a little longer to cook. Take from the pan and thinly slice. Put aside, keep hot. Heat the fat, add the chopped onion, brown, stir the flour into the fat, gradually add 2 cups (2½) of the stock, herbs, salt, sugar and vinegar. Stir to a thickish sauce and simmer 10 minutes, add the sliced lungs and heart and cook a further 10 minutes. Serve with bread dumplings (see page 107).
(Drink: beer)

FRANCONIAN SAUSAGE (*Blaue Zipfel*)

4–6 large Bratwurst
2 onions, sliced
salt to taste
1 tablespoon (1¼) sugar
1 bay leaf
1 cup (1¼) vinegar
1 clove

Into 2 pints (2½) of water put all the ingredients (except Bratwurst) and bring to the boil. Boil for 5 minutes, add the sausages and simmer for 15 minutes. Serve with some of the stock with onion and good peasant bread.
(Drink: beer)

NURNBERG SAUSAGE (*Nürnberger Stadwurst*)

Whenever Nürnbergers go on a journey, particularly those who have never before been away from home, the first thing they ask for in a hostelry is *Stadwurst*. Even after a mere 3 hours' drive, they long for this delicacy from their home town. There is a white and a red *Stadwurst*. Helpings of a quarter of a pound each are cut in large rings. Only the best pork with fresh seasoning is used in these sausages. If you have tried *Stadwurst* you will understand why Nürnbergers have lost their hearts to it.

Nor must we forget *Ochsenmaulsalat* (ox mouth or lips salad) commonly known as *Stadratslippen* (town councillor's lips). The cold cooked mouth or lips is thinly sliced and mixed with oil and vinegar, salt, pepper and sliced onions. It is left for a day and then served with black bread or fried potatoes.

SHIN OF VEAL (*Kalbshaxe*) – the national dish of Bavaria

One shin is sufficient for 2–3 servings. Salt it lightly and roast in a medium oven. Add small veal bones to the joint, so that the sauce is really rich. Baste the meat frequently, so that it is succulent. Later allow it to become crisp on the outside. Serve with mixed salad or mixed vegetables.
(Drink: beer)

BAKED SHIN OF VEAL (*Gebackene Kalbshaxe*)

Stew gently in stock as for beef. Separate the meat from the bone and leave to go cold. Cut in thick slices, toss in flour, and fry till golden in deep hot fat. Serve with a potato salad.
(Drink: beer)

ROAST VEAL (*Kalbsbraten*)

Season, lard, salt lightly and roast a joint either from the leg, fillet or loin of veal. Mix the gravy with a cream sauce and add sour cream. Serve with salads, mushrooms, cauliflower or other vegetables, bread dumplings or *Spätzle*.
(Drink: light white wine)

BAVARIAN CHAMOIS (*Gemskeule, wie Bayern sie lieben*)

1 leg of chamois
salt
**mixed onion, carrot and
   celery, sliced**
sugar
1 piece Hamburg parsley
4 juniper berries
2 cloves
1 lemon, sliced
1 cup (1¼) herb vinegar
**2 slices black bread,
   crumbled**
hot meat stock
½ cup (⅔) sour cream

As this dish may take up to 5 hours to cook it is advisable to prepare it a day in advance. Sprinkle the meat lightly with salt, put in a large baking pan, add the onion, carrot, celery, sugar, parsley, juniper berries, cloves and lemon. Heat the vinegar and pour it over the meat, sprinkle with the bread, cover the pan and roast in a moderate oven until the meat is tender. Baste frequently with meat stock. When tender take the meat from the pan, put aside but keep hot. Rub the sauce through a sieve, return to the pan on top of the stove, bring to a gentle boil, add the cream and stir. Serve the meat with the sauce separately with side dishes as for roast veal above.
(Drink: a light red wine)

VEGETABLES

BAVARIAN CABBAGE (*Bayerisches Kraut*)

2 lb. white cabbage, shredded

1½ oz. (3 tablespoons) pork fat

1 tablespoon (1¼) sugar

½ small onion, diced

1 slice bacon, diced

1 small apple, diced

pinch salt, pepper and caraway seeds

1 cup (1¼) hot meat stock or water

2 tablespoons (2½) white wine

1 tablespoon (1¼) vinegar

Heat the fat until very hot, add the sugar and brown it, then add the onion, bacon and apple and simmer a few minutes. Add the cabbage and seasoning, stir and add the stock. Cover and cook slowly – 1 to 1½ hours. Just before serving, stir in the wine and vinegar. If preferred, the cabbage can be simmered in a casserole in the oven.

WHITE OR RED CABBAGE SALAD (*Weiss oder Rotkohlsalat*)

2 lb. white or red cabbage, shredded

salt

2–3 slices bacon, diced

caraway seeds and sugar

2 tablespoons (2½) vinegar

2 tablespoons (2½) oil

Mix the cabbage with salt and knead. Brown the bacon in a pan. Sprinkle sugar and caraway seeds to taste over the cabbage, add vinegar and oil, mix well and leave to stand. Garnish with the bacon. A little sour cream may also be added to the salad.

Old cabbage should be lightly boiled but still crisp.

BREAD DUMPLINGS (*Semmelknödeln*)

8 stale rolls

½ pint (1¼ cups) warm milk

2 eggs, beaten

salt

1 oz. (2 tablespoons) fat

1 onion, diced

finely chopped parsley

Slice the rolls and put into a bowl. Mix the milk with the eggs and salt and pour over the bread. Heat the fat, fry the onion and parsley. Add to the bowl and mix well. Leave until the bread is soft, stir, but not too well, the bread must be recognizable. Shape the dough into round dumplings, drop into boiling salted water and cook for 15–20 minutes according to size. When they float they are ready.

YEAST DUMPLINGS (*Hefenknödeln oder Dampfknödeln*)

yeast dough (page 26)
1 cup (1¼) milk
1 oz. (1¼ tablespoons) butter
1 tablespoon (1¼) sugar

Make small dumplings from the dough. Arrange these in a greased roasting pan. Leave to rise. Boil the milk, butter and sugar together and pour it into the pan, along the sides, not over the dumplings. Cover with a cloth, then a lid and cook on top of the stove over a moderate heat for 30 minutes. Serve with a vanilla sauce, apple purée or any stewed fruit.

Yeast dumplings are served as soon as they are ready, preferably with cold sauce or fruit.

LITTLE CAKES FOR CHURCH FESTIVALS (*Kirchweih-küchle*)

From a yeast dough form balls 2 oz. in weight, then pull them so that they become dumb-bell shaped. Put them in deep hot fat and fry till golden brown. Drain and toss in sugar.

(They say that it is best to draw out the dough over the knees. That is why peasant girls always have such clean knees at Church Festivals!)

Finally, a word about the most renowned speciality of Nürnberg:

SPICE CAKE (*Lebkuchen*)

The word *Lebkuchen* comes from *Libum* – a flat cake. For 700 years these cakes have been baked at Christmas time and the whole year round; but the high season for them is naturally Christmas. At first, when they were baked in the monasteries, sugar was unknown in Europe. But here in Nürnberg were the beehives of the Holy Roman Empire and of its

Emperor. Flour and spices were mixed with the honey and *Lebkuchen* were made from them.

The confectioners who specialized in making these cakes were called *Lebküchner*. As early as 1645 they had formed themselves into a Guild. When the Franks went to settle in Silesia, traitors to the profession went with them and introduced *Lebkuchen* to Silesia. Later they were known there as *Pfefferküchler*, and today their descendants have travelled once again with their recipes and now bake their Silesian *Lebkuchen* in West Germany.

There are two kinds. Those which are made on wafers (rice paper) and are either round or square are called *Elisenlebkuchen*; the others, the brown ones, are called *Lebkuchen*. Packed in tins decorated with views of the town, they are sent all over the world.

At the Christmas Market in Nürnberg they are offered for sale under the wings of tinsel angels. Next to them stand the stiff, gay little *Zwetschgenmännla*, whose heads are made of nuts and their bodies from dried plums.

Cookery in Swabia

The Swabian's lament: How well ordered this world
would be if only one could drink one's food.

First let me admit that I am embarrassed and as you read on the reason
will become apparent. When I was still at school I used to bicycle into
Stuttgart to visit a friend whose mother cooked me my first *Maultaschen*,
who scraped my first *Spätzle* from the pastry-board and even let me taste
the scraps from the oven. She introduced me to *Laugenbrezel* and to wine,
and to this day she is a gifted cook. I realize now that it was she who en-
couraged my ambition to learn to cook.

My wife, however, is a Swabian from a long line of Swabians. Hence my
dilemma. She cooks and bakes as only her countrywomen can, but this
entails an inherent danger for me. Had she cooked every day I should have
burst long ago. Her *Maultaschen* and her *Gaisburger Marsch* are so
delicious that all promptings to moderation go unheeded. I believe I
sweat with pleasure when they come to the table, and it is small comfort
that they say only the healthy sweat while eating!

Her baking is just as good, whether she makes *Hefenzopf* or apple or plum tarts with crumble and plum cordial. The recipe, as she reminds me, came from her grandmother, as is the custom of her country. And what my wife is, so are her fellow Swabians. They love cooking and would not dream of its being beneath them. Even the most distinguished Swabian families are proud that the mistress of the house herself cooks for her family and guests. I have never yet heard a Swabian complain about having too much work in the kitchen. She enjoys it all and cooks with pleasure. Just as it would never occur to a Swabian to speak High German, however long he might have been away from home – even if he had been many years abroad – so it would never occur to a Swabian woman to deny her heredity and withdraw from her position at the stove. They do not wish to appear different from what they are. They do not like frippery; they are too honest. And here we have the character of Swabian cooking – it is honest, down to earth. I know of no district in Germany, although good cooking is appreciated everywhere, where so much value is placed on it as in Baden-Württemberg, broadly known by its old name of Swabia. But the reasons for this, if they are to be analysed, may lie elsewhere. The closeness of Switzerland and France have added variety to the menus: but above all the rich produce of the land itself and the wines of Stuttgart, Heilbronn, Neckartal, Remstal and Bottwartal, to name only the most important, have made for fine cooking. Where wine is made, cooking is better than elsewhere: look at France!

But what good would the basic essentials be, if woman's love were not present to transform these ingredients with care and skill into national dishes?

Sometimes uninformed people complain that the meals are monotonous, that the men cling to what they are used to and want no change. Every Sunday they eat roast pork with *Spätzle* (noodles) and salad. This is true, but they are right. Have you ever been privileged to share the Sunday roast pork – in a family circle? If not, then you must think again.

In the course of my life I have, thank God, already shared a few pork dinners in Swabian style. Destiny has spoilt me and I have discovered the following explanation for their excellence. This roast is a piece from the neck, the shoulder or the leg; sometimes still with the skin on, when it is called *Schwärtelbraten*. The butchers know exactly which cut to offer, and have done for years. The meat is cut correctly, well hung and handled. The butchers add the collection of bones that go with it, chopped small, so that the gravy will be tasty. The housewife always puts her joint in the same meat tin. She knows when she must push it into the hot oven. Dinnertime is about 12.30 p.m. The children come out of church, father comes from his drink. Everybody welcomes the savoury smell of the roast, drifting in from the kitchen. As the roast slowly cooks with its attendant onions, spices and bones, the housewife scrapes the *Spätzle* from the board. Then they are rinsed in cold water and lying in the strainer, she slices the potatoes finely into a bowl, ready to make a potato salad which should be both juicy and piquant. With it she will serve a green salad or a herb salad, perhaps with finely diced onion. When these side dishes are ready, she will look at the gravy, still having a little time. Meanwhile she fries thin *Flädle* (pancakes) in a deep pan. On the board they are cut as fine as angels' hair, before being placed in a warm dish. Now she peeps at the roast, quickly bastes it – then cut the skin into squares like a small chessboard, leaving it to crispen. No more basting now. The joint lies on the rack and the gravy is finished. The bones are taken out, but the pieces of onion remain, so that the gravy tastes strongly of pork and the tongue receives yet another sensation from the roasted onions.

The meal is likely to begin with hot *Flädlesuppe*. The finely chopped chives in the broth are spring green and remind one of the garden. When the empty soup plates are carried out, the side dishes come in. The *Spätzle* either come straight from hot water, in which case they are not so rich, or are browned in butter in a frying pan. Then come the salads and finally the roast and the gravy. All conversation is silenced. Everyone helps himself liberally, and how good the *Spätzle* and salad taste with the roast. No one who has once experienced it will lightly forget it. No hotel, even if it is of international standing, no master chef can imitate this meal. He too would have licked his fingers, had he been one of the party.

This, therefore, is why so many Swabians are homesick on Sundays for their roast pork when they are away from home. Now, however, let us turn to the recipes.

First, a few soups. The Swabian places great value on them and no modern diet can restrain him from them. In the end it pleases him to be called *Suppenschwab*, and who is to gainsay him, for soups of all kinds are always welcome to Germans, just as much in summer as in winter.

SOUP

BRAIN SOUP (*Hirnsuppe*)

1 lb. ox, calves' or pigs' brains
2 oz. (4 tablespoons) butter
1 small onion, diced
2 tablespoons (2½) flour
4 pints (5) hot meat stock
2 egg yolks, beaten
4 tablespoons (5) cream
salt, pepper
½ cup (⅔) white wine
chopped parsley

Warm the brains in warm water then leave in fresh warm water for 10 minutes. Drain and skin. Heat the butter, add the onion, fry a few minutes, add the brains and simmer for 5 minutes. Sprinkle with flour, stir until smooth, then add the boiling stock. Whisk until the soup is smooth, then cook gently for 10 minutes. Mix the eggs with the cream, add salt and pepper to taste. Stir the wine into the soup, add parsley and finally the egg and cream mixture. Stir quickly but do not let the soup boil.

BREAD SOUP (*Brotsuppe von Metzelsuppe*)

Metzelsuppe is the stock in which sausages have been boiled. The more they break and their contents scatter in the stock, the better the stock. To make this particular soup, sippets of stale rye bread are place in a tureen and the stock poured over it. Each plate of soup is garnished with chopped fried onions and sprinkled with grated nutmeg and garlic salt.

BLACK FOREST POTATO SOUP (*Schwärzwalder Kartoffelsuppe*)

1 lb. potatoes, sliced
4 slices fat bacon, diced
2 carrots, 3 tomatoes,
  1 stick celery, 1 leek,
  2 onions, all chopped
6 pints (7½) hot stock
butter
cubed black bread
chopped parsley

Fry the bacon until the fat runs, add the vegetables including the potatoes and after 10 minutes the stock. Cook slowly until the vegetables are soft. Heat enough butter to fry the bread cubes until crisp, add to the soup, sprinkle with parsley and serve.

The soup may be sieved before the bread cubes are added; if the soup seems thin, liver sausages may be added or 2 egg yolks beaten in a cup of sour cream.

(Drink: beer)

GAISBURG BROTH (*Gaisburger Marsch*)

This soup has been named after the Stuttgart suburb of Gaisburg. It is also called the 'Marriage of potatoes and noodles' (*Spätzle*, see page 121) or 'Potato slices and noodles'.

5 pints (6¼) strong meat
  stock
1 lb. beef
1 lb. tiny noodles
  (*Spätzle*) (page 120)
1 lb. potatoes, sliced in
  inch-long strips
2 onions, diced
1 oz. (2 tablespoons) butter
finely chopped parsley

The stock is made in the usual manner with carrots, cloved-onions, bay leaf, leek and celery, and with the 1 lb. of beef. It is then strained and the beef cut into thin strips when cool.

Bring the strained stock to the boil and boil the potatoes without letting them disintegrate. Add the meat and the *Spätzle*. Bring to the boil remembering that home-made noodles take only a few minutes to cook. In the meantime, heat the butter and fry the onions until brown. Add to the soup and sprinkle with parsley just before serving.

(Drink: beer)

FISH

LAKE CONSTANCE FISH MEUNIÈRE (*Bodenseefelchen Müllerin*)

1 small Felchen – a Lake Constance white fish
5 oz. (6 tablespoons) butter
flour
salt
lemon juice and slices
chopped parsley

Clean the fish and slash the skin diagonally on both sides. Heat the butter. Toss the fish lightly in flour and fry in the hot butter. When it is brown and crisp take from the pan, place on a hot plate and sprinkle lightly with salt, parsley and lemon juice. Quickly reheat the butter and pour it foaming hot over the fish. Garnish with slices of lemon and serve with boiled potatoes or a potato salad and a little mayonnaise.
(Drink: Lake Constance white wine)

BLACK FOREST TROUT (*Forelle aus dem Schwarzwaldbächen*)

1 trout per person
bouillon

For each 2 pints (2½) of bouillon, use 1 tablespoon (1¼) salt; 1½ tablespoons (2) vinegar; 1 onion; 1 bay leaf, and a little sugar. Bring to a gentle boil then simmer for 30 minutes.

Lay the trout in the stock, making sure they are covered. Bring to a slow boil then simmer 10 to 15 minutes or until the head fin can be pulled off easily. Drain and serve with boiled potatoes, sprinkled with chopped parsley and garnish with wedges of lemon.
(Drink: white wine from Remstal or Baden)

A master chef told me his special method with trout. He never throws away the stock. If more trout are to be used, he adds enough white wine to the stock to cover the fish and more seasoning.

BADEN PIKE (*Hecht auf Badische Art*)

4 lb. pike
1 oz. (2 tablespoons) butter
1 onion, diced
2–3 slices fat bacon, diced
¾ pint (2 cups) sour cream
4 tablespoons (5) grated cheese
4 tablespoons (5) fine breadcrumbs

Do not wash the pike too much, but if it seems muddy soak it for some hours in lemon or vinegar-flavoured water. Remove the scales and bones and cut the flesh into long pieces of about 4 in. Melt the butter in a casserole, add the fish, sprinkle with onion and bacon, add the sour cream, then the cheese and breadcrumbs. Bake in a moderate oven for 20 to 30 minutes. Serve with boiled potatoes tossed in butter, sprinkled with chopped parsley.
(Drink: Baden white wine)

Baden has a reputation both for its fish dishes and its wines.

MEAT

BRAWN SET IN A PLATE (*Tellersulz*)

strips of different kinds of cooked pork meats, sliced hard-boiled eggs, gherkins, chopped tomatoes or cooked sliced carrot
2 pints (2½) strong meat stock, flavoured with a little vinegar and white wine
6 gelatine leaves or 2 envelopes gelatine

Soak the gelatine leaves in cold water for 10 minutes. Bring the stock to the boil, add the gelatine and stir until it dissolves. Leave in a cold place until it begins to set.

Arrange the pieces of pork with the other ingredients in soup plates. Cover with aspic and leave in a cold place to set. Turn out to serve with roast potatoes or rye bread.

BOILED BEEF (*Gekochtes Rindfleisch*)

Served with boiled potatoes, carrots, horseradish sauce, pickled gherkins and *Spätzle*.
(Drink: beer)

Fine soups
(*Edle Süppchen*)

SMALL MEAT PASTIES (*Maultaschen*)

This is the Queen of Swabian recipes, but has nothing to do with large-mouthed people. *Maultaschen* are not unlike the smalled filled envelopes of pasta named 'ravioli'. They are so often served in Swabia that many butchers offer them for sale ready prepared on certain days of the week. But anyone who likes to prepare the filling herself can buy the dough ready made at the bakers and spare herself some of the effort.

Dough:

1 lb. (4 cups) plain (all purpose) flour

4 eggs, lightly beaten

salt

Filling:

¾ lb. raw ground meat, mixed veal and pork

¾ lb. washed, finely chopped spinach

1 onion, finely chopped

3–4 thick slices bread, soaked in milk until soft and squeezed dry

2 eggs, beaten

1 cup (1¼) finely chopped parsley

Garnish:

diced fried onions

Sieve the flour on to a board and make a well in the middle. Add the eggs and salt and knead to a dough, adding a little water if required. Knead vigorously until the dough is smooth. Cut into 4 equal parts and roll into 4 rectangles 8 × 10 in.

Combine the remaining ingredients and divide into 4 portions. Spread each piece of dough with the filling. Roll these lengthways, like a sausage, making sure the edges are firmly secured. Make dents with the hand every 2 in. and then cut through with a plate, not with a knife. (You can always recognize a Swabian if he takes a plate to cut the dough.) Press the edges firmly to seal them. Cook the the *Maultaschen* for 20 minutes in boiling salted water, take from the pan with a slotted spoon, place on a hot dish and sprinkle with the fried onion. Serve with mixed salads or a potato salad.

On Maundy Thursday, a meatless fast day, almost every family in Würtemberg has *Maultaschen*. Spiteful people say that this is because meat is smuggled in under the spinach. I prefer to believe that it is in accordance with the tradition of Maundy Thursday (Gründonnerstag) that something green be brought to the table.

Roast pork with crackling, dumplings and red cabbage (*Swartelbraten mit Klössen Rotkraut*)

SWABIAN ROAST MEAT (*Schwäbischer Rostbraten*)

This is not beef roasted in an oven, but fillets sliced, salted, floured and quickly browned on both sides in fat, sliced onions added to the pan and then covered and cooked until the meat is tender. The meat is taken from the pan with the onions and sour cream added to the gravy to make a sauce. This is poured over the meat which is served with seasonal salads, *Spätzle* and sometimes white cabbage.

A variation is to lay a slice of well-browned lean bacon and two small sausages (*Bratwürste* if possible) on the meat.

This is a favourite dish of which the Swabians and one they never tire of eating.

(Drink: red wine)

GAME

BLACK FOREST VENISON (*Rehrücken Sschwarzwälder Art*)

4 lb. saddle of deer hung for 2 days, skinned and larded
2 oz. (4 tablespoons) butter
1 bay leaf
12 juniper berries
½ cup (⅔) brandy
½ cup (⅔) sour cream
1 pint (1¼) meat stock
pinch of cinnamon
1 tablespoon (1¼) lemon juice

Heat the butter in a pan, add the saddle and brown it well all over. Add the bay leaf, juniper berries, continue cooking 10 minutes, baste with the brandy. After 5 minutes add the sour cream, cover the pan and cook gently until the meat is tender but still 'pink' inside. Take it from the pan, add the stock, bring to the boil, cook 10 minutes, add cinnamon and lemon juice, then rub through a sieve. Serve the saddle with the sauce, *Spätzle*, mushrooms and bilberries.

(Drink: red wine from Kaiserstuhl or Uhlbacher Götzenberg)

NOODLES (Spätzle)

Shall we make *Spätzle* or eat the dough as it is?
It is respectable to eat with a fork;
but one gets more with a spoon!

If today we can truly speak of a national dish, then it is the *Spätzle* from Swabia. People look on Swabians as progressive, but as far as *Spätzle* are concerned the men of Swabia are conservative. They require 'their' *Spätzle* to be scraped from the board by hand. They turn down the use of mechanical aids such as scrapers. Where else in Germany would long and serious debates take place in the Town Council as to whether *Spätzle* should be made by hand or by machine in the Stuttgart Municipal Restaurant? Finding: There must remain at least one restaurant or hostelry in Stuttgart where hand-scraped *Spätzle* are available. Incidentally, there are a good many others besides; in fact, they are all over the place in Stuttgart, wherever the landlord or landlady is a Swabian with special knowledge of *Spätzle*.

Basic recipe for 8–10 servings:

1 lb. (4 cups) best white flour

4 eggs

1 teaspoon ($1\frac{1}{4}$) cooking salt

4 tablespoons (5) water

First put the flour in a bowl, then the eggs, salt and water. Beat with a wooden spoon until the dough is smooth and light and produces bubbles. (The dough can easily be beaten with an electric mixer with kneading attachment.) Put a small piece of dough (about 2 oz.) on a small damp board. Cut into strips, scrape off with a knife and slip them into lightly salted, fast boiling water. The board and the knife should be repeatedly dunked in the boiling water.

Let the *Spätzle* come to the surface of the water, take them out with a skimming ladle and put them into plenty of cold water. The starch is then dissolved, and they no longer stick together. Repeat this operation until all the dough is used; then put the *Spätzle* in a colander, drain and warm in hot fat, preferably butter. Now add either onion rings, diced onion; or breadcrumbs browned in butter.

(The scraping of the *Spätzle* can be made easier by the use of a small machine, the *Spätzleschwob*; otherwise the cooking and further handling remain the same.) *Spätzle* may be served as an accompaniment to stews, fricassees, goulash, or roast game with cream sauce.

GREEN NOODLES (*Grüne Spätzle*)

1 lb. (4 cups) flour
4 eggs
4 tablespoons (5) water
¾ lb. raw spinach, rubbed
 through a mouli-grater

Prepare as for basic recipe (page 121).

KEMPTENER CHEESE NOODLES (*Kemptener Käsespatzen*)

ingredients and
 preparation as in basic
 recipe plus:
1 cup (1¼) grated Swiss
 cheese
3 oz. (6 tablespoons) butter

Lay the warm *Spätzle* in layers in a soufflé dish, and sprinkle each layer with grated cheese and dots of butter. Top with grated cheese. Let the cheese penetrate the *Spätzle* by cooking in a warm oven for 15 minutes.

LARGE NOODLES (*Knöpfle*)

the same dough as for
 Spätzle

Put the dough through a sieve or colander with large holes. Prepare as for *Spätzle*.

NOODLE PANCAKES LUDWIG UHLAND (*Spätzle-Eierkuchen Ludwig Uhland*)

1 pint (2 cups) pancake
 batter
1 lb. cold noodles
fat for frying

Mix the pancake batter into the cold *Spätzle*. Put ladlefuls of the mixture in hot fat in a frying pan and cook as for thin pancakes.
Variations: Brown diced bacon or ham in the pan, and then pour the *Spätzle* pancake batter over the top.

NOODLES WITH SAUERKRAUT (*Spätzle mit Sauerkraut*)

Brown prepared *Spätzle* in fat until golden yellow and then spread over cooked *Sauerkraut*. Mix slightly.

VEGETABLES

ONION TART (*Zwiebelkuchen*)

In the golden autumn the Swabians relish their new wine. It is still murky and changes colour after 3–4 days, turning to the so-called feather-white. Something extra is needed for the fullest enjoyment of the wine and that something is this unsurpassable onion tart.

Dough:

1 lb. (4 cups) plain (all purpose) flour
3 egg yolks
4 oz. (¼ cup) lard
pinch salt, sugar
½ cup (⅔) lukewarm water
1 oz. fresh (1 cake compressed) yeast

Filling:

4 slices fat bacon, diced
2 lb. onions, diced
5 eggs
1 cup (1¼) sour cream
pinch salt
caraway seeds to taste

Prepare the dough as on page 92, using lard instead of butter. Let it rise once, then roll it out finger-thick and line a baking pan. Press the dough edges up to a height of about ¾ in. Let the dough rise again.

Fry the bacon until crisp, take out 2 tablespoons (2½) and put aside. Fry the onions in the bacon fat, let them soften but not brown. Cool slightly then spread them over the dough. Beat the eggs with the cream, add salt and pour the mixture over the onions, sprinkle with remaining fried bacon and caraway seeds. Bake in a hot oven until the filling is set and the pastry a golden brown, about 30 minutes.

POTATO DUMPLINGS (*Buabaspitzle*)

1 lb. potatoes
2–3 eggs, beaten
4 tablespoons (5) plain (all purpose) flour
salt, nutmeg to taste

Cook the potatoes in their skins in salted water until soft. Drain, cool, peel and rub through a sieve. Mix with the remaining ingredients to a smooth dough. Break off pieces and roll into cigar-like shapes, narrowing to a point at both ends. Cook gently in boiling salted water for 5 minutes or until they float. Take out with a slotted spoon, drain well and serve with *Sauerkraut*, roast meat and gravy. They can also be left until cool, browned in hot fat and served with a salad or apple purée.

CAKES

CINNAMON STARS (*Zimtsterne*)

9 egg whites
1 lb. (4 cups) powdered sugar
2 teaspoons (2$\frac{1}{2}$) powdered cinnamon
grated rind and juice
1 lemon
1 lb. unblanched almonds, ground
extra powdered sugar for dusting the pastry board

Beat the egg whites until very stiff, gradually beat in the sugar and continue beating until the mixture is so stiff it can be cut with a knife. Beat in the cinnamon, lemon rind and juice. Put aside 1 cup (1$\frac{1}{4}$) of the mixture. Add the almonds. Sprinkle a board lightly with sifted powdered sugar. Pat or roll out the mixture about $\frac{1}{4}$ in. thick and cut with a star cutter. Place these on a greased baking (cookie) sheet and glaze the top with the reserved mixture. Bake in a slow oven 20 minutes and take while still warm from the baking sheet.

It is important that the glaze should remain white.

SWABIAN CHRISTMAS CAKES (*Springerle*)

Also called anise cakes, these may rightly be considered the original Swabian Christmas cakes or cookies. They are stamped in a wooden mould into quaint designs and figures. The name probably comes from the fact that in cooking, the cakes rise to half their height again, i.e., spring up.

50–60 cakes (cookies):

1 lb. (4 cups) plain (all purpose) flour
5 eggs
1 lb. (2 cups) sugar
grated rind 1 lemon
1 tablespoon (1$\frac{1}{4}$) brandy
pinch hartshorn salt or baking powder
1–2 tablespoons (1$\frac{1}{4}$–2$\frac{1}{2}$) crushed aniseeds

Beat the eggs with the sugar for 1 hour or 10 minutes in an electric beater. Add the lemon rind and brandy. Sift and gradually add the flour and hartshorn salt until the dough is stiff. Knead the dough and leave 2 hours, and then roll it out $\frac{1}{4}$ in. thick.

Flour a *Springerle* mould (or several biscuit moulds of different shapes) and press it hard over the dough to get a good imprint, also so the shapes come out cleanly. Separate the figures and lay them on a greased tin sprinkled with the aniseed. Leave for 20–24 hours. Bake slowly until the lower part is slightly yellow but the top remains white. Keep in a cool, not too dry, place for at least 4 weeks to soften and become mellow.

Do not make more than 2 lb. of dough at a time as it dries out too easily.

SWABIAN BISCUITS (COOKIES) (*Schwabenbrötli*)

$\frac{3}{4}$ **lb. (3 cups) plain (all purpose) flour**
8 oz. (1 cup) butter
8 oz. (1 cup) sugar
8 oz. (1$\frac{1}{3}$ cups) ground almonds
pinch salt
1 tablespoon (1$\frac{1}{4}$) cinnamon
grated rind 1 lemon
2 eggs, beaten
1 egg yolk, well beaten
chopped almonds, sugar crystals

Work the first 8 ingredients together. Leave in a cool place for 1 hour. Roll out $\frac{1}{8}$ in. thick and cut with a glass into half-moons. Leave overnight. Brush with egg yolk, sprinkle with chopped almonds and sugar crystals, place on a greased baking (cookie) sheet and bake in a moderate oven for 15–20 minutes.

Before we leave the Swabian paradise, may I say just a little more about the wines of Württemberg. Germany is blessed with good wine. The white wines are among the best in the world. The Württemberg wines have improved more in quality since 1945 than any others in the whole country. It has nothing to do with local patriotism if I maintain that the best white Württemberg wine comes today from Weikersheim in the Tauber Valley. Connoisseurs rightly say of it that, when they drink it, it is as if an angel were passing.

French people who have dined with me and drunk a *Zweifelsberg* from Brackheim with the meal – the favourite wine, incidentally, of former President Heuss – have assured me repeatedly that they have never drunk such a good red wine in Germany, and no one can deny that the best red wine in the world is made in France.

In the Black Forest we must make one further digression to the famous
distilleries. Cordials and fine spirits are distilled from crisp cherries,
quantities of wild raspberries and egg-shaped plums. It is thanks to these
cordials that the Black Forest *Kirschtorte* can be made.

Finally, we must allow ourselves to accept a small *Schnaps*, a noble
spirit, made from wild mirabelles. One can then take just one more slice
of Black Forest bacon, knowing that a raspberry or plum cordial will help
to digest it.

Anyone who has read these lines will ask for directions about where he
may obtain these dishes. The traveller need only go to the local hostelries.
A good guide book will show the inns in town and country where Swabian
cooking is available, and the directions may be relied upon. Cooks who
have learned their trade in Württemberg are proud of their regional specialities. They prepare them with devotion, and have been awarded gold
medals for them at international cooking exhibitions.

In many hostelries the chef himself does the cooking, helped by his en-
tire family. Usually the landlady of an inn cooks as well as any housewife;
and in a private house one is usually well catered for. The luckiest man,
of course, is one who is received into a Swabian family for whom the dishes
are prepared with real joy, and served with local wine. He will certainly not
be disappointed and will surely allow that I have not exaggerated my
praise of Swabian cooking.

Cookery in the Rhineland

We are on the citadel at Klopp, high above Bingen am Rhein. By good luck it is so agreeably warm that we can sit in the open air and enjoy a bottle of *Binger Schwätzerchen* with our conversation, while at the same time admiring the lovely view towards Rüdesheim and the left bank of the Nahe. In such surroundings it is a pleasure to discuss Rhenish food.

Rhine, happily enough, rhymes with wine, but at this moment we also have the Moselle, the Nahe, the Saar, the Aar and the Palatinate to consider. For many miles around we are surrounded by noble wines. The golden wine is king here and the foods which best set it off are local specialities which harmonize with it.

Down in Bad Dürkheim there is an impressive *Wurstmarkt*, another folk festival which, while less gigantic than the *Oktoberfest* at Munich, is still considerable in terms of wine drunk and sausages polished off. The good wine on the sunny slopes is a fine accompaniment to good fish, and eels from the Moselle and salmon from the Rhine are the pick of them. The people of Cologne give nicknames to their dishes, comprehensible only to themselves and very baffling to the stranger; one must learn by enquiry and experience. Carnival is of course the greatest celebration of their year, and in Cologne, as in Aachen, mussels cooked in white wine are particularly prized, washed down with a good *Kölsch*, a specially fermented beer resembling the Berlin *Weisser*. Another oddity is *Kölscher Kaviar* (Cologne Caviare), a highly misleading name since in fact it consists of one platter containing home-made black pudding, a rye roll, a pat of butter and a handful of spring onions. This, with a glass of local beer, is the native's idea of Paradise.

Meanwhile, let us change glasses and enjoy a bottle of *Binger Rosengarten* which will stimulate our appetite so that we can enjoy our lunch and give thought to the recipes of the Rhineland:

SOUP

BREAD DUMPLINGS IN PEA SOUP (*Weckklösse in grüner Erbsensuppe*)

4 pints (5) green pea soup
6 bread rolls soaked in water and squeezed dry
2 slices fat bacon, diced
1 onion, diced
chopped parsley
nutmeg, salt, pepper
2 eggs, well beaten

Dry the rolls in a hot frying pan until they no longer stick to the pan. Add the bacon and onion and cook 10 minutes longer. Take from the pan, add parsley (to taste), seasoning and eggs. Knead the mixture well and form small dumplings. Heat the soup and add the dumplings. Or cook the dumplings in boiling salted water, drain, place in soup plates and pour hot soup over them. ⟨Drink: beer)

SWEET AND SOUR BREAD SOUP (*Brotsuppe*)

½ lb. white bread
½ lb. black bread
4 cups (5) apple juice
4 tablespoons (5) raisins
5 egg yolks
2 tablespoons (2½) sugar
pinch cinnamon
juice 1 lemon
2 cups (2½) white wine

Soak the bread overnight in half the apple juice, bring next day to the boil. Rub through a sieve. Thin with remaining juice so that the bread is crumbly. Add the raisins. Beat the yolks with the sugar until frothy, add cinnamon, lemon juice and wine. Mix well, stir into the soup but do not further cook.

SOUR MILK SOUP (*Saure Milchsuppe*)

Whisk as much sour milk as required until smooth, add sugar, ground cinnamon to taste, and grated or diced black bread.

GREEN BEAN SOUP (*Grüne Bohnensuppe*)

1 lb. green beans
½ lb. potatoes
4 pints (5) meat stock
2 slices fat bacon, diced
1 onion, diced
2 tablespoons (2½) flour
½ cup (⅔) sour cream
chopped parsley

Wash and slice the beans, peel and chop the potatoes. Cook in the stock until tender. Fry the bacon, brown the onion, add the flour and stir well, adding enough of the stock to make a thick sauce. Stir this into the soup, add the cream and sprinkle with parsley.

RHINELAND ONION SOUP (*Rheinische Zwiebelsuppe*)

1 lb. onions, sliced
3 pints (3¾) meat stock
1 lb. hot boiled potatoes
salt, pepper
1 tablespoon (1¼) vinegar
3 slices fat bacon, diced
½ cup (⅔) sour cream
chopped marjoram
chopped parsley

Cook the onions in the stock until soft. Rub the potatoes through a sieve and add to the soup. Season with salt, pepper and vinegar. Fry the bacon until brown and sprinkle it over the soup. Stir in the sour cream, sprinkle lightly with marjoram and parsley and serve at once. (Drink: white wine)

On special occasions a welcome dish is lentil soup or a soup made of haricot beans or peas.

Serve lentil soup with smoked sausage, bean soup with Bologna sausage, and warm the sausages either by bringing them to the boil in the soup or by tossing them quickly in a frying pan. Serve pea soup with *Sauerkraut*.

Andudel also goes well with these soups. At pig-killing the cleaned intestines are cut into pieces about 20 in. long and laid one above the other, seasoned with salt and pepper, until a thick skinless sausage is produced. Pickle for 4–5 days, dry for 4–5 days more and smoke for 14 days. *Andudel* derives probably from *andouille*, a type of French sausage.

(Drink: beer)

FISH

BAKED SALMON (*Salm in Alu-Folie*)

salmon steaks	Brush a large piece of aluminium foil
olive oil	with olive oil. Place it in a baking pan on a
diced onion	rack and cover the bottom of the pan with
chopped parsley	hot water. Place the onion and herbs in
dill	the foil and gently steam in a hot oven
sage	until the onion is soft. Lay the salmon
salt	steaks on top of the onion, sprinkle with
	salt, wrap the foil over them and continue
	to bake for about 15 minutes in their own
	juice. Serve with parsley butter and
	boiled potatoes.

FRIED SALMON (*Salm gebraten*)

Thin salmon steaks are marinated, seasoned, tossed in egg and bread-crumbs, and fried till golden in olive oil. Serve with vegetable salad in mayonnaise, or with a green salad.

GRILLED SALMON (*Salm von Rost*)

Marinate ¾ in. thick salmon steaks 2 hours in olive oil. Sprinkle with salt. Make the grill very hot and cook the steaks 5 minutes on either side, basting with oil at intervals. Turn the steaks and finish with 2 more minutes on either side. Serve with onion or parsley butter and boiled potatoes sprinkled with chopped parsley.

POACHED SALMON (*Gekochter Lachs*)

salmon steaks	Bring the water with the seasonings and
2 pints (2½) water	vegetables to a slow boil. Simmer for
2 tablespoons (2½) vinegar	20 minutes. Add the salmon steaks, bring
salt	once to the boil, lower the heat so that
1 bay leaf	the liquid just trembles and cook for
2 cloves	15 minutes. The fish should be pink and
6 peppercorns	firm. Serve with melted butter or
small piece celery	Hollandaise, Béarnaise or Mousseline
1 carrot	sauce, very hot boiled potatoes and crisp
a little chopped leek and onion	fresh green salad.

RHINE SALMON (*Rheinsalm*)

Medium-sized fish are the most favoured. The steaks are cut before the fish is cleaned. Today it is possible to buy fine steaks already cut, which are most economical.

SALMON IN WHITE WINE WITH MUSHROOMS (*Lachs in Weisswein mit Champignons*)

salmon steaks
butter
sliced onion
salt
chopped parsley
white wine
Hollandaise sauce

All ingredients are to taste. Heat enough butter to fry the onion until soft but not brown. Add salt and parsley. Lay the salmon steaks on top, pour white wine in to almost cover the fish. Cover with foil and poach in a hot oven 15 minutes. Take from the pan, thicken the fish stock with Hollandaise sauce. Cover the fish with the sauce and serve with fried mushrooms, asparagus and rice.

BAKED SALMON (*Lachs, gebraten am Stück*)

1 moderate-sized salmon
salt, pepper
4 oz. ($\frac{1}{2}$ cup) butter
juice 1 lemon
1 cup ($1\frac{1}{4}$) sour cream

Scale and clean the salmon, wipe it dry. Rub with salt and pepper and place in a baking pan. Add a little salted water and pour the butter and lemon juice over the fish. Bake in a moderately hot oven until tender. Take from the pan, put on a hot plate. Stir the cream into the fish gravy, bring once to the boil, pour over the fish. Serve with boiled potatoes.

SALMON MAYONNAISE (*Lachs-Mayonnaise*)

cold poached salmon
salt, sugar
diced onion
lemon juice
lettuce leaves
mayonnaise
hardboiled eggs, halved
sliced tomatoes

Skin and bone the fish and slightly crumble the flesh. Season with salt: add sugar, onion and lemon juice to taste. Arrange on lettuce leaves, add mayonnaise and garnish with the eggs and tomatoes.
(Drink: red or rosé wine)

CHUB (*Alant*)
allow ¾ lb. chub per
  portion
salt
lemon juice
beaten egg
fine breadcrumbs
fat or oil
sour cream

Clean the fish, rub with salt and lemon juice. Leave for 1 hour. Roll in egg and breadcrumbs and fry in very hot fat till brown and crisp on both sides. Heat some sour cream in another pan, add the fat in which the fish was cooked, season, stir and pour the sauce over the fish. Serve with a potato salad.
(Drink: a light Saar white wine)

EEL WITH TARTARE SAUCE (*Aal in Tartarsauce*)
eel, cut into pieces 3 in.
  long
salt
beaten egg
fine breadcrumbs
oil or fat
mayonnaise
chopped pickled gherkins
capers
chopped hardboiled egg
mustard
paprika

Clean and skin the eel and cook in simmering liquid until tender, about 30 minutes. Take from the pan, leave until cold, add salt, then roll in egg and breadcrumbs and fry in hot oil until a golden brown. Mix the remaining ingredients together to make a Sauce Tartare. Serve the eel with the sauce separately and with potato salad. This dish is a speciality of the Saar.
(Drink: white wine)

MUSSELS IN WHITE WINE (*Muscheln in Weisswein*)
1 lb. cleaned mussels
1 onion, finely chopped
2 oz. (4 tablespoons) butter
salt, pepper
1 cup (1¼) white wine

Gently fry the onion in butter in a large pan for 5 minutes. Add the mussels, salt, pepper and wine. Cover and cook until all the mussels have opened, about 10 minutes. (Discard any which remain closed.) Serve the mussels in soup plates. When eating the mussels, remember 'fingers before forks'.
(Drink: white wine)

MÜLHEIM DRIED COD (*Möllmsche : Stockfisch vom Mülheim*)

2 lb. dried salted cod
salt, pepper
1 onion stuck with 2 cloves
and 1 bay leaf
2 lb. potatoes
slices of bacon
sour cream or milk
mustard

Soak the fish 24 hours. Put into unsalted water with the salt, pepper and onion, bring to the boil, then simmer 20 minutes. Meanwhile peel and boil the potatoes in salted water. Fry the bacon. Combine the fish and potatoes in a shallow bowl. Pour the sour cream over the top, add mustard and cover with bacon.
(Drink : white wine or beer)

SOUSED HERRINGS (*Heringstip*)

salted herrings
sliced onion
vinegar
allspice
sour cream

Arrange fillets of well-washed salted herrings in an earthenware pot in layers with onion, vinegar and allspice. Pour sour cream over the top. Leave for 2 days. Serve with boiled potatoes.
(Drink : beer)

MEAT

MUTTON CUTLETS (*Hammelkotelett*)

2–3 cutlets per serving
salt
egg
breadcrumbs
fat
anchovy butter or
parsley butter

Salt the meat, toss in egg and breadcrumbs and fry till golden. Spread anchovy butter or parsley butter on top. Serve with fried potatoes, peas or cauliflower.
(Drink : red wine)

TURNIPS WITH LAMB (*Weisse Rüben mit Lammfleisch*)

2 lb. peeled turnips
1 lb. lamb, cubed
1 oz. (2 tablespoons) fat
salt
1 lb. potatoes, diced
milk

Cut the turnips into small cubes. Heat the fat in the pan, add the turnips, fry for 5 minutes, add the meat and salt and cook gently for 30 minutes, adding just enough water to prevent burning. Add the potatoes and a little milk and cook until the potatoes are soft.

ROAST LEG OF MUTTON WITH MUSTARD (*Gebratene Hammelkeule mit Senf*)

8-10 servings:

1 small leg of mutton without the end bone
salt
mustard
cornflour
sour cream

Hang the leg of mutton for 8 days. Salt lightly, spread thickly with mustard, leave to stand in a cool place for 3 days. Roast the joint and thicken the gravy slightly with cornflour and add sour cream. Serve with green beans, boiled potatoes or *Klösse*.
(Drink: red wine)

RHINELAND SPICED BEEF (*Rheinischer Sauerbraten*)

4 lb. beef, preferably topside or silverside
¼ lb. salt pork or fat bacon
3⅓ pints (4) vinegar, or half vinegar and half red wine
salt
sugar
3 cloves
6 juniper berries
1 bay leaf
3 oz. (6 tablespoons) fat
a little sliced onion
celery and leeks
chopped parsley
1 tablespoon (1¼) tomato purée
3 slices black bread or gingerbread

Lard the beef with the pork. Place in a bowl. Bring the vinegar, salt, sugar, cloves, juniper berries and bay leaf to the boil and pour at once over the meat. Leave 5 days, turning it once a day. Drain thoroughly. Heat the fat in a large pan, brown the meat all over. Add the marinade, the vegetables, parsley and tomato purée. Cook gently until the meat is tender.

Take the meat from the pan, keep hot. Add the bread to the stock; when soft, rub the stock through a sieve, making sure the bread and vegetables come through as well. The sauce must be spicy and sweet-sour and a little extra red wine may be added. Serve with noodles, potato dumplings or *Spätzle*. Stewed apple rings, prunes or raisins or chopped almonds are added as a garnish. Serve the sauce separately.

In the neighbourhood of Düren pork is prepared in the same way.
(Drink: red wine)

Asparagus and lobster cocktail
(*Spargel Cocktail mit Hummer*)

VEAL ROLLS (*Kalbsrouladen*)

4 veal fillets
flour
½ lb. ground pork
fried onions, chopped
parsley, anchovy
salt, pepper
2 eggs, beaten
2 oz. (4 tablespoons) butter
1 pint (1¼) meat stock
1 tablespoon (1¼) cornflour
(cornstarch)
½ cup (⅔) sour cream

Pound the fillets until thin but unbroken. Place on a floured board. Mix together the pork, onion, parsley and anchovy, salt, pepper and eggs. Spread the fillets with this mixture, roll up and tie with thread. Roll in flour. Heat the butter, add the rolls and brown them all over. Carefully pour in the stock, round the sides so that it does not go over the rolls. Cook gently until tender, about 40 minutes, turning the rolls from time to time. Take out the rolls, place on a hot dish. Mix the cornflour with water to a thin paste, stir into the stock, cook until it thickens. Add the cream. Serve with buttered noodles or puréed potatoes.
(Drink: white wine)

CALF'S HEAD IN TOMATO SAUCE (*Kalbskopf in Tomatensauce*)

1 calf's head, cleaned
and chopped
stock
2 tablespoons (2½) vinegar
1 onion stuck with 2 cloves
1 bay leaf
1 oz. (2 tablespoons) butter
1 onion, diced
2 tablespoons (2½) tomato
purée
2 teaspoons (2½) cornflour
(cornstarch)
Madeira to taste

Simmer the calf's head in stock with the vinegar, onion and bay leaf until tender. Place the meat in a shallow dish. Keep hot. Heat the butter, add the onion and when soft add the tomato purée. Gradually add 2 cups (2½) meat stock from the calf's head, bring gently to the boil. Mix the cornflour with water to a thin paste, stir into the boiling stock. Cook until it thickens. Sieve and flavour with Madeira. Pour the sauce over the meat, serve with sliced hardboiled eggs, gherkins and boiled potatoes.
(Drink: red wine)

RHINE SUCKING PIG (*Rheinisches Spanferkel*)
The word *Ferkel* indicates a sucking pig. The term *Span* comes from

Strawberries, peaches and pineapple in champagne
Erdbeeren auf Pfirschen in Sektbad und Ananas

Middle High German, where it means the teat. Today the word *Spanferkel* is of real culinary significance. When one hears the word, one thinks of the crisp, brown dish of the name: it is a favourite dish. Here is the recipe for Stuffed Sucking Pig.

1 freshly slaughtered sucking pig 3–6 weeks old
salt, pepper
2 oz. (4 tablespoons) butter
3 onions, chopped
parsley, thyme, chopped
¾ lb. veal
½ lb. lean bacon
liver, heart, kidneys of the pig
3 rolls soaked in milk and squeezed dry
3 eggs
nutmeg
Madeira
melted butter
beer

Rub the pig with salt and pepper. Heat the first quantity of butter and fry the onions, parsley and thyme. Grind the veal, bacon, liver etc., bread, onions, herbs, mix together, bind with the eggs and flavour with nutmeg and Madeira. Stuff this mixture into the pig and sew it up. Cut out a small flap on both sides of the neck and tuck the forefeet in them. Sprinkle with salt and lay the pig on a rack (in a baking pan) so that both back legs can lie flat, pressed outwards. A piece of wood should be used to hold the back feet apart and another in the mouth to keep it open. Wrap the ears and tail in foil so they do not become exposed to excess heat.

Brush the pig with melted butter and beer and place in a hot oven. Baste frequently with hot butter, with gravy from the pig, and beer. When the pig is tender, between 2 and 3 hours depending on its size, use a large sharp heavy knife to carve it; a pair of poultry shears will also help.

Basting meat with beer is a well-tried German trick to make sure that the meat is crisp and evenly browned.

For the sake of expediency, the pig is often roasted separately and the stuffing made according to the recipe above but cooked in a cake tin. Carving is then much simpler. In this case one serves a slice of stuffing with each helping.

Serve with any of the following:

1. Bread dumplings and mixed salad;
2. Bread dumplings cooked and allowed to become cold, then sliced and

made into a salad with diced onions, oil and vinegar (an old Bavarian recipe);

3. Mixed salad;
4. Red cabbage with potato dumplings; or
5. *Füllsel-Kartoffeln*, a speciality from Bad Kreuznach, where sucking-pigs become available from the middle of September, and throughout the new wine season.

(*Füllsel-Kartoffeln*)

Boil a good quantity of potatoes, not letting them become too soft. Peel them and cut into small cubes. Fry in a pan with onions and un-cooked stuffing made from the following: lean pork, the inside of the sucking pig, seasoned with salt, pepper, nutmeg and marjoram. The potatoes should be well flavoured by the fine aroma of the stuffing, but should not disintegrate.

6. Hot cabbage salad with bacon (*Warmer Krautsalat mit Speck abgeschmeckt*)

(Drink: In Bavaria beer of various kinds is favoured as an accompaniment to sucking pig; and above all, a good *Schnaps*. In the Kreuznach region, they like a clear *Schnaps* and good wines; and in particular, new wine. It will be quite apparent that the delicious flavour of the sucking pig, and the aroma of roasting which pervades the house, requires not one but several *Schnaps*.)

There are further splendid ways of stuffing a sucking-pig:

1. with normal sausage meat, seasoned with thyme, marjoram and plenty of chopped parsley.
2. with apples cored and sliced and then mixed with currants, a little sugar and lemon juice.
3. with raw *Sauerkraut*, mixed with small sausages, lean slices of bacon and juniper berries.
4. with a bread stuffing, made from soaked white bread, squeezed out and minced, then mixed with eggs and seasoning.
5. with rice: Patna rice cooked for about 10 minutes mixed with gently fried onions and saffron.

Any stuffing may, as has already been mentioned, be made fairly solid, which will make carving easier.

ROAST SUCKING PIG (*Spanferkel vom Rost*)

When the pig comes from the butcher it will be opened out fairly flat. Salt and pepper it as it comes, brush it with oil and beer and roast it either in the oven or over an open fire.

The accompaniments to this dish should be sour to aid digestion. The same goes for the choice of drinks: a *Schnaps*, or preferably several, will be indispensable.

POULTRY AND GAME

JUGGED HARE (*Tippehas*)

1 hare, boned and cut in
   large pieces
1 lb. fat bacon or pork,
   sliced
3 onions, sliced
½ lb. black breadcrumbs
salt, nutmeg
1 clove garlic, chopped
2 cloves, 1 bay leaf
5 crushed juniper berries
1 cup (1¼) meat stock
2 pints (2½) red wine

Arrange the hare, bacon, onions and breadcrumbs in layers in a casserole, sprinkling each layer with salt and freshly grated nutmeg, and dispensing the garlic, cloves, bay leaf and juniper berries in between. Add the stock and wine, cover the pan and cook in a slow oven until the hare is tender. Serve with potato purée or dumplings. (Drink: red wine)

VEGETABLES

POTATO CAKES (*Reibekuchen*)

2 lb. peeled potatoes
3 eggs
salt to taste
hot fat

Grate the potatoes in warm water – this keeps them white. Drain and dry in a cloth; mix with the eggs, add salt. Drop in tablespoonfuls into a pan of hot fat – not for deep frying – and fry the cakes on both sides until crisp and brown. Serve hot with apple purée or compôte, or the Rhineland speciality *Äpfelkraut*, a kind of thick unsweetened jam. (Drink: beer and *Schnaps*)

They can also be eaten cold, sprinkled with sugar and every housewife has her own variation of this dish, e.g.:

1. Add grated, cooked potatoes.
2. Add grated onions.
3. Season with nutmeg.
4. Add cream or milk and thicken with flour.
5. Add peeled, cored and grated apple.
6. Add rolls soaked in milk, then squeezed dry.

The *Rievkoucke*, as it is called in Cologne, is an everyday dish and also appears at every folk festival and fair; like a sausage it can be eaten in the hand without a knife and fork. It is part of our folk life. Wherever a German Merchant Navy ship is sailing, potato cakes are served every Thursday.

PURÉE OF TURNIP TOPS (*Stielmus*)
This dish is made from the stalks of young turnips.

2 lb. turnip tops
1½ oz. (2 tablespoons) pork fat
1 oz. (2 tablespoons) butter
1 tablespoon (1¼) flour
½ cup (⅔) milk
salt, nutmeg to taste

Pull off the leaves (these can be used as spinach) and wash the stalks. Cut into 3 in. lengths. Heat the fat, add the stalks, a little water and cook until tender. Heat the butter, add the flour, stir to a roux, add the milk and cook to a thick sauce. Add salt and freshly grated nutmeg and pour the sauce over the stalks. Serve with lamb.

STRING BEANS (*Schnippelbohnen oder Fitzebohnen*)

1 lb. green beans
1 oz. fat
meat stock
salt

Wash and break the beans into short lengths. Heat the fat, add the beans, fry a minute or so, add stock to cover, season and cook until tender.

HEAVEN AND EARTH (*Himmel und Erde*)

2 lb. boiled potatoes
2 lb. stewed apples
salt, sugar to taste
1 lb. black pudding, sliced
fat bacon, diced

Separately rub the potatoes and apples through a sieve. Mix, add salt and sugar and reheat. Fry the black pudding and bacon until crisp. Serve on top of the potato-apple mixture.
(Drink: beer)

BISCUITS

RHINELAND SHORTCAKE BISCUITS (*Rheinischer Spekulatius*)

100 biscuits:

1 lb. flour
2 tablespoons (2½) baking powder
1 cup (1¼) sugar
1 packet vanilla sugar
¼ lb. (½ cup) butter, softened
pinch ground cardamon
cloves, salt
1 teaspoon (1¼) cinnamon
2 eggs, beaten
milk

Sieve the flour and baking powder together and on to a board. Make a well in the centre, add the sugar, vanilla sugar, butter, spices and eggs and mix to a firm dough. A little milk can be added if required. Knead quickly and leave covered for 20 minutes in a cool place.

Roll out the dough to a thick sheet and stamp with biscuit cutters – if the dough does not come out clean, either add more flour to the dough or to the cutters.

Arrange the biscuits on a greased baking sheet and bake for 15 to 20 minutes in a hot oven.

CHEESE

CHEESE WITH VINAIGRETTE DRESSING (*Burebahnhof*)

2 small Mainz cheeses
1 tablespoon (1¼) oil
2 tablespoons (2½) vinegar
salt, pepper, mustard

Slice the cheeses. Make a dressing with the remaining ingredients and pour this over the sliced cheese. Serve with beer.

Many people like to add 2 tablespoons (2½) of diced onions.

This type of cheese salad is also made in other parts of Germany using Emmentaler, Tilsiter, Edamer and other similar cheeses.

The Best of German Food

THE COLOGNE FOOD FAIR

Every other year Cologne holds the ANUGA, or Food Fair. It is one of the greatest displays of its kind to be held anywhere in the world, and exhibitors from even the most distant countries come to show their wares in this old cathedral city on the Rhine. A visit to the serried stalls of the Fair is a trip round the world. In this context, however, we will confine ourselves to the German section.

'*Aus deutschen Landen frisch auf den Tisch*' – from the German country-side fresh to your table – runs the motto for this survey of German cooking, and a very persuasive survey it is. The daily food of a nation is first and foremost drawn from its own soil. Even though international trade has led to sizeable imports, the basic pattern remains the same. Wherever one lives, the tendency is to eat what is grown locally and to cook it in the traditional manner of the area. German cooking is not so celebrated as Chinese or French cooking but it is nevertheless good and it rewards study.

Let us look a little more closely at the German section of the Fair. In the centre of it the market gardeners have built up their display into a splendidly colourful still-life, with snow-white cauliflowers set among the varying greens of leek, savoy and the cabbage which yields the famous *Sauerkraut*. These contrast agreeably with the red tomatoes, carrots, peppers and beans. Close by are splendid asparagus, as much admired by foreigners as are our celery, beets, onions and potatoes.

Equally interesting is the work of our bakers who display the regional specialities of the whole country. German bakers who emigrated to America had little trouble in becoming well-to-do. Here they not only exhibit bread of many shapes and colours, but also their skill as pastry-cooks, and we can inspect *feuilleté* pastries, tarts and a variety of little tidbits which have been handed down and improved over centuries of skilled handicraft. The bakers' stand is dominated by a magnificent specimen of the *Baumkuchen*, and at its foot lie the many different sorts of Christmas cakes and cookies which are so much part of that season in every German home. Honey, eggs and sugar are combined in many other ways.

In the cool rooms are many fresh and appetizing sides of pigs, calves, lambs and steers from which high quality roasts, hams and sausages will be made, and in as many different varieties as there are varieties of bread and pastry. German butchers are world renowned and although the technical apparatus has altered, the native recipes have hardly done so down the centuries. Not for nothing have the North Americans christened their beloved hot sausage a 'Frankfurter'.

Nearby there is the seafood display, drawn from the products of the North Sea and the Baltic. From lobster to mussel, from sole to bass, everything is fresh from the water. Perhaps the herring deserves a special mention, for who has not enjoyed it grilled or as rollmops or Bismarck herring? Our neighbours in Scandinavia make great use of it and we have even developed one form of it for curing hangovers. Alas, most of us have suffered from one at one time or another, and experience which will have taught the wise the beauty of moderation in all things!

Next come the tables displaying wine, with their attendant girls in peasant costume dispensing sample tastings. It is wise, between sips, to eat a cheese sliver from the Allgäu or some other district, for there is an enormous choice of cheeses and they marry well with the wine. The problem is where to start. There stand the slim green and brown bottles of Rhine, Moselle, Nahe, Ruwer, Saar and Ahr wines. Beside them the *Bocksbeutel* of Franconia, the *Würzburgers*, the Eschendorfer *Lump* and many another. Afterwards there are the Baden wines from the Kaiserstuhl to consider, along with the Württembergers growing along the slopes of the river Tauber. Nor must we overlook the sparkling wines whose capital is the city of Wiesbaden. Here is an opportunity to study how much in the way of wine Germany has to offer, not only to Germans but to the world.

Gold medals have been awarded not only to our wines but also to our beer which, apart from quenching many a thirst at home, is also a major export. Complementing beer comes *Schnaps*, and perhaps at this point of our survey we should drink one. There is ample choice. Brandy – and the name of Asbach is widely known – is perhaps the most celebrated. It consoles the stomach after rich food and is a very present help in troubles of the private sort. The *Klaren* – clear spirits from the north and west – share their virtues with the fine Geister and Wässerli, distilled from many fruits both wild and cultivated, which come from the Black Forest and elsewhere. To return to our visit, however, first a *Schnaps* and then a beer.

Germany is the brewers' and the beer-drinker's paradise. Hardly a town fails to have its brewery. Everyone swears by his particular favourite, be it from Munich, Nürnberg, Kulmbach, Dortmund or Bremen, to name only a few of the great ones. The best plan, though, is to drink the local beer, wherever you happen to be, for the same reason that it is rather pointless to drink Moselle in Württemberg or Rhine wine in Munich. Profit by – and take your pleasure in – the specialities of kitchen and cellar which are offered you locally. With this thought in mind I am going to suggest that you accompany me on journeys which I have made recently. Your journeys of the future may well be much the same as these, and I offer the next sections as modest companions to the traveller. May your journeys be happy ones, and your nights tranquil.

THE ROMANTIC ROAD

In an earlier chapter I quoted a saying from a *Weinstube* in Würzburg, and in this very city our journey begins, a journey of discovery through friendly landscapes, villages and towns, a journey which will not necessarily lead us only to castles, walled cities and immortal works of art but also to inns and *Weinstübe* where we can dine as did emperors and kings, poets and painters of the past. People nowadays drive much too fast along these roads. In the old days it was a voyage, a long and difficult voyage, from the north southwards to the sun. It would have been an affliction for anyone, had it not been for the hostelries along the road where comfortable beds and plenty of food and drink were to be found. Even today, many a

house has survived war and the ravages of time; the old inn-signs swing
over the door, window-boxes brighten the façade and at the heavy oaken
tables one can sit down to eat and drink the abundance of the neighbouring
countryside.

Let us then begin our journey in Würzburg, now recovered from the
wounds of the last war, smiling once more its gay and baroque smile. The
men of Franconia draw. their reserves of strength from the local wine;
their two patron saints, it is said, are St Kilian and the *Frankenwein*. One
has only to take a few sips of *Stein* or *Leisten* in the Juliusspital or the
Bürgerspital for the spirits of Balthasar Neumann, Tiepolo and the other
great craftsmen in iron, glass and stone to stand at one's side. Already as
Hofrat Goethe took pleasure in *Bocksbeutel* and used to accompany it with
the flat pastry known as *Blatz* which is only to be found hereabouts.
The splendour of the wine tends rather to outshine the enjoyment of mere
food but one should make a point of not missing the crisp and golden
Meerfischle which go so well with a glass of light beer from the Würzburger
Hofbräu.

Along the route we shall encounter widely differing styles of cooking,
from Franconia, Württemberg, Swabia and the Allgäu, which is related
to the cooking of Bavaria. This makes for a particularly varied journey. In
Bad Mergentheim, our first stop out of Würzburg, one is already in
Württemberg and so one is in Weikersheim and Creglingen. A roast joint
of beef with onions and potatoes should still our hunger here. An equally
good alternative would be *Maultaschen* (see page 119) in a spicy bouillon
or cooked with butter and onions. At the time of the vintage the new wine
is accompanied by the celebrated onion cakes, cooked with bacon fat and
caraway. Every bride from Württemberg has to know how to bake these.
On the slopes above the Tauber grows the *Tauberwein*. In Markelsheim it
is stored in the huge vats of the Winzer Co-operative. This wine has a
certain affinity to the wines of Franconia, but a style of its own. In Weikersheim the traveller can combine a visit to the castle of Hohenlohe with a
wine-tasting in the cellars where wine from the princely vineyards can be
sampled. In the old days this wine would be drunk to celebrate the con-
clusion of the hunt, in the biggest Renaissance hall in Germany beneath
the roof of this castle.

In Creglingen, too, wine from the Tauber is to be had. The traveller
should pause here to admire Tilman Riemenschneider's altar in the
Herrgottskirche. After this one leaves Württemberg and sets off into 'the
land of the Franks'. From far away one sees the towers of the Free Imperial

City of Rothenburg ob der Tauber; the kitchens and cellars hold many treasures for the visitor. Here one is greeted by the sight of the local *Bratwurst*, rough in texture, highly spiced with herbs, served brown and crisp. The best drink to accompany these is a cool glass of beer from the Rothenburg brewery (which has been quenching the town's thirst since 1724). Carp, too, are baked with great skill in Rothenburg, and one can go further and fare worse than eat a piquant veal salad. The carp, however, is split in half, dipped in a mixture of egg and semolina and then baked in hot fat. The fins and the tail must become as crisp and brittle as the thinnest glass. The better to digest it, one should preface this dish with a glass of Franconian *Zwetsch*, the strong honest brandy made from our local plums. If anyone still needs refreshment after the carp, let him order coffee and a 'Snowball', a pastry which is formed in a special iron mould, baked in hot lard and well sprinkled with icing sugar.

During the Thirty Years War, Rothenburg was saved from destruction by the *Meistertrank* of its burgomaster who, to the amazement of the enemy, lowered a three-litre jug without drawing breath. If this form of non-stop drinking is hardly to be recommended, let no one fail to have a few sups of Tauber or Franconian wine which is readily available in many a pleasant inn.

The next two places on our journey, Feuchtwangen and Dinkelsbühl, are still in Franconia. Here the *charcuterie* is to be recommended, particularly the splendid liver sausages and black puddings which are so well set off by *Sauerkraut*. Our road leads on to Nördlingen where the roast goose with *Klösse* (see page 81) is especially good. The local geese are particularly delicate and tasty. No one will protest if you take a crisp wing or leg in your fingers and clean it up as you would at home. In Harburg an der Wörnitz one can enjoy a lovingly prepared sausage salad washed down by a beer from the Prince Wallenstein Brewery. One need only take time to look out over the landscape from the citadel to realize how closely soil, food and drink are interwoven with man and his work.

By way of Donauwörth this romantic journey leads on to golden Augsburg, so closely bound up with the history of the banking Fuggers who through boldness and hard work earned great wealth and made their city's fortune. One can say of the Augsburgers that they have never had a bad meal in their life. Here one can eat genuine Swabian food in all its glory. Augsburg also boasts one particular speciality which is not to be had elsewhere, the *Donauschüll*, a sort of pike from the Danube which is served in many forms. With it beer or wine go perfectly. The great importance attached in this town to the pleasures of the table is emphasised by an excellent cookbook written by the worthy Frau Sophia Juliana Weileri. It has been through no fewer than fourteen editions since 1810.

Travelling outward, the next goal is Landsberg, where the *Gockerl* taste so good with a green salad. If one is lucky one may be given a brook trout *au bleu* fresh out of the Lech. If one is out of luck then a fine fish dinner is sure to be available in Schongau, and trout are also to be had there, very delicate and scented.

From here it is no great distance to the magic castles of Bavaria. Here the Allgäu begins, with its lush meadows and the chain of the Alps on the horizon. The white clouds and blue skies of this country are repeated in the colours of the Bavarian flag. Milk, butter, cheese and cereals are the staple diet and fish from the many lakes and streams are superbly prepared. *Käsespatzen*, the local cheese pastries, are worth tasting; and in the town of Füssen Debrziner, a splendid sausage, must be eaten. In Füssen the traveller reaches the end of this romantic road. Lucky is the man who finds time to use his eyes and palate to enjoy the lovely landscape through which he has travelled and to appreciate the other gifts of God which he has now made his own. As the poet, Gottfried Keller said:

Trinkt, o Augen, was die Wimper hält,
Von dem goldnen Überfluss der Welt!

THE FORTRESS ROAD

One of the handsomest roads in Germany is called the Burgenstrasse, the Fortress Road, which, starting on the Rhine at Mannheim, leads up the valley of the Neckar through the former territory of the Hohenlohe family into Franconia, and ends at Nürnberg. The road is certainly well named; but let no one be entirely distracted from the gastronomic pleasures which it has to offer. First it sets off through the reassuring countryside of Baden where the wines of the Palatinate are at one's elbow. The galaxy of wines available justify nibbling at the local pretzels, crisp, brown and sprinkled with coarse salt. One can safely go on toying with these without ruining one's appetite for more solid fare.

In these old townships along the Neckar one should allow oneself the pleasure of a *truite au bleu* with melted butter and potatoes well sprinkled with parsley. Here, too, a saddle of venison is not to be despised, brought in from forests rich in game. Many a village draws its name, many a coat of arms its blazon from this source – Eberbach and Hirschhorn for example.

With saddle of venison, which of course demands a creamy sauce, one should serve cranberry sauce and handmade *Spätzle* straight from the board, into boiling water and finally, for good measure, well tossed in butter. Wine goes well with it, for instance a Götzenberger, which grows on the slopes outside the fortress town of Hornberg. Those who prefer beer will also find cause for admiration, for master brewers abound in this part of the world.

From the fields below the proud castle of Horneck, the peasants provide wonderful gherkins which they pickle in an immemorial formula of sweet-and-sour vinegar. The corncobs of Gundelsheim are also to be recommended in their season as a refreshing garnish to hot beef or smoked ham.

The further one drives towards Heilbronn, the more the influence of Swabian cookery becomes apparent. Here, crisp from the oven, the traveller finds the pastries, meats, soups and other specialities of that notable cuisine which has been described already in the Swabian chapter of this book and which is scarcely overshadowed even by the wine which is provided so abundantly on these fortunate hillsides. A slightly *pétillant* white wine, a Weissriesling, comes from here, and a delicate red called Trollinger. Here the wine is not served in the usual *viertel* (quarter litre) glasses with stocky stems, but simply poured out, as it were, on draught. In the huge cellars of the Hohenlohe princes at Oehringen the local wine matures in vats each larger than its neighbour. The largest of all has been converted into a little tasting chamber and it is a great honour to be invited into this miniature room. One of the oldest houses making *Sekt* has for centuries drawn on these cellars.

In the Hohenlohe country, a splendid one for wine, Künzelsau can offer its *Kocherperle* and Ingelfingen its *Ingelfinger Gold*.

A peak point – in the truest sense of the word since the road climbs steadily into the mountains – on this Burgenstrasse is the *Residenz* of the Princes of Hohenlohe-Langenburg. In the shops of the neighbouring craftsmen *Wibele* are for sale which have a special connection with the *Residenz*. The name derives from a master confectioner, Jakob Christian Karl Wibel, who in the eighteenth century founded a baker's and confectioner's business in Langenburg. The original recipe from which even today *Wibele* are made, is carefully guarded. Its origins go back to the reigning prince of the period who liked something sweet on his bedside table at night. Wibel was charged with providing it. One night his servant patronized another baker and the prince was far from pleased and immediately commanded that in future only *Wibele* were acceptable; and so the

little pastries were christened. The court at Langenburg was well known
then as it is to this day, for its hospitality, and the distinguished guests
of that era took to the *Wibele* and arranged to have them sent to their own
courts, with the result that Meister Wibel became Purveyor to half the
courts of Europe. The royal and princely warrants still hang in the
Café Bauer, as the former Café Wibel is now called. Today as long ago,
kings and queens can still eat *Wibele*.

The Burgenstrasse crosses our previous route in Rothenburg and then
runs on through typical Franconian scenery to Ansbach and Lehrberg,
to its goal at Nürnberg, a city not only celebrated for Albrecht Dürer and
its art treasurers but also justly renowned for its food. Here the best of all
Nürnberg dishes, little *Bratwürste*, are grilled over a charcoal fire and are
eaten accompanied by *Sauerkraut* in which the black pearls of the pepper-
corn gleam like juniper berries. In spring these sausages go well with a
salad of asparagus or hop-shoots. Another speciality is Nürnberg's
sharp-tasting salad of calf chaps, marinaded in spring onions, a little salt,
oil and vinegar, helped down by a beer from the world-famous brewery.
Another typical Franconian delicacy is baked carp, which we have
described before. The Nürnbergers claim to prepare this dish better than
anyone. To round off this culinary expedition we should mention three
more internationally known Nürnberg specialities, classics of the baker's
art – *Pfefferkuchen, Elisenkuchen* and *Mandelbaum Kuchen*. In the early
Middle Ages the nomads had the secret of these recipes, using honey from
their own bees and herbs from distant lands. Not for nothing used
Nürnberg to be known as the 'treasure-chest' of Germany.

EPILOGUE

Here I should like to add a brief epilogue to this part of the book. Just as
a painter captures a landscape on canvas and a poet sets it down on paper,
so I too have tried to sketch a description of what my countrymen eat and
drink in their different localities. I had obviously to be selective in my
choice of recipes, so that there is still room for exploration and discovery!
The most important dishes have, however, found room here and will, I
hope, give the reader an impression of the country and its people. I hope
that I shall prove to have been a good counsellor and guide to the German
scene.

PRIVATE THOUGHTS ON COOKERY

'He who can cook will survive, but the world is a good cook's oyster for
everyone must eat to live and everyone prefers to eat well.'

A cook who sets himself the task of realizing new ideas must, like a painter,
a writer or a composer, be creative. A new dish which is not to be found in
a cookbook may be compared with a composition based round a new motif.
It is created in the same way as any other work of art, with the aim of
giving pleasure. It was well said that there is nothing new under the sun;
yet the world has changed since Ancient Greece and the new artists have
stood upon the shoulders of their forerunners to perfect, refine and even
to change what was already ready at hand.

I chose the profession of cook because I enjoyed eating and my mother's
kitchen was a fairyland for me, but before I became first a cook and then
a chef I had a long apprenticeship. I gathered experience in small restaurants, big hotels, and fashionable resorts, in railway dining cars and
on the great ocean liners of the Norddeutscher Lloyd in which I sailed the
seven seas. On my travels I looked into the kitchens of other countries and
put together my own personal collection of cookbooks. I shall never cease
to learn and to experiment, in accordance with the spirit of the times.

The particular quality of my own recipes stems from the belief that
people today cannot cope with heavy meals, that dishes should be un-
complicated, easy to digest, attractive to look at and quick to prepare.
Modest helpings are best because, for instance, motorists should not
overtax their stomachs and women pay more attention than ever to their
figures. I aim to fight against the traditions which for decades have
dominated eating and drinking. If someone wishes to drink white wine
with dark meat or red wine with fish, let him do so. I find in this no lack of
education but an expression of personal taste. Certainly at formal banquets the classical marriages of food and wine are continued, but often
enough I have known a guest to slip outside at some point in the pro-
ceedings in search of a quick glass of beer. It would be reasonable were he
able to order it at table.

There are chefs, too, who hold that women know little about cooking.
I am not of this persuasion, and am reminded in this context of something
which happened to me in Hong Kong. In that city I ate in a restaurant
whose proud boast was that it was the second best in the world. Being
interested, and having eaten a splendid meal, I asked the chef which he

considered to be the very best in the world. He smiled and said: 'the best cooking is at home'. I feel that the housewife does need expert help. Certainly she does not have to make money out of her skills, but her trouble should be reduced to a minimum and her meals slanted in the modern way with an eye to the contentment and health of her whole family. This task, of helping housewives with their cooking, has been a great joy to me, and still is. I speak to them on the radio, I cook for them on television and I write for them in magazines and illustrated papers. To them I have directed most of my cookbooks. Countless letters seem to indicate that I have been of service to them and this gives me courage to go on in my own chosen way.

Publicity has never played such an important role as today. In pictures and sound, television exploits it, just as the magazines do with their bright photographs of food products. The best photographers are employed to make the most expensive productions on behalf of this or that brand. I myself have collected and tested many of them, have prepared copy for them, written brochures and handed on new discoveries to others. A pleasant and rewarding task!

It is undeniable that since the war a certain American influence has made itself felt, not only in Germany but in Europe generally, in forms of speech, fashion, music, dancing and naturally, eating. Some of my older colleagues strove against this influence from America on German cooking. I have tried to extract what was best from this material and in my recipe section quite a number will be found (for instance asparagus cocktail) which I brought back from journeys to the U.S.A. Many combinations of meat with fruit, and indeed many and varied recipes pleasing to the eye and taste, stem from American cooking.

At the ANUGA – the Food Fair – at Cologne, and at other exhibitions, it has fallen to my lot to prepare special dishes, salads and samples. On many a day I have made five thousand or so, with temporary equipment in little kitchens with glass walls through which a ceaseless flow of spectators would gaze. This is no easy exercise, though a necessary one for launching new dishes. Talking of which, it is worth giving a thought to the number of new fruits and vegetables which have begun to be imported into Germany in the last ten years. The Siebenburgers and Sudeten Germans brought us paprika shoots, the Italians brought *finocchio* and artichokes, from Israel came aubergines and avocados, and so forth. It has delighted me to find them generally available in our markets and to introduce them to our housewives so that they may become regular fare at home as well as in international hotels.

Many manufacturers, particularly of noodles and macaroni only concerned themselves – until some fifteen years ago – with producing and selling, until the day when sales began to lag through foreign and particularly Italian, competition. Their public relations men advised them to make clear to the public what could be made of their products, and that more could be done with them than to boil them in salt water and serve them as a dreary accompaniment to something else. Here, too, I was able to help by trying out noodles in new combinations. New packaging, with recipes and bright colour-photographs led to remarkable demand. The same has applied to such diverse products as Bols liqueurs and bananas. Not only have new types of food and drink intrigued me, but also their preservation in refrigerators and deep freezes. I have written a number of articles on this subject but only after careful tasting in my own kitchens in order to come up with the best answers.

One of the most important questions, nowadays, in the housewife's mind is 'what shall I cook tomorrow?' It used to be 'what shall I wear?' If, for my part, I can help to keep the art of good cooking alive then I shall be very happy in the knowledge that I shall not have worked to no purpose. My hope is that I may succeed in enriching your daily fare with the recipes which follow. I wish my readers, therefore, success at the cooker, good appetite, and above all, much enjoyment.

Recipes by Hans Karl Adam

HORS D'OEUVRE

ASPARAGUS COCKTAIL HANS KARL ADAM (*Spargel Cocktail Hans Karl Adam*)

The ingredients for this recipe are all 'as required'.

3 stalks asparagus per portion
lemon juice
tomato ketchup
brandy
thick mayonnaise
cooked lean ham
pineapple slices
salt
lettuce
sliced tomatoes
hardboiled eggs, sliced
chopped parsley

Mix a little lemon juice, tomato ketchup and brandy into the mayonnaise.

Cut the asparagus (stewed or canned) into small pieces and cut the ham and pineapple into thin strips. Mix with the asparagus and lightly salt. Tear the lettuce leaves into small pieces, arrange these in glass bowls. Add asparagus, ham and pineapple and cover with the sauce. Garnish with asparagus tips, tomato, hardboiled egg and parsley. An unusually good delicacy for arousing the appetite.

ASPARAGUS COCKTAIL GABI (*Spargel Cocktail Gabi*)

Ingredients are as required.

3 stalks asparagus
cooked chicken and ham
lettuce
sliced hardboiled egg
Remoulade sauce
flavoured with Madeira
and whipped cream
chopped tomatoes

Cut the asparagus (stewed or canned) into small pieces; the chicken and ham into thin strips. Arrange with the remaining ingredients as in previous recipe. Cover with the sauce and garnish with asparagus tips and tomatoes.

ASPARAGUS COCKTAIL WITH LOBSTER (*Spargel Cocktail mit Hummer*)

Add a little port wine to a thick mayonnaise sauce until it is of pouring consistency. Allow 3 stalks of asparagus (stewed or canned) per portion: mix with diced cooked lobster meat and arrange as in previous recipes, with lettuce and cover with the sauce. Garnish with asparagus tips, lobster meat, chopped parsley or as in illustration facing page 134.

APPLE SALAD OXI (*Äpfelsalat Oxi*)

1 cooked ox tongue
dessert apples
salt
lemon juice
mayonnaise
mustard
tomato ketchup
hardboiled egg
sour cherries, stoned
lettuce
parsley

Cut the tongue into medium-thick slices. Peel and core the apples and chop into fairly small pieces. Sprinkle with salt and lemon juice. Flavour a really thick mayonnaise with mustard and ketchup, mix this with the chopped apples. Arrange the smaller slices of tongue on a flat dish. Pile the apple salad on the slices of tongue, then place the larger tongue slices on top. On the top of each 'pocket' place a slice of hardboiled egg and on the yolk half a cherry. Garnish with lettuce and sprigs of parsley.

CHICKEN LIVER PASTE AUNT HEIDE (*Geflügelleberpaste Tante Heide*)

1 lb. chicken livers,
   cleaned
$\frac{1}{4}$ lb. fat sliced bacon
1 small onion, diced
salt, pepper
grated nutmeg
pinch each rosemary and
   thyme
1 tablespoon ($1\frac{1}{4}$) chopped
   parsley
2 oz. (4 tablespoons) butter
$\frac{1}{2}$ cup ($\frac{2}{3}$) cream
$\frac{1}{4}$ cup ($\frac{1}{3}$) brandy
$\frac{1}{4}$ cup ($\frac{1}{3}$) Madeira

Gently fry the bacon until the fat runs, add the chicken livers, cook these gently until firm but not dark. Add the onion, continue cooking gently for 15 minutes. Put all this through the fine blade of a grinder. Add the seasoning, nutmeg and herbs. Mix thoroughly, blend in the butter, cream, brandy and Madeira. Fill the paste into a jar, cover and put into the refrigerator to become as firm as butter. Spread hot slices of toast thickly with the paste which has an unbelievably good aroma.

The liver paste, which is best left overnight before using, can be moulded into small individual containers if preferred. (Drink: dry sherry)

KARILLA FRIED BREAD (*Toast Karilla*)

4 thick slices white bread,
   fried on both sides in
   butter
3 oz. (6 tablespoons) butter
$\frac{3}{4}$ lb. mushrooms, sliced
salt
juice $\frac{1}{2}$ lemon
4 eggs, well beaten
$\frac{1}{2}$ cup ($\frac{2}{3}$) cream,
   stiffly whipped
1 teaspoon ($1\frac{1}{4}$) chopped
   chives
1 teaspoon ($1\frac{1}{4}$) chopped
   parsley
1 teaspoon ($1\frac{1}{4}$) mild
   paprika pepper

Arrange the bread in a shallow baking dish. Heat the butter, add the mushrooms, sprinkle with salt and lemon juice and cook for 3 minutes. Pour the eggs over the top and allow to curdle over a low heat. Spread this mixture over the bread and bake in a moderate oven for 10 minutes. Season the cream, add the chives and parsley. When serving put a blob of cream on to each slice of fried bread and sprinkle with paprika. Serve with a green salad.

(Drink: sparkling white wine)

HERRING COCKTAIL (*Herings Cocktail*)

4 pickled herring fillets
juice 1 lemon
2 cartons yoghourt
mustard to taste
3 egg yolks, well beaten
salt, pepper
2 tomatoes, peeled,
    chopped and pipped
chopped parsley

Thinly slice the herrings and sprinkle with lemon juice. Divide between 4 cocktail glasses. Cover with the following sauce: mix the yoghourt with mustard, egg yolks, salt, pepper and the tomatoes. Pour the sauce over the herrings, sprinkle with chopped parsley and serve with toast and butter.

SAVOURY MEAT FRITTERS (*Kräuterkugeln in Bierteig*)

Beer batter:
5 oz. (1¼ cups) plain (all
    purpose) flour
½ cup (⅔) light beer
salt
2 egg yolks, beaten
2 egg whites, stiffly beaten
1 tablespoon (1¼) oil
Filling:
1¼ lb. finely ground pork
3 eggs, beaten
1 medium-sized onion,
    diced
2 tablespoons (2½) chopped
    parsley
1 tablespoon (1¼) chopped
    dill
1 teaspoon (1¼) chopped
    chervil
salt, nutmeg
6 tablespoons (7½) fine
    breadcrumbs
fat for frying
2 large onions, sliced

Sieve the flour, add the beer and beat until smooth. Add salt and egg yolks and beat with a wire whisk. Fold in the egg whites and the oil. Leave for 30 minutes. The beer causes the batter to slightly ferment but it also mellows it. The batter should be thicker than for pancakes.

Mix the meat with the remaining ingredients, except the sliced onions and fat. Make small balls from the mixture and lay them on a board sprinkled with breadcrumbs to prevent their sticking. Heat plenty of fat for deep frying. Quickly fry the onion rings until crisp, take from the pan, drain and put aside but keep hot. Dip the meat balls into the batter and fry them in the same fat until a golden colour.

Serve the meat balls with the onion scattered over the top.

MUSHROOM CAKES (*Champignonplätzchen*)

1 lb. mushrooms
**4 tablespoons (5) maize
flour**
4 eggs, well beaten
**2 tablespoons (2½) chopped
parsley**
salt
juice 1 lemon
3 slices fat bacon, diced
2 large onions, diced
oil for deep frying

Clean the mushrooms and chop coarsely with a knife on a board. Put them into a bowl, add the flour, eggs, parsley, salt and lemon juice. Fry the bacon until it becomes transparent, add the onions and continue frying until golden. Slightly cool. Mix with the mushrooms. Heat the oil. Take tablespoonfuls of the mixture and fry until golden all over. Drain and serve with boiled long grain rice and a green salad.

Instead of lemon juice, a dry white wine or a light beer may be used in the same quantity.

(Drink: white wine or light beer)

ONION AND POTATO CAKE JOSÉ (*Kartoffelpfannkuchen mit Zwiebeln José*)

**1 lb. onions, finely
chopped**
2 lb. boiled potatoes
½ cup (⅔) wine vinegar
½ cup (⅔) water
salt
1 tablespoon (1¼) sugar
1 bay leaf
2 cloves
nutmeg
5 eggs, beaten
flour
fine breadcrumbs
fat for frying

Simmer the onions with the vinegar, water, salt, sugar, bay leaf and cloves until they are soft and the liquid absorbed. Discard the bay leaf and cloves. Rub the potatoes, while still hot, through a sieve, season with salt and nutmeg and mix with the onions. Add 3 eggs and, if the potato mixture seems too soft, and potatoes vary in texture, add enough flour to thicken it. The mixture should be dry but easy to work. Make small flat cakes from the mixture, similar to fish cakes, toss in flour, coat with the remaining beaten eggs and roll in breadcrumbs. Heat a fair quantity of fat and fry the potato cakes until golden on both sides. Serve with a green and a tomato salad.

(Drink: beer)

MORNING DEW SALAD (*Salat Morgentau*)

1 lb. red peppers
½ lb. fresh peaches
6 oz. smoked ham,
  thinly sliced
4 hardboiled eggs
4 large tomatoes
1 tablespoon (1¼) dry
  mustard
1 tablespoon (1¼) sugar
1 teaspoon (1¼) salt
5 tablespoons (6¼) herb
  vinegar
4 tablespoons (5) olive oil
4 tablespoons (5) water
lettuce
chopped parsley

Wash the peppers, slice off the tops, discard the seeds and cores. Slice and place in a bowl. Dip the peaches in boiling water and peel off their skins. Stone and thinly slice.

Cut the ham into strips. Slice the eggs. Peel, seed and thinly slice the tomatoes. Stir the mustard, sugar, salt, vinegar, olive oil and water together for 5 minutes to make a sharp sauce. Combine the peaches, ham, eggs and tomatoes with the peppers, add the sauce and stir gently Leave for 10 minutes.

Turn into a salad bowl lined with lettuce leaves, sprinkle with parsley and serve with toast.

When fresh peaches are not available, use instead peaches preserved in water or in a very light syrup, and thoroughly drained.

(Drink: tomato juice)

SAUSAGE MEAT RISSOLES (*Ballettklösschen*)

1½ lb. sausage meat,
  preferably half pork,
  half veal
3 eggs
5 tablespoons (6¼) sour
  cream
12 thin slices streaky bacon
12 thick slices apple,
  cut in rounds

Beat the eggs with the cream, mix with the sausage meat. Make 12 oval rissoles from the mixture with a tablespoon, repeatedly dipping both hands and spoon into cold water.

Lay the bacon on the bottom of a baking tin (one with a high rim) and place an apple ring on each, with a rissole on top of this. Bake in a very hot oven for 20 minutes. The rissoles must be very firm when cooked.

Serve the rissoles on a bed of potato purée, still lying on the bacon and apple rings.

(Drink: Württemberg Schiller wine)

SOUSED HERRINGS AUNT ANNI (*Eingelegte Heringe Tante Anni*)

Allow 1–2 herrings per person for a supper dish. They must be salt, fleshy herrings; this is important as they are to be pickled.

8 herrings

4 large onions

4 tablespoons (5) herb vinegar

1 tablespoon ($1\frac{1}{4}$) sugar

4 large apples

2 large carrots

4 medium-sized pickled gherkins

1 tablespoon ($1\frac{1}{4}$) dry mustard

3 tablespoons ($3\frac{3}{4}$) oil

1 carton yoghourt

1 cup ($1\frac{1}{4}$) sour cream

Wash the herrings under cold running water; leave overnight in plenty of cold water, completely submerged, and in a cold place.

On the following day carefully drain off the water, remove the heads and skin. The skin will come away easily if you take a sharp kitchen knife and, using the point, start at the tail and pare away lightly; in a minute it will be possible to draw the skin right off to the head. When this is done, take a coffee spoon, bowl downwards, and gently loosen the fillet from the backbone, starting at the dorsal fin. Then cut straight down the fish to obtain clean herring fillets. It is possible (in Germany) to buy fresh herring fillets, but you pay more; or often obliging fishmongers will fillet the herrings for a customer. Wash the fillets in cold water and dry them in a cloth. Wrap in foil and put aside until required.

Peel the onions, cut into thin rings and cook in vinegar and half the sugar until they are just soft, about 5–8 minutes. They must not disintegrate. Allow to cool in their liquid. Peel, core and quarter the apples and thinly slice or grate. Wash the carrots and gherkins, grate or slice as for the apples.

Place a glass or earthenware bowl on a cloth so that it does not slip and make the sauce. First put in the mustard, the remaining sugar and the oil. Stir slowly, the oil should make the sauce as smooth as velvet. Add the yoghourt and cream, stir, and at this point add the onions in their vinegar, the apples, gherkins and carrots. Taste for flavour, the sauce should have a sharp, sweet-sour flavour. If necessary, add extra sugar or vinegar.

Put a layer of the sauce at the bottom of a bowl (preferably one with a lid), then a layer of herring fillets. Add more sauce, then again herrings and continue in this way until all is used up. Make sure there is sufficient sauce to spread over the top layer of herrings. Cover the bowl and leave in a cool place until the following day. Serve with boiled potatoes, sprinkled with parsley.

(Drink: beer)

STEAK TARTARE FOR LADIES (*Steak Tartar für Damen*)

1 lb. lean beef
salt, pepper
½ teaspoon (⅔) mild paprika pepper
1 teaspoon (1¼) dry mustard
1 teaspoon (1¼) tomato ketchup
juice 1 orange
4 tablespoons (5) brandy
4 newly laid egg yolks
2 pickled gherkins
2 medium-sized onions
4 anchovy fillets
1 tablespoon (1¼) capers
1 tablespoon (1¼) chopped parsley
lettuce, sliced tomatoes

Put the meat through the finest blade of a grinder – it must be completely free of fat or gristle. Add salt, pepper, paprika, mustard, tomato ketchup, orange juice, brandy and 2 egg yolks. Very finely chop the gherkins, 1½ onions and the anchovy fillets. Finely chop the capers. Add these ingredients to the meat mixture and mix thoroughly, then shape into a thick flat loaf or cake. Make two wells in the middle of the mass and place one egg yolk in each indentation. Slice the remaining ½ onion into thick rings and dip these in chopped parsley. Lay them like a wreath round the egg yolks. Garnish with lettuce leaves and sliced tomatoes and serve with rye bread and butter.

(Drink: *Doornkaat* and 'fizzy' beer)

STUFFED CUCUMBERS WITH CREAM (*Gefüllte Gurken in Rahm*)

2–3 large fat cucumbers
salt
vinegar
1 lb. (2 cups) Patna-type rice, boiled and left until cold
3 eggs, beaten
3 tablespoons (3¾) chopped dill
grated nutmeg
slices of Bologna sausage
1 cup (1¼) cream
1 tablespoon (1¼) cornflour (cornstarch)
½ cup (⅔) milk
3 oz. (6 tablespoons) butter
white cocktail onions

Wash the cucumbers and cut into 3 in. lengths. Peel, but let a few strips of peel remain. Cook in salted water flavoured with the vinegar for 10 minutes. Drain in a sieve. Cool and scoop out the centres leaving a reasonably thick 'wall'. Take 3 cups of rice, mix with the eggs, add a little dill, salt and grated nutmeg to taste. Fill this into the pieces of cucumber and lay them in a baking dish. On each piece of cucumber place a slice of sausage. Bake for 20 minutes in a hot oven. Meanwhile gently bring the cream to the boil. Mix the cornflour with the milk to a paste and stir this into the cream. Gently bring again to the boil, stirring all the time until the cream is thick. If it is too thick, add a little liquid from the cucumbers. Season lightly and add remaining dill. Heat the butter and quickly fry the rice. Season and spread a layer of rice in a serving dish. Place the hot cucumber on top and on each piece put a white cocktail onion. Serve with the sauce and remaining rice. (Drink: a light wine from the Palatinate)

STUFFED HAM HORNS (*Gefüllte Schinkenhörnchen*)

Slice lean ham or cooked gammon into very thin slices, allowing 1 slice per person. Form each slice into a horn shape and secure at one end with a cocktail stick. Fill with the following mixture: sliced hardboiled eggs, sprinkled with salt and lemon juice and covered in a thick mayonnaise mixed with finely chopped parsley or chives. Fill each ham horn with some of the mixture and arrange on a platter, garnished with sliced tomatoes and chopped lettuce. Serve with toast or rolls of white bread, and perhaps a glass of sherry.

SPRING SALAD (*Frühlingssalat*)

2 lb. fresh spinach
diced onion to taste
salt, white pepper
1 cup (1¼) mayonnaise
½ lb. Gruyère cheese,
grated
2 tablespoons (2½)
tomato ketchup

Thoroughly wash the spinach and scald it in hot water. Drain and sprinkle with cold water. Squeeze firmly with the hands and shape into round balls. Cut into finger-thick slices and arrange neatly in a bowl. Add the onion, salt and pepper. Put aside. In another bowl mix the mayonnaise, cheese and ketchup. Pour the sauce over the spinach.

Spinach, which is rich in mineral content and fat free, goes well with the rich mayonnaise. This unusual mixture can be served as a salad in its own right or filled into hollowed-out large tomatoes, oranges, grapefruit or apples. It is highly esteemed as an *hors d'oeuvre*.

When the salad is combined with ham or tongue, it makes an outstanding supper dish, served on slices of toasted white bread. Soft or hardboiled eggs also go well with it.

(Drink: light red wine)

TURKEY SALAD CUBA (*Truthahnsalat Kuba*)

1 lb. cold cooked turkey
meat
1 each red and green sweet
peppers
4 apples, peeled, grated
1 large onion, diced
2 tablespoons (2½) oil
1 tablespoon (1¼) vinegar
salt
1 teaspoon (1¼) anchovy
paste
1 teaspoon (1¼) sugar
½ cup (⅔) cream

Cut the meat into small cubes. Slice off the tops of the peppers, discard cores and seeds, cut the flesh into small pieces. Mix these 2 ingredients with the apples. Mix the onion, oil, vinegar, salt, anchovy, sugar and cream to make a dressing. Pour it over the turkey etc. Leave in a cool place 1 hour. Turn the salad into a salad bowl and garnish with sliced hardboiled eggs.

TURKEY SALAD JUGO (*Truthahn salat Jugo*)

1 lb. thinly sliced cold cooked turkey
3 apples, peeled
3 large pickled gherkins
10 large cooked cold boiled potatoes
juice ½ lemon
salt
1 teaspoon (1¼) sugar
1 cup (1¼) mayonnaise
1 tablespoon (1¼) German mustard
1 tablespoon (1¼) tomato purée
½ cup (⅔) sour cream

Thinly slice the apples, gherkins and potatoes and mix with the turkey. Sprinkle with lemon juice and salt and gently but thoroughly mix. Blend the mayonnaise with the remaining ingredients, pour this mixture over the turkey salad and leave in a cool place 1 hour. Arrange lettuce leaves in a salad bowl, add the salad and garnish with sliced tomatoes and quartered hardboiled eggs.

SEMOLINA DUMPLINGS EVELYN (*Griessnockerln Evelyn*)

Semolina seems to have gone out of fashion, yet it is so quick and simple to prepare. And the dishes that can be prepared from semolina are really wonderful. Semolina is easily digestible, satisfying in the pleasantest way and costs little. Here is a semolina recipe:

7 oz. (generous 1 cup) semolina
3 oz. (6 tablespoons) butter
2 eggs
salt, pepper
3 tablespoons (3¾) olive oil
4 slices bacon
1 lb. tomatoes, peeled
1 onion, finely chopped
¼ teaspoon (⅓) dried rosemary
1 cup (1¼) sour cream
3 oz. (1 cup) grated cheese

Cream the butter until frothy, beat in the eggs, add salt and pepper. Gradually beat in the semolina. Bring a large pan with plenty of salted water to the boil. With a teaspoon make small dumplings with the semolina mixture and drop them into the boiling water. Lower the heat and gently cook for 10 minutes, then lower the heat still more and simmer for 10 minutes. Time them carefully. Whilst the dumplings are cooking, rub a baking dish with oil and place the bacon and tomatoes in the bottom. Sprinkle lightly with salt and with the onion. Put into a hot oven for 5 minutes. Add the rosemary and the cream.

Drain off the dumplings, lay them on the top of the cream and sprinkle with the cheese. Bake in a medium oven until the top is a golden brown. Serve with a green salad.

SOUP

ASPARAGUS SOUP CONTI (*Spargelsuppe Conti*)

Combine good meat stock with asparagus juice* in equal quantities; bring to the boil. Mix cornflour (cornstarch) with cold milk to a thin paste (allow 1 oz. to 4 pints (5) stock). Stir the cornflour into the boiling stock and continue boiling, stirring all the while until the soup thickens. Add a trace of nutmeg and salt to taste. Take from the heat and beat in 2 egg yolks mixed with cream (to taste). Pour the soup into bowls, garnish each with asparagus tips, slivers of butter, finely chopped parsley and diced, peeled tomato.

An excellent variation: toss fresh tiny green peas and chopped asparagus in butter and use as a garnish.

ASPARAGUS SOUP GAKELI (*Spargelsuppe Gakeli*)

Mix good chicken stock and asparagus juice* in equal quantities; season with a little nutmeg and salt and simmer for a few minutes. Remove the soup from the heat; then stir in 1 egg per person and add plenty of chopped asparagus, and finally sprinkle with chopped parsley.

DUCHESS SOUP (*Herzoginsuppe*)

Make a stock by cooking celery, leeks, carrots, parsley etc. with chicken bones and water. Strain well, return it to the pan, season and simmer. Thicken it with cornflour (cornstarch) mixed with cream to a thin paste. It should be only lightly thickened. Bring to a slow boil then cook for 10 minutes. Meanwhile toss cooked chicken meat and chopped mushrooms in butter, adding a little sherry. Allowing 1 egg per person, mix in a bowl 3 tablespoons (3¾) of cream for each yolk used and pour this into the chicken soup, stirring all the while. Add slivers of butter, salt, a little grated nutmeg and a few drops of lemon juice to round off a delicious soup. Serve at once.

* Asparagus juice: the water in which asparagus has been cooked or the juice from canned asparagus.

CALCUTTA SOUP (*Kalkuttasuppe*)

1 can turtle soup
  (10 fl. oz.)
½ teaspoon (⅔) curry
  powder
1 teaspoon (1¼) cornflour
  (cornstarch)
2 egg yolks
1 cup (1¼) cream
chopped parsley

Heat the turtle soup with an equal quantity of water and the curry powder. Mix the cornflour with water to a thin paste, stir into the soup, bring to the boil and cook for 5 minutes, stirring all the time. Beat the egg yolks into the cream and stir into the hot soup. This makes a soup as mild and sweet as an evening in May. Pour into warmed soup bowls, add a pat of fresh butter and a dash of dry sherry. Garnish with strips of peeled tomato and sprinkle with finely chopped parsley.

GOURMET SOUP (*Feinschmeckersuppe*)

1 lb. stewing beef
herb vinegar
sugar
1 bay leaf
½ onion, sliced
2 juniper berries
3 allspice corns
2 cloves
2 oz. (4 tablespoons) fat
1 lb. onions, chopped
1 tablespoon (1¼) tomato
  purée
salt, pepper
1 tablespoon (1¼) cornflour
  (cornstarch)
1 teaspoon (1¼) paprika
  pepper
½ cup (⅔) cream
½ cup (⅔) brandy

Steep the meat for 4 days in the herb vinegar, adding a little sugar, the bay leaf, sliced onion, juniper berries, allspice and cloves. Make sure the meat is completely immersed.

Heat the fat, fry the chopped onions until soft, stir in the tomato purée and about 4 pints (5) hot water. Bring to a gentle boil, lower the heat and simmer. Take the meat from the marinade, cut into small pieces, add to the pan. Add salt and pepper and continue cooking until the meat is tender.

Mix the cornflour with water to a thin paste, stir into the soup and cook gently until the soup is thickened. Add the paprika and cream, bring once to the boil, add brandy and serve the soup with fresh bread rolls.

(Drink: beer)

GARDENER'S WIFE SOUP (*Gärtnerinsuppe*)

1 lb. leeks
1 lb. new potatoes
½ lb. onions
1 small head cauliflower
1 stalk celery
½ lb. carrots
2 oz. (4 tablespoons)
  fat bacon, diced
salt
6 pints (7½) meat stock
4 pairs smoked sausages
nutmeg
marjoram to taste
1 bunch parsley
1 bunch chives

Clean, wash and slice or chop the vegetables. Heat the bacon in a large pan, when the fat runs add the vegetables and salt to draw out the juices. Simmer 10 minutes, add the stock and continue cooking gently until the soup is thick. Slice the sausages, add to the pan – these need only heating. Add nutmeg and marjoram, parsley and chives, stir once and serve. Serve with fresh rolls or rye bread.

(Drink: beer)

HUNGARIAN GOULASH SOUP (*Ungarische Gulaschsuppe*)

A spicy goulash should be served every now and then in every household. With fresh rolls, it is not only a fine savoury meal, but also a favourite warming soup which may well be served at night to round off a party.

¾ lb. rump steak, cut
  into cubes
2 oz. (4 tablespoons)
  pork fat
½ lb. onion, sliced
3 tablespoons (3¾) tomato
  purée
salt, pepper
3 tablespoons (3¾) paprika
  pepper
4 pints (5) meat stock
1 tablespoon (1¼) cornflour
  (cornstarch)
1 teaspoon (1¼) caraway
  seeds, crushed
2 cloves garlic, finely
  chopped
1 lemon rind, grated

Heat the fat and gently cook the onion. Add the tomato purée, stir well and continue cooking for 5 minutes. Rub the meat with salt, pepper and paprika pepper, stir into the onion mixture. Cook for 30 minutes in a covered pan over a low heat or in a moderate oven. Bring the stock to the boil, stir this into the soup and gently cook another 10 minutes. Mix the cornflour with water to a thin paste, stir it into the soup and cook until it is thickened. Add the caraway, garlic and lemon rind. Serve at once. Red peppers may be added, after they have been seeded and cored and cut into thin strips. They are added to the pan at the same time as the onions and fried with them.

PROCESSED SOUPS WITH STYLE

We cannot but admit that the food industry puts on the market excellent ready-prepared products. They certainly make life easier for those who use them wisely. Among these products are soups in many forms; in packets, in cubes and in tins. They are economical and good. Housewives who have time will naturally prepare their own soups better according to their traditional methods. But for anyone who goes out to work and whose time is limited, these soups are invaluable. With a little imagination they can be so dressed up that no one would ever believe that they are not home-made. So here are a few small tips for using the most readily available soups.

CREAM OF VEAL SOUP (*Kalbrahmsuppe*)
Pour in 3 tablespoons (3¾) of white wine and add a few slivers of butter. Perhaps a few drops of lemon juice as well.

GOULASH SOUP (*Gulaschsuppe*)
Stir in a little finely grated lemon rind and caraway seeds.

HARICOT BEAN SOUP (*Bohnensuppe*)
Stir in tomato ketchup. Add small cubes of salt leg of pork.

MUSHROOM SOUP (*Pilzsuppe*)
Add a little white wine and cream. Perhaps also 2 tablespoons (2½) of mayonnaise.

OXTAIL SOUP (*Ochsenschwanzsuppe*)
Add a small glassful of brandy, Madeira, port or sherry – whatever is available in the house – sprinkling it in gradually.

PEA SOUP (*Erbsensuppe*)
Fry small cubes of white bread in butter; then fry slices of sausage in the same pan. Add to the soup just before serving.

QUEEN SOUP (*Königinsuppe*)
Place green peas and small chopped pieces of veal in the plates before adding hot chicken consommé.

SPINACH SOUP (*Spinatsuppe*)
Garnish with whipped cream, sprinkled lightly with grated nutmeg.

TOMATO SOUP (*Tomatensuppe*)
Fry small cubes of white bread in butter. Bring the soup to the boil, sprinkle grated cheese or chopped almonds on top; then decorate with blobs of unsweetened whipped cream or horseradish cream, and serve with the bread cubes.

VEGETABLE SOUP (*Gemüsesuppe*)
Add diced marrow from beef bones.

FISH

RED SAND COD (*Kabeljau Roter Sand*)

4 good-sized cod steaks
3 pints ($3\frac{3}{4}$) water
salt
5 peppercorns, crushed
1 onion stuck with 2 cloves
1 bay leaf
1 carrot, chopped
2 slices lemon
**1 bunch parsley, tied with
    thread**
Garnish:
sprigs parsley
lemon slices
tomato slices
3 oz. (6 tablespoons) butter
**1 tablespoon ($1\frac{1}{4}$) German-
    style mustard**

Simmer the water with the next 7 ingredients for 30 minutes. Cool, add the cod steaks, bring to a gentle boil, then again reduce the heat and cook until the fish is tender – make sure the fish is quite covered. Carefully take the fish from the liquid, place in a warm dish and garnish with sprigs of parsley, sliced lemon and tomato. Heat the butter over a low heat, add the mustard and cook until hot but not browned. Serve the fish with mustard butter sauce and boiled potatoes.

(Drink: a light white wine)

COD ZITRONENHEINI (*Kabeljau Zitronenheini*)

4 thick cod steaks
salt, pinch sugar
3 slices lemon
1 bay leaf
2 cloves
1 bunch parsley
juice ½ lemon
8 oz. (1 cup) butter
1 small onion, sliced
5 bananas, mashed with
** a fork**

Fill a deep pan with water, add salt, sugar, lemon slices, bay leaf, cloves and parsley. Boil it for 6 minutes so that an aromatic steam is given off. Sprinkle the fish lightly with salt and some of the lemon juice and place on a rack in the pan. Steam the fish for 20 minutes, covered. Melt the butter, fry the onion until soft, mix with the mashed bananas, add salt and the remaining lemon juice. This makes a thick sauce. Take the fish from the pan when tender, serve with the sauce and dry curried rice. (Drink: mild white wine)

EEL COOKED IN ALUMINIUM FOIL (*In Stanniolfolie Gekochter Aal*)

Allow 2 pieces of eel, each weighing about ¼ lb. per person. Sprinkle with salt. Put each piece into separate pieces of foil, previously well rubbed with oil. Sprinkle with finely chopped parsley and dill. Wrap up the eel pieces but not too tightly as the eel needs space in which to swell. Place in a baking tray and bake in a hot oven for 30–40 minutes. Serve the eel in the foil packages, each plate garnished with wedges of lemon and sprigs of parsley.
(Drink: white wine)

HALIBUT IN TOMATO AND ONION SAUCE (*Halibut in Tomatensauce mit Zwiebeln*)

4 large halibut steaks
olive oil
4 tablespoons (5) tomato
** purée**
2 onions, diced
trace of garlic
salt
lemon juice

Rub 4 squares of aluminium foil with olive oil. On each place 1 tablespoon (1¼) of tomato purée, some diced onion, garlic, salt and lemon juice. Lay the halibut steaks on top of this mixture and spread with the same mixture. Wrap up and bake in a medium oven for 30–40 minutes. Serve with plain boiled rice.
(Drink: rosé wine)

FILLETS OF SOLE IN MOSELLE SAUCE (*Seezungenfilets in Moselwein Sauce*)

8 sole fillets
butter
salt
2 tablespoons (2½) lemon juice
2 cups (2½) Moselle wine
1 tablespoon (1¼) cornflour (cornstarch)
milk
3 tablespoons (3¾) mayonnaise
sliced mushrooms to taste
1 can crab meat
8 stalks asparagus (stewed or canned), chopped

Well butter a baking dish and sprinkle with salt. Roll the fillets twisting them in the shape of a bow. Sprinkle with salt and lemon juice, add the wine and cover with greaseproof paper or foil. Cook in a moderate oven for 12 minutes. Take out the fish, put aside but keep warm. Mix the cornflour with milk to a thin paste. Stir this into the fish liquid, bring to the boil on top of the stove and cook gently until it thickens. Take from the heat and add the mayonnaise. In another pan heat a little more butter and fry the mushrooms until tender. Add the crab meat and asparagus. Arrange the fish in a warm serving dish, cover with the mushroom mixture and pour the wine sauce over the top. Serve with boiled potatoes tossed in butter.

FISH IN PUFF PASTRY (*Fisch in Blätterteig*)

about ½ lb. filleted fish
1 small onion, minced
chopped parsley
salt, pepper
grated nutmeg
1 lb. puff pastry
1 egg

Grind the fish or chop it finely and mix with the onion, parsley, salt, pepper and nutmeg. Roll out the pastry and cut into triangles, each 4 × 5 in. long. Place a fourth of the mixture on the widest part of the triangle. Roll up into a horn or cornet, paint with egg and bake for 15 minutes in a hot oven. Serve with tomato salad.

If liked, a few fried pieces of lean bacon may be added to the fish mixture. Another filling:
Crush skinned and boned herrings with a fork, season with salt and pepper and mix with a little curry powder and lemon juice; put about 2 oz. of the filling in each pastry horn and then prepare as in the previous recipe. Serve with cucumber salad.
(Drink: red Cinzano)

FISH CAKES (*Musikdampfer-Krusteln*)

1½ lb. cooked fish, boned
  and shredded
fat for frying
1 large onion, diced
salt
1 tablespoon (1¼) German-
  style mustard
1 tablespoon (1¼) tomato
  purée
1 lb. mashed potatoes
2 eggs, lightly beaten
flour
1 egg, well beaten
breadcrumbs

Heat a little fat and fry the onion until soft but not brown. Mix with the fish, salt, mustard and tomato purée. Blend into the mashed potatoes and bind with the lightly beaten eggs. Break off pieces of the mixture, shape into long sausages, place on a floured board and cut off lengths of about 2½ in. Roll in flour and the well beaten egg and then in bread-crumbs. Heat plenty of fat for deep frying and fry the potato cakes until golden. Serve with a green salad.

(Drink: beer)

SEA FISH STEAKS FLEURI (*Seefischsteaks Fleuri*)

1 lb. white fish
juice 1 lemon
salt
1 tablespoon (1¼) oil
2 tablespoons (2½)
  chopped parsley
fat for deep frying
Batter:
½ cup (⅔) beer
6 oz. (1½ cups) plain (all
  purpose) flour
salt, sugar
1 egg yolk, beaten
1 teaspoon (1¼) oil
2 egg whites, stiffly
  beaten

Cut the fish into steaks 1 in. thick. Place in a bowl, add lemon juice and salt. Mix the oil with the parsley, pour it over the fish and leave for 20 minutes.

Stir the beer into the flour until the mixture is smooth, add a pinch of salt, sugar, egg yolk and oil, beat well and leave for 10 minutes; then fold in the egg whites. Heat plenty of fat until hot. Holding the fish steaks on the end of a long fork, dip them into the batter and place them at once in the hot fat. (Take care, as the fat spits.) Fry the fish until golden, take it from the pan and place on a sieve or rack to drain. While still hot, arrange the fish on a hot dish, garnish with sprigs of parsley, sliced tomato and lemon. Serve with a potato salad, mixed with chopped tomatoes or orange.

(Drink: apple juice with soda water)

RICE AND FISH FOR SAILORS (*Fisch mit Reis für Seeleute*)

½ lb. (1 cup) long grain
   rice
½ lb. red mullet
salt, pepper
butter
lemon juice
3 oz. (6 tablespoons) fat
2 onions, diced
chopped parsley to taste
½ cup (⅔) milk
4 eggs
grated cheese to taste

Cook the rice in plenty of lightly salted bubbling boiling water for 20 minutes. Strain and wash in cold water. Place a layer of rice in a well-buttered casserole. Clean and chop the fish, spreading about one-third of it over the rice. Sprinkle with salt, pepper and lemon juice. Heat the fat and fry the onions until soft. Pour some of the onions and fat over the fish, sprinkle generously with parsley. Repeat this, but make sure a layer of rice tops the dish. Mix the milk with the eggs, beat well and pour it over the rice. Sprinkle well with cheese and bake in a moderate oven for about 25 minutes. Serve with a green salad. (Drink: beer)

SALMON WITH MUSSELS (*Lachs oder Salm mit Muscheln*)

4 salmon steaks
1 can mussels or oysters
butter
1 onion, thinly sliced
salt, lemon juice
white wine
1 cup (1¼) cream
2 tablespoons (2½)
   cornflour (cornstarch)
grated cheese
croûtons

Heat a little butter in a shallow pan, fry the onion until soft. Lay the salmon on the top, sprinkle with salt and lemon juice, add wine to cover. Cover the pan and cook gently for 15–20 minutes. Take the fish from the pan and place in a buttered baking dish. Put aside but keep warm. Drain the mussels and gently fry in a little hot butter. Add the cream and stir gently. Mix the cornflour with liquid from the salmon to make a thin paste, stir this into the mussels. Cook gently until the sauce has thickened, then pour it over the salmon. Sprinkle with cheese and brown in the oven. Cut up cubes of white bread and quickly fry them in hot fat. Serve the salmon with the croûtons in a bowl.

FRIED PERCH (*Gebackene Barschfilets Vierländer*)

1 lb. perch, cut into ½ in. slices, salted and sprinkled with lemon juice

2 oz. (4 tablespoons) butter

2 onions, diced

¾ lb. green peas, shelled

meat stock

½ lb. mushrooms, sliced

salt, nutmeg, sugar

1 tablespoon (1¼) chopped parsley

1 tablespoon (1¼) curry powder

4 tablespoons (5) flour

4 eggs, beaten

4 tablespoons (5) oil

lemon juice

slivers butter

Heat the butter and fry the onions until soft but not brown. Add the peas and a little stock (if using frozen peas cook them as directed on the packet). Add the mushrooms, salt, nutmeg and sugar to taste and parsley.

Cook gently. Mix the curry powder into the fish, sprinkle with flour, mix well and then add the eggs. Heat the oil, add the fish and fry over a moderate heat until a golden brown.

The egg and flour mixture surrounds the fish and forms a brown coat. The curry powder gives it a good flavour.

Arrange the fish (cooking time about 5 minutes) on a hot dish and sprinkle with lemon juice. Sprinkle with slivers of butter and serve with the onion, peas and mushroom mixture and long grained rice or boiled potatoes.

(Drink: white wine)

POULTRY AND GAME

CHICKEN CROQUETTES (*Geflügelkroquetten*)

Croquettes are small fried savoury cakes which must be very carefully prepared. The coating with breadcrumbs is very important. The mixture must be completely covered with egg white so that the breadcrumbs stick firmly. When the small cakes or rolls are put in the hot fat, the heat must immediately set the coating so that the cake does not burst and the precious filling escape.

This dish may be prepared on the day before it is to be eaten and then cooked just before serving.

1 lb. boiled chicken

¼ lb. mushrooms, fresh or canned

butter

celery salt

juice 1 lemon

2 cups (2½) chicken stock

2 tablespoons (2½) cornflour (cornstarch)

milk

salt

nutmeg

rosemary

¼ cup (⅓) white wine

3 egg yolks

flour

3 egg whites, stiffly beaten

breadcrumbs

fat for frying

Garnish:

lettuce

cocktail onions

small pickled gherkins

cheese

Finely chop the chicken and the mushrooms. Heat the butter, lightly fry the mushrooms and add the chicken. Season with celery salt and flavour with some of the lemon juice. Simmer.

Bring the stock to the boil. Mix the cornflour with enough milk to make a thin paste. Stir it into the boiling stock. Cook and stir the stock until it thickens. Add salt, nutmeg and rosemary to taste, a little lemon juice and the wine.

Take from the heat and let it cool. Beat the egg yolks and stir into the sauce. Pour the sauce over the pieces of chicken and mushrooms. Stir gently until blended.

Cover a baking (cookie) sheet with aluminium foil and paint with cold water. Spread the chicken mixture over the foil to a thickness of 1 in. Leave until cold, then cut into pieces 2 in. long × ½ in. wide. Roll the pieces first in flour, then in egg whites and finally in breadcrumbs – make sure the croquettes are completely and well-coated.

Heat the fat until hot and fry the croquettes until golden brown all over. Drain the croquettes and serve hot, garnished with lettuce, cocktail onions, gherkins and cubes of cheese. Serve with a remoulade sauce and a potato salad. (Drink: beer)

CHICKEN CASSEROLE (*Hühnerkasserole*)

4 servings:

2 chickens prepared for cooking
1 lb. carrots
1 lb. savoy cabbage
¾ lb. potatoes
1 lb. leeks
1 onion stuck with 2 cloves
1 bay leaf
6 pints (7½) meat stock
1 pint (1¼) white wine
salt, nutmeg
butter
parsley

Sauce:

2 oz. (4 tablespoons) butter
1 small chopped onion
2 tablespoons (2½) flour
¼ cup (⅓) cream
2 tablespoons (2½) finely chopped parsley

Wash the vegetables and slice or chop (see below). Put with the whole onion, bay leaf, meat stock and wine into a large pan and cook over a moderate heat (or in a moderate oven) for 25 minutes.

Add the chickens, sprinkled with salt and nutmeg and cook them for 25 minutes or until tender. Take from the pan, drain well, and place on a hot dish.

Drain off the vegetables, arrange these with the chickens and dot with slivers of butter. Sprinkle with chopped parsley and garnish with sprigs of parsley.

Keep hot while the sauce is prepared. Heat the butter, add the onion, cook until soft, then add the flour and stir until smooth. Gradually add enough of the chicken stock to make a thick sauce.

Immediately before serving, add the cream and parsley.

(The chickens should be ready for cooking, i.e. drawn and cleaned. If they have been frozen, they will need to cook for at least 20–30 minutes longer, but they can certainly be placed just as they are in the casserole.)

Meat stock may be made from cubes so that the chicken and vegetables will taste all the more savoury. If the vegetables are cooked before adding the chicken, they will give a better flavour to the meat. When one considers that chicken needs only 25 minutes cooking time, one realizes that the liquor in which it cooks must be full-bodied.

The vegetables must be tender but should not disintegrate. Only use the white part of a head of leek; choose carrots of even size. Clean the savoy cabbage and cut into four quarters. Cut away the stalks from each piece. It may well be cooked after 20 minutes, in which case it may be removed. Peel the potatoes and cook them whole. They will taste particularly good. Slice before serving. Add the white wine straight away to the meat stock. It will make the whole dish sparkling and piquant.

If any of the casserole remains after the meal, cut up all the ingredients and put them into the remaining stock. Then you will have a delicious soup ready for the next meal.

The preparation of the sauce is explained for those who enjoy a good sauce. The casserole is excellent even without the sauce. If liked, 2 dessert-spoonfuls mayonnaise may be added to the prepared sauce to make it particularly smooth and bland.

(Drink: white wine)

VENISON STEAKS WITH BLACK CHERRIES (*Rehlenden-schnitte mit Schwarzekirschen*)

8 venison steaks
1 cup (1¼) black sour or Morello cherries, cooked or canned
salt
3 tablespoons (3¾) oil
6 juniper berries, well crushed
4 slices fat bacon, diced
1 large onion, finely chopped
2 tablespoons (2½) flour
1 cup (1¼) sour cream
nutmeg
3 tablespoons (3¾) redcurrant jelly
butter
4 thick slices white bread

The meat should be cut from a haunch of venison which has been hung for at least 8 days. Carefully skin and lightly beat the steaks. Sprinkle with salt. Heat the oil and fry the steaks on both sides for about 3 minutes. Place on a warm dish and keep hot. Scatter the juniper berries over the top.

Pour off the oil, heat the bacon until the fat runs, add the onion and fry until soft. Add any gravy from the meat. Stir in the flour, blend thoroughly, then add the sour cream, whisking all the time. Simmer for 2 minutes, season with salt and nutmeg to taste and stir in the jelly.

Heat enough butter to fry the bread on both sides until brown and crisp. Place these on a warm flat dish, put a steak on top of each piece and cover with the sauce. Garnish with slices of orange and serve with buttered noodles and a tart jelly.

(Drink: red wine)

VENISON KEBABS (*Waldläufer Spieschen*)

Cut very small slices from a haunch of venison, each weighing about 1 oz. Spear these on skewers alternately with slices of lean bacon, mushroom

caps, pineapple cubes, and slices of green or red peppers. Fry quickly. Serve with buttered Patna rice, mixed with paprika and raisins.
(Drink: red wine)

VENISON HASH (*Wildhaschee*)

4 lb. venison, raw or cooked
2 slices fat bacon, diced
½ lb. onions, diced
2 tablespoons (2½) flour
salt, pepper
2 cups (2½) meat stock
½ cup (⅔) cream
½ cup (⅔) white wine
1 tablespoon (1¼) lemon juice

Fry the bacon until the fat runs, add the onion, fry until soft. Grind the venison, add to the pan and fry for 5 minutes, turning it round and round so that it is fried right through. Sprinkle in the flour, add salt and pepper and fry for 3 minutes, then gradually stir in the meat stock. Blend well and continue cooking for 30 minutes for cooked venison, and about 1 hour for raw. Just before serving, add the cream, wine and lemon juice, stir gently but well and serve at once with *Spätzle* (noodles).
(Drink: red wine)

VENISON LIVER FAVOURITE (*Rehleber Favorit*)

1 venison liver
½ lb. fat bacon
salt

The liver should be cleaned and kept at least 3 days in the refrigerator. Cut into finger-thick slices. Heat the bacon until the fat runs, fry the liver quickly on both sides. Sprinkle with salt and arrange on a hot dish. Serve with fried apple slices or fried bananas, or with cooked red cabbage with grapes or with mashed potatoes.

The following makes an excellent *hors d'oeuvre*. Garnish the fried liver slices with thin slices of fried bacon and halved fried or pickled mushrooms. Or the liver may be ground and made into a *pâté* for serving as a filling in hot *vol-au-vent* cases, in omelettes or in thin pancakes.
(Drink: red wine)

HARE PIE PRINCE OF HUNTSMEN (*Hasenpasteten Jägerfurst*)

1 lb. boned cooked hare
   meat
1 lb. puff pastry
¼ lb. fat bacon
1 large onion, diced
salt, nutmeg
4 juniper berries,
   crushed
2 tablespoons (2½) finely
   chopped parsley
½ cup (⅔) cream
¼ cup (⅓) Madeira
egg yolk

Divide the pastry in two portions, one piece slightly larger than the other. Roll into two thin rounds. Line a greased flan pan with the larger round. Spread this with the following filling:

Grind the meat with the bacon, mix with the onion, add salt, a grating of nutmeg, juniper berries, parsley and cream. Flavour with Madeira and, if the mixture seems too runny, add soft breadcrumbs.

Cover the filling with the second round of pastry and paint with egg yolk. Pinch firmly round the edges and make small holes in the top of the pie to let the steam escape. Bake for 30 minutes in a hot oven. Serve with a mixed salad.
(Drink: red wine)

HARE'S LIVER WITH MADEIRA (*Hasenlebermus mit Madeira*)

hares' livers
bacon
onions
salt and pepper
crushed juniper berries
cream
Madeira
marjoram

Fry the livers very gently with bacon and onions, making sure that they remain pink inside. Season with salt, pepper, marjoram and crushed juniper berries. Sieve or beat in an electric mixer. Mix with cream and Madeira, and serve on toast.

DUCK COUNT WALDERSEE (*Gebratene Ente Graf Waldersee*)

**1 duck, oven-ready
  weighing 4 lb.**
salt
thyme
½ lb. cooked noodles
**1 tablespoon (1¼) chopped
  parsley**
nutmeg
1 large onion, diced
4 tablespoons (5) honey
2 tablespoons (2½) beer
3 egg yolks, beaten
½ cup (⅔) cream
1 bay leaf
3 cloves
6 mandarin oranges
¼ cup (⅓) port
Garnish:
tomatoes
parsley

Cut the wings off the duck leaving enough skin to secure it firmly to the back. Salt lightly inside and out and rub a little thyme on the inside. Put the duck aside. Cook the heart, liver and gizzard until tender; skin the gizzard and slice it finely. Mix the noodles with the liver, heart and gizzard, some thyme, parsley, nutmeg and diced onion, half the honey and beer, egg yolks and cream. Push the filling into the duck and sew up the opening. Fill a roasting pan to a depth of 1½ in. with boiling water, add salt, bay leaf and cloves. Place the duck in the pan breast downwards and roast in a moderate oven for 1 hour. Baste frequently. Take the duck from the pan, place it on a rack and return it to the roasting pan, and continue cooking, letting it brown all over. Baste from time to time with a mixture of the remaining honey and beer. This will make the skin crisper. When the legs feel tender, the duck is ready. Take it from the pan, place on a warm dish and return it to the oven to keep hot. Strain off the water in which the duck was cooked and bring it to the boil. Peel the oranges, discard the pips and crush the flesh. Add this to the boiling gravy. Bring to the boil, add the port, rub through a sieve and serve hot in a sauceboat. Carefully remove the threads from the duck and cut the bird into 8 pieces. Slice the noodle stuffing fairly thickly and lay the pieces on one side of a hot platter. Arrange the duck pieces on the other side, breast upwards.

WILD DUCK WITH PINEAPPLE (*Wildente mit Ananas*)

1 wild duck, cooked
1 small can pineapple
  slices
¼ lb. fat sliced bacon
cornflour (cornstarch)
meat stock
½ cup (⅔) sour cream

Strip the meat from the duck in neat pieces. Put aside. Fry the bacon in a shallow pan until brown. Cover with the pineapple and add the meat. Cook gently for 10 minutes, take from the pan and place in a hot shallow serving dish, the duck meat at the bottom, the bacon and pineapple on top.

Make a sauce from the gravy in the pan, adding enough cornflour to thicken it and meat stock to dilute it until it is smooth and of a cream consistency, then add the cream. Pour the sauce over the duck and serve it with apple salad. (Drink: red wine)

TURKEY DUMPLINGS IN MUSHROOM SAUCE (*Truthahn-würfel in Pilzsauce*)

1 lb. cooked turkey meat,
  finely minced with:
3 rolls soaked in milk and
  squeezed dry
3 beaten eggs
salt, nutmeg to taste
chopped parsley to taste
meat stock or water
White sauce:
2 tablespoons (2½)
  cornflour (cornstarch)
cold milk
finely chopped cooked or
  canned mushrooms to
  taste
lemon juice to taste
grated nutmeg
3 tablespoons (3¾) thick
  mayonnaise

Mix the turkey and bread with the eggs, add salt, nutmeg and parsley. Knead the mixture well and make small dumplings. Bring a pan with plenty of stock to the boil, throw in the dumplings, bring to the boil, lower the heat and cook until they rise to the top of the liquid.

While the dumplings are cooking, make a sauce. Mix the cornflour with milk to a thin paste. Take about 3 cups (3¾) of the hot stock from the pan, bring this to the boil in another pan. Stir in the cornflour paste, bring to the boil, flavour with mushrooms, lemon juice, nutmeg and finally the mayonnaise. Stir until the sauce is smooth and thick. Drain the dumplings, turn into a serving bowl and pour the sauce over the top. Garnish with diced tomatoes and chopped parsley. Serve with boiled rice.

TURKEY AND RICE SISSI (*Truthahn mit Reis Sissi*)

**1 lb. cold turkey meat cut
    from the leg and
    coarsely ground**
oil
½ lb. onions, diced
**1 lb. sweet peppers, cut
    into strips**
**3 tablespoons (3¾) tomato
    paste**
salt, paprika pepper
3 pints (3¾) meat stock
**1 lb. (2 cups) Patna-type
    rice**

Heat a little oil and lightly cook the onions and peppers (cores and seeds discarded). After 10 minutes, add the tomato paste, stir well into the onion and peppers, then add the turkey meat. Season with salt and paprika and simmer. Bring the stock to a bubbling boil, add the rice and cook for 5 minutes. Stir in the turkey mixture, bring to the boil, taste for seasoning and continue cooking until the rice is tender and the liquid evaporated, about 15–20 minutes. Serve hot with a mixed salad.
(Drink: red wine)

TURKEY AND RICE *AU GRATIN* (*Truthahn mit Reis Gratiniert*)

Follow the previous recipe. Place the turkey and rice in a fireproof dish. Sprinkle on grated cheese mixed with breadcrumbs. Brown in a hot oven.

DICED TURKEY IN TOMATO RICE (*Truthahnwürfel mit Tomatenreis*)

**1 lb. cooked turkey meat
    cut into large dice**
salt
paprika pepper to taste
6 tablespoons (7½) oil
1 large onion, diced
**8 tablespoons (10) washed
    rice**
**2 tablespoons (2½) tomato
    paste**
**1⅔ pints (3 cups) boiling
    meat stock**

Sprinkle the meat lightly with salt and paprika. Pour the oil into a fireproof glass baking dish, add the onion and let it cook on top of the stove for 5 minutes (it is better to use asbestos over the direct flame). Add the meat, spoon the rice over the top together with tomato paste. Add the stock. Cover the pan tightly (first with a piece of cloth) with a lid and bake in a moderate oven for about 25–30 minutes or until the rice is tender and the liquid evaporated. Serve the rice in the dish in which it was cooked.

FRIED SLICES OF TURKEY AND POTATO PURÉE
(Gebackene Truthahnscheiben)

1 turkey breast
salt
1–2 eggs, lightly beaten
fine breadcrumbs
2 oz. (4 tablespoons)
  margarine
2 oz. (4 tablespoons)
  butter

Thinly slice the turkey breast, sprinkle with salt, dip into beaten egg, then in breadcrumbs. Press the coating on well with a knife blade. Heat the margarine and fry the turkey until a golden brown on both sides – 10 minutes. Pour off surplus fat, add the butter and finish cooking in butter. Serve with potato purée made with butter and cream. (Drink: red wine)

POTATO OMELETTE *(Kartoffelomelett)*

1 lb. potatoes
fat for frying
1 onion, diced
¾ lb. cooked chicken meat,
  diced
6 eggs
1 tablespoon (1¼) butter

Peel and dice the potatoes. Heat a little fat in a frying pan, add the onion, as these begin to brown, add the chicken meat. Lightly beat the eggs, heat the butter in a hot pan and make an omelette in the usual manner. Spread the potato mixture in the centre, fold the omelette over one side and slide it on a hot plate so that the overlap is downwards. Serve with a mixed salad. (Drink: beer)

CHICKEN PASTIES *(Geflügelpastetchen)*

1 lb. raw chicken meat,
  finely ground
salt, pepper
grated nutmeg
3 eggs, lightly beaten
1 lb. puff pastry
1 egg yolk, well beaten

Season the chicken meat with salt, pepper and nutmeg. Add the 3 whole eggs and mix well. Roll out the puff pastry and cut into squares 6 × 6 in. Put a portion of the ground meat on to each square. Wrap the pastry round the meat and press down the edges firmly. Paint the pasties with the egg yolk and bake in a hot oven until the pastry is a golden colour. Serve with mashed potatoes. (Drink: red wine)

CHICKEN PIROSCHKA (*Hähnchen Piroschka*)

2 chickens, oven-ready, each cut into 8 pieces
2 oz. (4 tablespoons) pork dripping
½ lb. fat smoked bacon, thinly sliced
¾ lb. mushrooms, sliced
½ lb. sliced leeks, white part only
salt
2 tablespoons (2½) paprika pepper
1⅔ pints (3 cups) meat stock
2 tablespoons (2½) cornflour (cornstarch)
milk
½ lb. skinned tomatoes, quartered
1 cup (1¼) sour cream
2 tablespoons (2½) chopped parsley

Heat the pork dripping, add the bacon, mushrooms and leeks, and cook for 10 minutes. Add the pieces of chicken, sprinkle lightly with salt and a little paprika pepper (leave some for later garnishing). Add the stock, cook gently for 15 minutes or until the chicken is tender. Take the chicken pieces out with a slotted spoon, place in a hot dish and keep hot. Mix the cornflour with enough milk to make a thin paste, stir it into the chicken stock, bring to the boil, stirring all the time. Add the tomatoes, bring again to the boil, add half the cream and pour the sauce while still hot over the pieces of chicken. Sprinkle with parsley and the rest of the red paprika. Add the remaining sour cream in blobs so that the Hungarian colours, green, white and red, may be seen.

Serve with fried rounds of potato dumplings or noodles boiled and tossed in butter.

(Drink: a sharp white wine)

CHICKEN RISSOLES (*Geflügelbällchen*)

1 lb. uncooked chicken meat
1 cup (1¼) cream
6 tablespoons (7½) plain (all purpose) flour
4 eggs, well beaten
butter
1 onion, diced
2 tablespoons (2½) chopped parsley
salt, nutmeg

Put the chicken meat through the fine blade of a grinder and mix with the cream, flour and eggs. Heat enough butter to fry the onion until soft, add the parsley, salt and nutmeg. Stir this mixture into the chicken batter. Heat enough butter to generously cover the bottom of a thick pan. Add the mixture in 'blobs' and fry until a golden brown on both sides.

Serve with spinach.

CHICKEN IN DIJON MUSTARD SAUCE (*Hähnchen in Senfsauce Dijon*)

1 chicken, oven-ready
2 tablespoons (2½) Dijon mustard
salt, pepper
2 tablespoons (2½) oil
1 sliced apple and onion
red wine
1 tablespoon (1¼) cornflour (cornstarch)
milk
Madeira
crushed garlic

Cut the chicken into 4 or 8 portions. Lightly sprinkle with salt and pepper. Heat the oil, add the chicken, apple and onion. Cook gently for a few minutes, add the mustard, stir this well into the chicken then add red wine to cover. Cover the pan and cook gently for 20 minutes. Take out the chicken pieces, put aside but keep hot. Mix the cornflour with milk to a thin paste, stir until thick, add Madeira and garlic to flavour. Pour over the chicken. Serve with buttered noodles.

CHICKEN KARLEMANN (*Hähnchen Karlemann*)

1 chicken, about 2 lb.
salt
3 tablespoons (3¾) oil
1 onion, diced
8 tablespoons (10) rice
1⅔ pints (3 cups) meat stock mixed with:
1 tablespoon (1¼) tomato paste
2 tablespoons (2½) paprika

Joint the chicken into 4 or 8 pieces. Sprinkle lightly with salt. Put all the ingredients into a casserole in the order given. Cover and place in a hot oven and cook for 30 minutes or until the chicken is tender. Serve the chicken in the casserole.
(Drink: beer)

CHICKEN BALLS WITH GREEN SALAD (*Geflügelbällchen mit Grünem Salat*)

½ lb. cooked chicken meat
1 small onion, diced
oil for frying
1 lb. cooked potatoes, sieved while still hot
salt, nutmeg to taste
2 oz. (⅓ cup) cornflour (cornstarch)
3 eggs, beaten
fine breadcrumbs

Finely grind the chicken and fry with the onion in a little oil. After 5 minutes add the potatoes, stir well, add salt and nutmeg. Take from the heat, beat in the cornflour and 2 eggs and leave until cool. Break off small pieces of the mixture and form into balls. Roll in the remaining egg and breadcrumbs and fry in hot oil until golden all over. Serve with green salad.

MEAT

ROAST LEG OF PORK AND RED CABBAGE (*Schwartel-braten mit Rotkraut*)

2 lb. leg of pork
2 lb. red çabbage,
 shredded
3 oz. (4 tablespoons) pork
 fat
1 large onion, sliced
3 cloves
2 bay leaves
salt
1 tablespoon (1¼) brown
 sugar
3–4 tart apples, chopped
2 tablespoons (2½) vinegar
1 tablespoon (1¼) red-
 currant jelly
1 onion stuck with 2 cloves
nutmeg, caraway to taste

First prepare the cabbage. Heat the fat, fry the onion until brown. Add the cabbage, cloves, 1 bay leaf, salt, sugar, apples, vinegar and water to cover the bottom of the pan. Stir and cook over a moderate heat for 2½ hours. Add the red-currant jelly just before serving.

Wash the meat, wipe it dry and rub lightly with salt. Place skin side down in a roasting pan with ½ in. hot water and bake in a hot oven until the skin has softened. Cut the skin in a criss-cross pattern. Add the onion stuck with cloves, 1 bay leaf, nutmeg and caraway. Continue roasting the joint until the meat is tender, basting often. Take the meat from the pan, keep hot. Strain the gravy, reheat it but do not thicken. Serve the pork with the red cabbage.

SMALL MEAT BALLS (*Kleine Fleischbällchen als Suppeinlage*)

1½ lb. mixed pork and veal
butter for frying
1 onion, diced
2 eggs
3 tablespoons (3¾) cream
3 tablespoons (3¾) soft
 breadcrumbs
2 tablespoons (2½) chopped
 parsley
paprika, salt, pepper
1 onion stuck with 2 cloves
1 bay leaf

Heat a little butter in a pan, gently fry the onion. Mix the meat, eggs, cream, breadcrumbs, fried onion, parsley, paprika, salt and pepper to taste. Knead to a firm paste, break off small portions and roll into small balls. Bring a pan with plenty of salted water (with the cloved onion and bay leaf) to the boil. Add the meat balls, bring to the boil, lower the heat and simmer for 20 minutes.

NECK OF PORK (*Schweinenackenstreifen*)

2 lb. best neck of pork
fat for frying
1 large onion, diced
caraway seeds
salt, white pepper
garlic
8 large apples, cored
German mustard
oil

Cut 8 slices of lean pork and beat until thin. Heat a little fat and gently fry the onion, sprinkle with caraway and salt. Fill this mixture into the apples. Rub the slices of meat with garlic, sprinkle with salt and pepper, spread with mustard and wrap round the apples, securing with toothpicks making sure the meat does not overlap in the middle. Put into an oiled baking pan and bake in a medium oven 10 minutes. Baste with the juices from the meat and continue cooking until the meat is tender and the apples soft but still firm. Serve with mashed potato.

PICKLED PORK RIBS WITH BEANS (*Pökelrippchen mit dicken Bohnen*)

2 lb. pickled pork ribs,
  still on the bone
2 packets frozen broad
  beans
1 carrot
1 stick celery
1 onion stuck with 2 cloves
1 bay leaf
4 slices streaky bacon,
  diced
1 large onion, diced
1 cup ($1\frac{1}{4}$) cream
1 tablespoon ($1\frac{1}{4}$) cornflour
  (cornstarch)
milk
salt, nutmeg
1 teaspoon ($1\frac{1}{4}$) chopped
  parsley

If the pork is salty, soak it for 1 hour. Put it into a pan with cold water, add carrot, celery, the cloved onion and bay leaf. Bring slowly to the boil, simmer for 2 hours.

Fry the bacon until the fat runs, add the diced onion and fry until soft but without changing colour. Add the beans as they come from the packet, without previous thawing. Pour over them a little of the stock from the meat and cook until tender. Add the cream. Bring to a gentle boil. Mix the cornflour with milk to a thin paste. Stir into the beans, bring to the boil, let the liquid thicken, add salt, nutmeg and parsley. Turn into a serving dish. Take out the meat, separate the ribs and place them on the beans. Serve with boiled potatoes.

(Drink: beer)

HAM AND BANANAS MAJORCA (*Schinkenbanane Mallorca*)

lean ham slices
4 large bananas, peeled
butter
juice 1 lemon
German mustard
1 lb. boiled long grain
　　rice
salt, nutmeg to taste

Rub the inside of a shallow earthenware baking dish with butter. Sprinkle the bananas with lemon juice – this prevents their going brown. Lay the ham slices on a board and spread each well with mustard. Place 1 banana on top of each slice and roll up. Place the ham rolls side by side in the baking dish, cover with foil and bake in a hot oven for about 15–20 minutes or until the bananas are soft. Meanwhile heat 3–4 tablespoons of butter in a shallow pan and quickly fry the rice, adding salt and nutmeg. Turn the rice into a shallow dish, place the ham rolls on top and garnish with sprigs of parsley and quarters of tomatoes.

Instead of rice, the rolls can be placed on top of creamed potatoes and served with spinach.

(Drink: red wine)

HAM ROLLS SIRIKI (*Schinkenrouladen Siriki*)

8 large thin slices ham
German mustard
1 oz. (2 tablespoons) butter
½ lb. boiled Patna-type
　　rice
4 tablespoons (5) mango
　　chutney
salt to taste
1 onion, diced
2 tablespoons (2½) tomato
　　purée
½ cup (⅔) sour cream

Lay the slices of ham out on a table and spread with German mustard. Heat half the butter, quickly fry the cooked rice and mix with the mango chutney, add salt. Pile a little of this mixture in the middle of each ham slice and roll up. Heat the remaining butter, gently fry the onion in a pan without a handle, add the purée and the cream. Bring to the boil, add the rolls with the closure downwards and cover the pan with foil. Bake in a hot oven for 20 minutes. Serve in the pan with a celery salad and sliced tomatoes.

(Drink: white Cinzano)

FILLET STEAK WITH SWEET PEPPER AND MUSHROOM SAUCE (*Rinderlendenschnitte mit Paprika-Champignons*)

4 fillet steaks
butter
1 large onion, finely chopped
1–2 sweet peppers, sliced
1 lb. mushrooms, cleaned and sliced
salt
juice 1 lemon
1 cup (1¼) cream
1 tablespoon (1¼) cornflour (cornstarch)
1 tablespoon (1¼) chopped parsley
3 tablespoons (3¾) mayonnaise
olive oil
crushed garlic
4 slices white bread
port

First prepare the sauce. Heat 3 oz. (6 tablespoons) of butter and fry the onion until soft but not brown. Add the peppers and, as they begin to soften, add the mushrooms. Sprinkle with salt and lemon juice and after 10 minutes add the cream. Cook this gently until it comes to the boil. Mix the cornflour with water to a thin paste. Stir this into the mushrooms etc., and cook gently until the sauce thickens. Add the parsley and mayonnaise. Put aside but keep warm until required.

Soak the steaks in olive oil for 3 hours. Heat several tablespoonfuls of oil in a frying pan until it smokes. Add the steaks and fry them 4 minutes on each side so that they are almost crusty outside, but still pink inside. Baste frequently with the hot oil. Pour off the oil and fry the steaks in butter for the last few minutes – this improves the flavour of the meat.

Before serving, sprinkle the meat lightly with salt and rub with crushed garlic.

Toast the bread, place it on a hot dish. Sprinkle the toast with port. Place the steaks on top. Pour the gravy from the meat into the sauce, add port to flavour and spread the sauce over the steaks. Serve with potato croquettes.

This is an unusual method of cooking steaks, and it is essential that really tender fillet steak is used.

(Drink: a light red wine)

RUMPSTEAK KELLERMEISTER (*Rumpsteak Kellermeister*)

**4 rumpsteaks, each with
   slight incisions made
   into the skin on the
   outside**
8 large onions, halved
sugar, salt to taste
½ pint (1¼ cups) white wine
**1 tablespoon (1½) cornflour
   (cornstarch)**
½ cup (⅔) sour cream
**1 teaspoon (1¼) chopped
   parsley**
2 egg yolks
**½ lb. mushrooms, fresh or
   canned, chopped**
3 tablespoons (3¾) olive oil
butter

Put the onions into a pan, add sugar, salt and white wine and cook gently until soft. Mix the cornflour with the sour cream to make a thin paste – add more sour cream if required. Add it to the onions, let the mixture thicken, then add the mushrooms and bring it all gently to the boil. Stir in the chopped parsley and mix in the egg yolks. The sauce must be thick, white and savoury. Put aside, keep warm but do not allow it to cook further.

Heat the oil in a pan until it smokes, add the meat and brown it well on both sides, basting with the hot oil so that the steaks remain juicy. After 4 minutes cooking on both sides, pour off the oil. Add butter – quantity as liked – and finish cooking the steaks. Place the meat on a hot dish, cover with the onion sauce and pour the hot butter from the pan over the top. Garnish with lettuce and quartered tomatoes. Serve with boiled potatoes, sliced and warmed in butter and sprinkled with chopped dill.
(Drink: a light red wine)

CALF'S BRAIN WITH EGGS (*Hirn mit Ei*)

1 large calf's brain
**3 oz. (6 tablespoons)
   butter**
4 eggs
salt, pepper

Wash the brain and remove all the skin. Cook it in salt water for 15 minutes. Drain. Heat half the butter in a shallow pan until very hot. Slice the brain into 4 equal slices. Fry these on both sides until brown. Place on a flat dish, put aside but keep hot. Heat the remaining butter in the same pan and carefully fry the eggs. Place an egg on each slice of brain. Sprinkle with salt and pepper. Serve with boiled potatoes.

CALF'S SWEETBREADS ROLLED IN ALMONDS
(Kalbsmilcher-Schnitzel in Mandelkleidchen)

1 lb. cooked sweetbreads
   sliced when cold
salt
2 eggs, beaten
2 oz. (⅓ cup) almonds,
   blanched and finely
   chopped
butter for frying
1 lb. cooked rice
1 cup (1¼) cooked peas
nutmeg
chopped parsley

Sprinkle the sliced sweetbreads lightly with salt, coat with beaten egg and roll in the almonds. Press the almonds well into the sweetbreads with the blade of a knife. Heat plenty of butter, add 2 or 3 slices of sweetbreads and brown quickly on both sides – take care the almonds do not brown too much, 2 minutes on either side should be enough. Keep the sweetbreads warm until all are fried. Serve with *risi-e-bisi*. For this, toss the cooked rice in hot butter, add the peas, season with salt, nutmeg and chopped parsley.

Risi-e-bisi is a dish of Italian origin, where it is regarded as a very thick soup, oddly enough eaten with a fork. The quantity of peas should equal that of the rice. The rice and the peas should be throughly mixed.

(Drink: sparkling Moselle)

FRIED LIVER *(Gebratene Kalbsleber)*

1½ lb. skinned calf liver,
   cut in ½ in. thick slices
salt, pepper
flour
1 egg, beaten
breadcrumbs
butter or oil for frying

Sprinkle the liver with salt and pepper, roll in flour, dip into beaten egg and roll in breadcrumbs. Press down with the blade of a knife so that the breadcrumbs stick well. Heat butter or oil in a pan, add the liver, fry it quickly and serve slightly underdone. Arrange the slices of liver on a hot dish.

They can be served with fried onions but if so these should be put on one side of the liver and not on top, for the juice of the onions will soak through the coating and spoil it. Garnish with parsley and serve with a potato salad.

(Drink: rosé wine)

CALF'S HEART MIRAMAR (*Kalbsherz Miramar*)

2 calf's hearts
salt
buttermilk
2 strips larding bacon
2–3 slices fat bacon,
  diced
2 onions, sliced
1 large pickled gherkin,
  sliced
$\frac{3}{4}$ pint (2 cups) meat stock
1 tablespoon ($1\frac{1}{4}$) cornflour
  (cornstarch)
milk
4 anchovy fillets, chopped
2 tablespoons ($2\frac{1}{2}$) capers
1 teaspoon ($1\frac{1}{4}$) sugar
$\frac{1}{2}$ cup ($\frac{2}{3}$) sour cream

Carefully wash the hearts, cut away the walls of the large blood vessels but leave the fleshy part intact. Soak the hearts for 10 minutes in salted water or, if liked, 3 days in buttermilk. This helps to tenderize the meat. Drain the hearts and cut into fairly even flat slices. Lard these with larding bacon.

Heat the diced bacon in a pan, add the onions, fry for 5 minutes, add the slices of heart. Sprinkle lightly with salt, cover and cook 5 minutes. Add the gherkin and meat stock. If the hearts have been steeped in buttermilk, this may be used as well.

Take out the pieces of heart, keep warm. Mix the cornflour with milk or water to a thin paste. Stir this into the gravy with a wire whisk. Add the anchovies, capers, sugar and finally the sour cream. Bring gently to the boil, continue slow boiling until the sauce has thickened. Serve the sliced hearts with the sauce poured over them and with boiled puréed potatoes or buttered noodles with chopped cooked tomatoes.

An equally interesting way of cooking calf's heart is to use onions and peeled tomatoes instead of anchovy fillers and capers, and sour cream instead of buttermilk. The sour cream is used, of course, in making the sauce. If preferred, the heart can be simply cut into half instead of sliced. In this method of cooking, as tomatoes are used in the sauce, they are not served as an accompaniment; wide noodles are preferred. The heart is sprinkled with lemon juice.

STUFFED VEAL CUTLETS (*Gefüllte Kalbskoteletts Burgtheater*)

4 fair-sized veal cutlets,
  on the bone
salt
½ lb. mushrooms
1 tablespoon (1¼) chopped
  parsley
2 slices fat bacon, diced
1 small onion, diced
flour
4 tablespoons (5) olive oil
1 cup (1¼) sour cream
1 tablespoon (1¼) tomato
  purée
1 tablespoon (1¼) cornflour
  (cornstarch)
milk or water
½ cup (⅔) white wine

Slightly flatten the cutlets and make a large incision to resemble pockets in each. Sprinkle lightly inside with salt. Coarsely chop the mushrooms. Fry the bacon, add the onion and mix with the mushrooms and parsley. Push a little of this mixture into each 'pocket'. Sew up the opening or secure with cocktail sticks. Sprinkle lightly with salt and toss in flour. Heat the olive oil, brown the cutlets on both sides, until crisp on the outside and tender and juicy inside.

Put the rest of the mushroom mixture in a fireproof dish, add the sour cream and tomato purée, stir well, add the cutlets and the oil in the pan, cover and cook for 25 minutes in a hot oven. Arrange the cutlets on a hot dish. Reheat the sauce, add if available a little meat stock. Mix the cornflour with water to a thin paste, stir this into the gravy. When the sauce has thickened, flavour with white wine. Pour the sauce over the cutlets, garnish with sprigs of parsley and quartered tomatoes. Serve with buttered spaghetti sprinkled with grated cheese.
(Drink: a mild red wine)

MEAT PIE (*Altburgermeister Nuschhappen*)

1 lb. puff pastry
4 thin slices pork fillet
4 thin slices beef fillet
4 thin slices lamb fillet
salt, pepper
2 slices fat bacon, diced
1 oz. (2 tablespoons) butter

Divide the pastry into 2 portions, roll into rounds one larger than the other. Place the smaller round on a flat baking sheet and on top of this place the meat. Sprinkle with salt and pepper. Fry the diced bacon in the butter, add the onion, when this is soft, add the chicken livers,

1 onion, sliced
½ lb. chicken livers, ground
nutmeg
1 tablespoon (1¼) chopped
    parsley
1 egg yolk

nutmeg and parsley. Fry another 5 minutes, then spread this mixture over the slices of meat. Paint round the edge of the pastry with egg. Cover with the larger pastry round, press the edges down firmly. Paint the top of the pie with remaining egg, cover with foil and bake in a hot oven for 10 minutes. Take off the foil and bake another 10–15 minutes.

MEAT BALLS (BEEFBURGERS) UNCLE OTTO (*Deutsches Beefsteak Onkel Otto*)

1 lb. meat (half beef, half
    pork) finely ground
fat for frying
1 onion, finely chopped
3 tablespoons (3¾) chopped
    parsley
2 rolls soaked in milk
salt, pepper, nutmeg
2 large onions, sliced

Heat a little fat in a pan and fry the chopped onion until soft, add the parsley. Beat the meat in a bowl with 3 tablespoons (3¾) water. Squeeze the rolls dry, add to the meat with the fried onion, salt, pepper and nutmeg. Heat a little more fat in the same pan. Brown a test meat ball for about 4 minutes on each side. If it holds its shape, all is well; if not, mix in an egg to bind the mixture. Heat some more fat. Make the meat balls, repeatedly dipping the hands into cold water so the mixture does not stick to the fingers. Flatten the meat balls on a board and then fry in the hot fat for 4 minutes on each side.

In another pan heat more fat and fry the onion rings until brown and crisp, drain. Arrange the meat balls on a hot dish and scatter the fried onion rings on top. If liked, a poached egg may be placed on each meat ball. Garnish with thick slices of tomato on which a twist of smoked salmon has been placed or a strip of anchovy fillet. Serve with a green salad or green vegetable, or fried or boiled potatoes.

GLORIFIED POTATO CAKES (*Verputzte Kartoffelwürstchen*)

1 lb. potatoes cooked in
   their skins and peeled
4 tablespoons (5) flour
salt, nutmeg to taste
2 eggs, beaten
fat
1 onion, chopped
1 teaspoon (1¼) parsley,
   chopped
½ lb. sausages, chopped
1 cup (1¼) meat stock
2 tablespoons (2½)
   tomato purée
2 teaspoons (2½) cornflour
   (cornstarch)
milk or water

Rub the potatoes while still hot through a sieve, quickly add the flour, salt, nutmeg and eggs and mix with a wooden spoon to a dough. Heat a little fat, lightly fry the onion, parsley and sausages. Mix into the potato dough. Make small balls from the potato mixture and put on a floured board so they do not stick. Bring plenty of lightly salted water to the boil, add the potato balls, bring to the boil and cook for 5 minutes. Drain.

Prepare a tomato sauce. Heat the stock, add the tomato purée. Mix the cornflour with milk to a thin paste, stir this into the tomato sauce and cook gently for 5 minutes. Place the potato cakes in a greased fireproof baking dish, cover with the sauce, sprinkle with cheese and brown in a hot oven.
(Drink: a mild red wine)

VEAL IN A MUSTARD CREAM SAUCE (*Kalbswürfel in Sahne-Senfcreme*)

1 lb. chopped veal
1 oz. (2 tablespoons) fat
1 small onion, diced
salt, pepper and
   paprika pepper
1 tablespoon (1¼) German
   mustard
1 cup (1¼) white wine
2 teaspoons (2½) cornflour
   (cornstarch)
milk
sour cream to taste

Heat the fat and fry the veal until brown. Add the onion and continue frying. Add salt, pepper, paprika and mustard. Stir gently, add the wine and cook slowly for 10 minutes. Mix the cornflour to a thin paste with milk, stir it into the sauce. Bring to the boil, simmer for 5 minutes, finally add sour cream and serve with boiled Patna-type rice, tossed in hot butter.
(Drink: a light white wine)

HARICOT BEANS IN CREAM (*Bohnen in Sahne*)

1 lb. haricot beans, soaked overnight
2–3 slices fat bacon, diced
1 small onion, diced
1 sweet pepper, thinly sliced
½ lb. potatoes, sliced
2 tablespoons (2½) tomato purée
1 pint (1¼) hot meat stock
½ cup (⅔) sour cream
2 tablespoons (2½) chopped parsley

Drain the beans. Fry the bacon until the fat runs, add the onion, pepper and potatoes. Turn into a casserole, add the tomato purée and beans and cover with stock, and continue cooking in a slow oven until the beans are tender. Stir in the sour cream and sprinkle with parsley.

ROTHENBURG TAUBER SAUSAGE ROLLS (*Rothenburger Tauberpastetchen*)

puff pastry
sausage meat for filling
1 egg yolk, well beaten

Roll out the prepared puff pastry and cut into triangles. Place a little of the sausage meat on each triangle and roll into horns or cornet shapes. Place these on a greased baking sheet, paint with egg and bake for 15 minutes in a hot oven. Serve with salad.

ALMOND COATED MÉDAILLONS (*Médaillons in Mandelrock*)

tender veal and pork
salt
nutmeg
egg
finely chopped almonds, blanched
butter for frying

Médaillons of meat (sometimes also fish) are small tender pieces of meat cut into shapes of medallions, small, round and flat for good presentation. In this recipe the meat is seasoned with salt and nutmeg, coated in egg, rolled in almonds and gently fried until tender in butter. Only superbly tender meat can be used in this manner, as too long cooking will burn the almonds. Serve with boiled Patna-type rice and green salad.
(Drink: wine)

LAMB STEAKS WITH CARAWAY POTATOES (*Lammsteak mit Kümmelkartoffeln*)

4 lamb steaks
4 tablespoons (5) oil
1 lb. potatoes, peeled and
  very thinly sliced
salt, pepper
1 large onion, diced
1 tablespoon (1¼) caraway
  seeds
½ cup (⅔) grated cheese
¾ pint (2 cups) sour cream
1 clove garlic, peeled and
  pounded with salt and
  pepper
2 oz. (4 tablespoons) butter
4 slices smoked ham, cut
  into strips
½ lb. button mushrooms
chopped parsley
8 eggs, well beaten and
  flavoured with celery
  salt
4 tablespoons (5) chopped
  chives

Rub the inside of a baking dish with oil. Add the potatoes in layers, sprinkling each layer lightly with salt, diced onion, caraway seeds and cheese. Pour half the oil over the top and the sour cream. Cover and bake gently in a hot oven for 30 minutes or until the potatoes are soft. Serve the potatoes in the dish in which they were cooked. After the potatoes have been cooking for 10 minutes, start to prepare the meat.

Beat the steaks until thin. Rub with the garlic. Heat the remaining oil and fry the steaks 5 minutes on each side or until brown and tender. Take from the pan, heat half the butter and lightly fry the ham. Take from the pan, fry the mushrooms, season with salt and pepper. Sprinkle with parsley. Place the ham at the bottom of a casserole, add the mushrooms, parsley and the lamb steaks. Put into a slow oven. Heat the remaining butter in another pan and scramble the eggs. Spread these over the meat and sprinkle with cheese. Garnish with sliced tomatoes.

(Drink: a mild red wine)

SWEETS AND DESSERTS

ICE-CREAM WITH HOT FRUIT SAUCE (*Eis mit heisser Fruchtsauce*)

First prepare the sauce: dissolve 4 tablespoons (5) granulated sugar in a shallow pan over a moderate heat until it dissolves and becomes a golden brown. Add halved strawberries, sliced peaches (from skinned and stoned fresh fruit) or pineapple cubes. Leave the fruit to simmer in the syrup for 5 minutes, then add a glass of brandy or liqueur. Pour the sauce over the ice-cream immediately before serving. If fresh fruit is not available, thin a fruit jam and flavour it with brandy.

FRUIT SALAD IN HOT WINE SAUCE (*Kühler Fruchtsalat im heissen Weinschaumbad*)

fruit in season
juice 1 lemon
2 eggs
sugar to taste
2 teaspoons (2½) cornflour (cornstarch)
1 cup (1¼) white wine

There is no one recipe for making a good fruit salad. Imagination and above all, available ingredients are decisive. A mixture of apples, oranges, bananas, pears, with fresh or bottled strawberries, peaches or cherries usually succeeds admirably. To flavour such a salad, use lemon juice and caster sugar and a sweet liqueur such as apricot brandy, a few drops of Kirsch or raspberry cordial. It is attractive to serve a fruit salad on a bowl packed with crushed ice. At the last moment a hot sauce, such as the following can be poured over it.

Beat the eggs thoroughly with the sugar and cornflour. Very slowly add the wine and blend it with care. Pour the sauce into a pan and beat it over a low heat until it thickens. The heat must not be too great or the eggs will curdle.

PÊCHES FLAMBÉES (*Flammende Pfirschen*)

4 large peaches, stoned and halved
8 slices pineapple
½ lb. marzipan
1 tablespoon (1¼) apricot brandy
4 tablespoons (5) Curaçao

If possible, use fresh peaches, otherwise bottled may be used but well drained. Lay the pineapple on a dish and the peach halves, hollow-side uppermost, in the centre of the rings. Beat the marzipan with the apricot brandy and fill the mixture into the peach halves. Warm the Curaçao, ignite it at table and pour over the peaches.

APPLE FROST OR SNOW (*Rauhreif-Äpfeln*)

4 large apples
juice 1 lemon
vanilla sugar
1 cup (1¼) whipped cream
1 tablespoon (1¼) apricot
  brandy
2 tablespoons (2½)
  almonds, roasted
glacé cherries

Peel and core the apples and cut into thin slices. Sprinkle at once with lemon juice to keep them white. Flavour with vanilla sugar. Mix the brandy with the cream and pour this over the apples. Gently mix.

Spoon into glass dishes and garnish with the almonds and glacé cherries. This quickly prepared, delicious pudding can also be made from quinces, bananas or sliced preserved ginger.

MARZIPAN APPLES (*Marzipan-Äpfeln*)

4 large apples
marzipan
almond essence
raisins
butter
1 cup (1¼) white wine
hot apricot jam
brandy
glacé cherries

Peel and core the apples and fill the cavity with marzipan well blended with almond essence and raisins. Butter a casserole and half fill it with white wine. Place the apples in it, cover with foil and bake in a hot oven until the apples are tender. Take from the casserole, put into a serving bowl and spread with hot apricot jam. Sprinkle with brandy and garnish with cherries and, if available, a few fresh leaves from an apple tree.

BAKED BANANAS (*Überbackene Bananen*)

4 large bananas
butter
lemon juice
powdered cinnamon
sugar
4 eggs, separated
icing (powdered) sugar
4 tablespoons (5) Curaçao

Slice the bananas in halves lengthwise and lay in a well-buttered shallow baking dish. Sprinkle lightly with lemon juice, then with cinnamon and sugar to taste. Bake the bananas in a hot oven until almost tender.

Meanwhile beat the egg whites to a stiff foam. Beat the egg yolks with sugar to taste until stiff, fold in the yolks and spread this mixture over the bananas. Dredge with icing sugar, return the bananas to the oven. Brown. Warm the Curaçao and pour it over the bananas at table. Ignite and serve the bananas while still flaming. Instead of Curaçao, a good quality rum or brandy may be used instead.

(Drink: Madeira)

RHUBARB CREAM (*Rhubarber in Eigelbschaum*)

1 lb. young rhubarb, stewed
4 egg yolks
3 oz. ($\frac{1}{3}$ cup) sugar
2 tablespoons ($2\frac{1}{2}$) brandy
2 tablespoons ($2\frac{1}{2}$) apricot brandy
1 cup ($1\frac{1}{4}$) whipped cream
vanilla
glacé cherries

Pour the rhubarb over a sieve and let the juice run through, then either put the pieces through a food mixer or crush well with a fork.

Beat the egg yolks with the sugar. Add the brandy and the apricot brandy. Beat the cream until stiff and lightly flavour with vanilla sugar. Add the egg yolk foam to the cream. Fold in the rhubarb and serve in individual dishes, garnished with a glacé cherry.

OMELETTE ALSTERBLICK (*Omelett Alsterblick*)

3 eggs
butter
2 sliced bananas
1 tablespoon ($1\frac{1}{4}$) honey
1 teaspoon ($1\frac{1}{4}$) orange juice
2 tablespoons ($2\frac{1}{2}$) grated chocolate
vanilla sugar
good quality rum

Heat a little butter in a pan, lightly fry the bananas. Keep hot. Make a 3-egg omelette in the usual manner, pile the fried banana in the middle. Add the honey, orange juice and chocolate. The heat of the omelette will be enough to dissolve the honey and the chocolate and provide a marvellous flavour.

Fold the omelette over, slide on to a warm plate and sprinkle with vanilla sugar. Warm the rum, ignite it in a spoon and pour while still flaming over the omelette.

CREAM CHEESE OMELETTE (*Quark-Omelett*)

2 tablespoons (2½) cream
  cheese
vanilla sugar
1 tablespoon (1¼) raisins
lemon juice
milk
½ oz. (1 tablespoon) butter
3 eggs, lightly beaten
sugar

Mix the cheese with a little vanilla sugar, raisins, lemon juice and enough milk to make a thick cream. Heat the butter in a pan, add the eggs and make an omelette in the usual manner. When it is half set, spread it with the cheese mixture. Fold over both sides and slide on to a dish, sprinkle with sugar and lemon juice and serve at once.

The omelette can be flambéed with rum as in previous recipe.

STRAWBERRIES, PEACHES AND PINEAPPLE IN CHAMPAGNE (*Erdbeeren auf Pfirschen in Sektbad und Ananas*)

sliced fresh pineapple
fresh peach halves
cream, whipped
strawberries
sugar
sweet chilled champagne

Lay the slices of pineapple in a wide shallow dish; in the middle of each slice place half a peach, fill this with whipped cream and top with a whole strawberry, sprinkle with sugar. Add enough champagne to cover the pineapple. Garnish with pineapple leaves and the skin and serve at once.

Comparative Cookery Terms and Measures

BRITISH MEASURES	AMERICAN MEASURES	APPROXIMATE METRIC MEASURES
Liquid Measures		
1 teaspoon	1¼ teaspoons	6 c.c.
1 tablespoon	1¼ tablespoons	17 c.c.
1 fluid ounce	1 fluid ounce	30 c.c.
16 fluid ounces	1 pint	·480 litre
20 fluid ounces, or 1 pint	1¼ pints	·568 litre
1¾ pints	2 pints	1 litre
1 quart or 2 pints	2½ pints	1·136 litres
1 gallon or 8 pints	10 pints	4·544 litres

British Standard Measuring Cup is equivalent to 10 fluid ounces
American Standard Measuring Cup is equivalent to 8 fluid ounces

BRITISH	AMERICAN	METRIC
Solid Measures		
1 ounce	1 ounce	30 grammes
16 ounces or 1 lb.	16 ounces or 1 lb.	500 grammes
2 lb., 3 ounces	2 lb., 3 ounces	1 kilogram

British and American Equivalent Ingredients

BRITISH	AMERICAN
Icing sugar	Confectioners' sugar
Cornflour	Cornstarch
Sultanas	White raisins
Rusk crumbs	Zwieback
Single cream	Light cream
Double cream	Heavy cream
Bicarbonate of soda	Baking soda
Scone	Biscuit
Soft brown sugar	Brown sugar
100 per cent wholemeal flour	Graham flour
Digestive biscuits	Graham crackers
Butter or margarine	Shortening
Other vegetable fats	Soft shortening
1 oz. cooking chocolate	1 square chocolate
$\frac{2}{3}$ oz. bakers' yeast, or	
3 level teaspoonfuls dried yeast	1 cake yeast
Okra	Gumbo
$\frac{1}{3}$ oz. powdered gelatine, or 1 level tablespoonful	1 envelope gelatine
Caster sugar	Granulated sugar
Biscuit	Cookie or Cracker
Minced meat	Ground meat

Throughout this book English measurements are given first: the American equivalent follows in brackets

Vintage Chart

YEAR	CLARET	BURGUNDY	WHITE BURGUNDY	SAUTERNES	RHONE	RHINE	MOSELLE	CHAMPAGNE	PORT	LOIRE
1945	7	6	–	6	7	–	–	5	7	–
1946	1	1	–	2	5	–	–	–	–	–
1947	5	6	–	6	6	–	–	6	7	–
1948	5	5	–	5	4	–	–	–	7	–
1949	6	5	–	5	7	–	–	6	–	–
1950	5	3	–	6	6	–	–	–	6	–
1951	0	1	–	2	4	–	–	–	–	–
1952	6	5	5	6	6	5	4	7	4	–
1953	6	5	4	5	6	7	6	6	–	–
1954	4	3	1	2	7	2	2	–	6	–
1955	6	5	4	6	6	5	4	6	7	–
1956	0	1	1	2	5	1	1	–	–	–
1957	5	5	5	4	7	4	4	–	5	–
1958	4	3	4	4	5	5	5	–	6	–
1959	6	7	6	6	6	7	7	7	–	6
1960	4	1	1	3	6	2	2	–	7	2
1961	7	7	7	5	7	5	4	7	–	5
1962	6	5	6	6	6	3	3	6	5	4
1963	1	4	3	2	5	3	2	–	7	1
1964	6	7	7	5	6	6	7	7	–	7
1965	0	1	2	2	5	1	1	–	4	1
1966	6	7	7	6	6	6	6	–	7	5
1967	5	5	7	5	6	5	4	–	6	6
1968	1	1	1	0	5	1	1	–	–	3

0 = No Good   7 = The Best

Fresh Food in its Best Season

	JANUARY	FEBRUARY	MARCH	APRIL	MAY	JUNE	JULY	AUGUST	SEPTEMBER	OCTOBER	NOVEMBER	DECEMBER
MEAT												
Beef							x	x	x			
Beef, stall-fed	x	x	x	x								
Grass lamb						x	x					
House lamb	x	x										x
Mutton	x	x	x	x	x	x	x	x	x	x	x	x
Pork	x	x								x	x	x
Suckling-pig	x	x	x									
Veal	x	x	x	x	x	x	x	x	x	x	x	x
POULTRY												
Chicken	x	x	x	x	x	x	x	x	x	x	x	x
Duck	x	x	x	x	x	x	x	x	x	x	x	x
Duckling					x	x						
Goose	x								x	x	x	x
Guinea-fowl		x	x	x	x	x	x	x				
Muscovy duck	x	x	x							x	x	x
Turkey	x				x	x	x	x	x	x	x	x
GAME												
Blackgame								x	x	x		
Capercailzie								x	x	x	x	
Golden plover	x								x	x	x	x
Grouse								x	x	x	x	
Hare	x								x	x	x	x
Partridge	x								x	x	x	x
Pheasant	x									x	x	x

	January	February	March	April	May	June	July	August	September	October	November	December
GAME (*continued*)												
Snipe	X									X	X	X
Venison	X	X	X							X	X	X
Wild duck	X								X	X	X	X
Wild goose	X									X	X	X
Wild pigeons and doves	X	X						X	X	X	X	X
Wild rabbit	X	X						X	X	X	X	X
Woodcock	X								X	X	X	X
FISH												
Bass	X	X	X	X	X	X	X	X	X	X	X	X
Bream	X	X	X	X	X	X	X	X	X	X	X	X
Brill				X	X	X	X	X	X			
Carp		X	X									
Cod	X	X								X	X	X
Dab			X	X	X	X	X	X	X	X		
Eel	X	X				X	X	X	X	X	X	X
Flounder			X	X	X	X	X	X	X			
Grayling									X	X	X	
Grey mullet	X	X	X	X	X	X	X	X	X	X	X	X
Haddock	X	X	X	X	X	X	X	X	X	X	X	X
Hake			X	X	X	X	X	X	X			
Halibut	X	X	X	X	X	X	X	X	X	X	X	X
Herring			X	X	X	X	X	X	X			
John Dory	X	X	X	X	X	X	X	X	X	X	X	X
Lamprey	X	X										
Lemon sole			X	X	X	X	X	X	X			
Mackerel			X	X	X							
Pike	X	X	X					X	X	X	X	X
Pilchard			X	X	X	X	X	X	X			
Plaice			X	X	X	X	X	X	X			
Red mullet						X	X	X	X	X	X	X
Rock salmon	X	X	X	X	X	X	X					X
Salmon		X	X	X	X	X	X	X	X			
Salmon trout		X	X	X	X	X	X	X	X			

	JANUARY	FEBRUARY	MARCH	APRIL	MAY	JUNE	JULY	AUGUST	SEPTEMBER	OCTOBER	NOVEMBER	DECEMBER
FISH (*continued*)												
Sardine	x	x	x	x	x	x						
Skate	x	x	x	x	x	x	x	x	x	x	x	x
Smelt	x	x	x	x					x	x	x	x
Sole			x	x	x	x	x	x	x			
Sprat										x	x	
Sturgeon	x	x	x	x	x	x	x	x	x	x	x	x
Trout	x	x	x	x	x	x	x	x	x	x	x	x
Turbot	x	x	x	x	x	x	x	x	x	x	x	x
Whitebait	x	x	x	x	x	x	x	x	x	x	x	x
Whiting	x	x	x	x	x	x	x	x	x	x	x	x
CRUSTACEANS												
Crab	x	x	x	x	x	x	x	x	x	x	x	x
Crawfish	x	x	x	x	x	x	x	x	x	x	x	x
Crayfish	x	x	x	x	x	x	x	x	x	x	x	x
Lobster	x	x	x	x	x	x	x	x	x	x	x	x
Prawns	x	x	x	x	x	x	x	x	x	x	x	x
Shrimps	x	x	x	x	x	x	x	x	x	x	x	x
MOLLUSCS												
Mussel	x	x	x	x					x	x	x	x
Oyster	x	x	x	x					x	x	x	x
Scallop	x	x	x	x					x	x	x	x
FRESH VEGETABLES												
Artichoke, globe						x	x	x	x			
Artichoke, Jerusalem	x	x									x	x
Asparagus					x	x	x					
Bean, broad					x	x	x					
Bean, French						x	x					
Bean, haricot						x	x					
Bean, runner							x	x	x			
Beetroot	x	x	x							x	x	x
Broccoli										x	x	x

FRESH VEGETABLES (continued)

	JANUARY	FEBRUARY	MARCH	APRIL	MAY	JUNE	JULY	AUGUST	SEPTEMBER	OCTOBER	NOVEMBER	DECEMBER
Brussels sprout	x	x								x	x	x
Cabbage	x	x	x	x				x	x	x	x	x
Cabbage, red	x	x	x							x	x	x
Cabbage, savoy	x	x								x	x	x
Carrot				x	x	x	x	x				
Cauliflower						x	x	x	x			
Celery	x									x	x	x
Chestnut	x	x	x								x	x
Cucumber						x	x	x	x			
Curly kale								x	x	x	x	x
Endive	x	x	x	x					x	x	x	x
Leek	x	x	x	x							x	x
Lettuce					x	x	x	x	x			
Mushroom								x	x	x		
Onion	x	x	x	x	x	x	x	x	x	x	x	x
Onion, spring				x	x	x						
Parsnip										x	x	x
Pea						x	x					
Potato	x	x	x	x	x	x	x	x	x	x	x	x
Potato, new						x	x					
Pumpkin						x	x	x		x	x	x
Radish						x	x	x				
Rhubarb				x	x	x						
Sea kale									x	x	x	
Shallot								x	x	x		
Spinach			x	x	x	x	x	x	x	x		
Swede	x									x	x	x
Sweet corn							x	x	x	x		
Tomato					x	x	x	x	x			
Turnip	x									x	x	x
Vegetable marrow						x	x	x	x			
Watercress	x	x	x	x	x	x	x	x	x	x	x	x

FRUITS

	JANUARY	FEBRUARY	MARCH	APRIL	MAY	JUNE	JULY	AUGUST	SEPTEMBER	OCTOBER	NOVEMBER	DECEMBER
Apple, cooking	x	x	x	x								

FRUIT (*continued*)

	JANUARY	FEBRUARY	MARCH	APRIL	MAY	JUNE	JULY	AUGUST	SEPTEMBER	OCTOBER	NOVEMBER	DECEMBER
Apple, eating	x	x	x						x	x	x	x
Apricot					x	x	x	x	x			
Blackberry							x	x	x			
Blueberry							x	x				
Cherry						x	x	x				
Crabapple								x	x			
Currant						x	x					
Damson								x	x	x		
Gooseberry						x	x	x	x			
Green fig									x	x		
Greengage							x	x				
Loganberry								x				
Medlar											x	
Melon					x	x	x	x	x			
Nectarine							x	x				
Peach						x	x	x				
Plum							x	x	x			
Quince										x		
Raspberry						x	x	x				
Sloe									x			
Strawberry					x	x	x	x				

Index

The International
Wine and Food Society

The Wine and Food Society was founded in 1933 by André L. Simon, C.B.E., as a world-wide non-profit-making society.

The first of its various aims has been to bring together and serve all who believe that a right understanding of wine and food is an essential part of personal contentment and health; and that an intelligent approach to the pleasures and problems of the table offers far greater rewards than the mere satisfaction of appetite.

For information about the Society,
apply to the Secretary,
Marble Arch House,
44 Edgware Road, London, w.2.